Contemporary American Women Writers

Narrative Strategies

Catherine Rainwater and
William J. Scheick, Editors

THE UNIVERSITY PRESS OF KENTUCKY

Earlier versions of "A Bibliography of Writings by Cynthia Ozick," by Susan Currier and Daniel J. Cahill, and "A Bibliography of Writings by Anne Redmon," by Catherine Rainwater, appeared in *Texas Studies in Literature and Language* 25 (1983): 313-21, 364-66, and are reprinted by permission of the publisher.

Scholarly publisher for the Commonwealth, serving Bellarmine College, Berea College, Centre College of Kentucky, Eastern Kentucky University, The Filson Club, Georgetown College, Kentucky Historical Society, Kentucky State University, Morehead State University, Murray State University, Northern Kentucky University, Transylvania University, University of Kentucky, University of Louisville, and Western Kentucky University.

Editorial and Sales Offices: Lexington, Kentucky 40506-0024

Library of Congress Cataloging in Publication Data
Main entry under title:
Contemporary American women writers.

Includes bibliographies.
Contents: Ann Beattie, the art of the missing / Carolyn Porter—Grace Paley, chaste compactness / Ronald Schleifer—Annie Dillard, narrative fringe / William J. Scheick—[etc.]
1. American fiction—20th century—History and criticism—Addresses, essays, lectures. 2. American fiction—Women authors—History and criticism—Addresses, essays, lectures. 3. Narration (Rhetoric)—Addresses, essays, lectures. 4. American fiction—Women authors—Bibliography. I. Rainwater, Catherine, 1953—   . II. Scheick, William J., 1941—   .
PS379.C66   1985   813'.54'099287   85-9116
ISBN 0-8131-1558-2
ISBN 0-8131-0168-9 paperback

Contemporary
American
Women
Writers

For Doris S. Rainwater & Irene L. Scheick

CONTENTS

Introduction

Catherine Rainwater & William J. Scheick

In 1970, a signal year in the development of the women's movement, Kate Millett published her cornerstone study, *Sexual Politics.*[1] This book codified the patriarchal views of women and of female experience expressed in modern literary classics—all works by male authors. Since 1970, owing at least in part to feminist awareness generated by works such as Millett's and others which appeared at approximately the same time,[2] ever-growing numbers of female writers have arisen on the contemporary scene and contributed poetry and fiction which contradict the once nearly monolithic patriarchal vision of women—and women writers—characterizing modern literature. Inspired by this appearance of unprecedented numbers of women authors, many of whom self-consciously struggle against the force of sexist literary tradition, is an intriguing and controversial question regarding the traditional or nontraditional status of works by women: Can female authors be said to participate in a literary tradition which has consistently disfranchised and misrepresented women; or has this very disfranchisement and misrepresentation brought about the total displacement of women artists from tradition to the extent that their works depart radically in form and content from those of their male counterparts? As the many recent attempts to discover a distinctly feminist poetics suggest, feminist scholars continue to ponder this question.

Although the question remains open, many feminists agree and much evidence suggests that the distinctively different traits of literature written by women lie in its content, point of view, and perspective on experience, human values, and sensibility; certainly women writers of recent years have contributed more convincing female narrators and characters than have male writers throughout history. Fewer distinctive differences between works by male and female authors so far have been detected in genre and overall construction; that is to say, male and female writers alike tend to observe or violate many of the same generic norms and to employ the same figurative, structural, and rhetorical devices. Often, women writers do seem to manage these norms and devices in ways uncommon or even unprecedented in works by men. If the ten contemporary women writers included in this study apparently do not work within some completely separate poetics or set of literary conventions, their fiction certainly expands and revises the forms and devices they employ to convey feminist messages ranging from conservative to radical. Many feminist scholars have already done much to show what is new or transformative in the content of works by women. In putting together this volume, therefore, we have emphasized narrative technique or craft over content precisely because we wished to illuminate some of the ways in which present-day women artists are reshaping many of the apparently inescapable elements of tradition and thus are making this tradition more their own.

This volume originated as a companion to an earlier work of ours that had much the same purpose. *Three Contemporary Women Novelists: Hazzard, Ozick, and Redmon,* published in the summer of 1983 as a special issue of *Texas Studies in Literature and Language,* was likewise meant to direct attention toward a few contemporary women novelists who, in our estimation, merited recognition but who as yet had not attracted adequate critical interest. Not surprisingly, we found difficult the task of choosing only three such writers from the growing number of noteworthy contemporary female authors. Choosing only ten such authors for inclusion in this volume again presented a considerable challenge.

Deciding to focus our second study exclusively on American women writers helped us to narrow our field of choice and imparted an overall coherence to an otherwise quite diverse body of literature by contemporary women. We believe, moreover, that the works of the authors we have selected exhibit varied and intriguing approaches to narrative management and that they do so in a way that indicates the importance of these writers to the continuing development of American literary tradition. Indeed, many of the critical essays here included suggest essential as well as incidental connections between these women writers and their male and female American precursors: Carolyn Porter observes connections between Ann Beattie and

Henry James, Sherwood Anderson, and Ernest Hemingway; William Scheick, between Annie Dillard and Henry David Thoreau; Catherine Rainwater, between Anne Redmon and Flannery O'Connor; Mary Robertson, between Anne Tyler and Eudora Welty; and Linda Wagner, between Toni Morrison and William Faulkner. Such observable connections, even when they are only marginally relevant to the interpretation of the texts at hand, strongly suggest that, however revolutionary a writer's politics and themes may be, the weight of tradition to some extent shapes the expression of ideas.

In attempting to clarify and elaborate upon the place of women artists in American literary tradition, we have tried to select a group of artists whose works generally represent the aesthetic issues that confront contemporary American women writers for whom narrative technique is a more or less conscious concern. The essays we have here assembled include diverse discussions of writers such as Toni Morrison and Marge Piercy, whose feminist messages are contained within relatively conventional forms, and Annie Dillard and Maxine Hong Kingston, whose works might best be described as transgeneric—Dillard's incorporating elements of the novel as well as of the Thoreauvian personal-philosophical essay, Kingston's employing and revolutionizing the conventions of the novel as well as of the autobiography. Also included are essays on the works of Anne Tyler, Grace Paley, Ann Beattie, Cynthia Ozick, Alice Walker, and Anne Redmon, writers whose art proffers an array of narrative techniques ranging from the more or less traditional to the decidedly innovative. Redmon, for example, adapts a classical musical form to literary purposes. Tyler, as Mary Robertson shows in her essay on the family novel, employs an ostensibly conventional narrative formula but manages the narrative so as to subvert the expectations that the family novel evokes in the reader.

Not only do the authors themselves present a variety of narrative strategies, but the critics whose essays appear in the volume define the term "narrative technique" in a variety of interesting ways. Similarities and differences in these definitions perhaps account for some fortuitous and interesting continuities that emerge between the various essays on the works of our ten authors. The first four articles concern themselves with what is omitted from narratives and with important tensions between surfaces and depths in the texts of the writers they treat. Carolyn Porter discovers in Ann Beattie's "art of the missing" a deliberately fashioned metonymic narrative technique that reveals a "vision of a world in a state of lack." Porter shows how Beattie develops a fictive universe replete with objects, characters, and settings signifying depths that are conspicuously absent from postmodern experience as well as surfaces that are perhaps all too clearly present. Ronald Schleifer concentrates on Grace Paley's tendency to exalt plenary experience, to focus on surface details of life and human interaction, and to avoid plumbing the depths of experience. Such a tendency, he argues, reveals Paley's intention to preclude the narcissistic search for "meaning beyond meaning" that characterizes, Paley believes, patriarchal philosophy and fiction. William Scheick, writing on Annie Dillard, discovers the "narrative fringe" or liminal space of the text where Dillard attempts to conjoin the phenomenal (what can be seen and verbalized) with the noumenal (what lies beyond language), and to evoke in the reader something akin to a "conversion experience." Finally, Catherine Rainwater discusses the ways in which Anne Redmon's "fugal" novel orchestrates narrative voices and interstitial silences to involve the reader in an active process of completing the meanings suggested by the voices but lying finally in the shared human silences beyond words.

In the next two essays authorial violation of generic norms and disruption of readers' expectations are discussed. Ellen Pifer observes Cynthia Ozick's use of surface disruptions, dislocations, and discontinuities. According to Pifer, Ozick employs many of the gamelike tricks of the postmodern antinovel, but instead of the nihilism characteristic of this form, Ozick offers a "deeply orthodox vision of reality." Mary Robertson shows how Anne Tyler deliberately manages implausibility in the family novel to disrupt her readers' expectations of orthodox family alignments.

Two more essays are concerned with the development of feminist consciousness and identity through the use of language. Elizabeth Fifer shows how Alice Walker's characters in *The Color Purple* emerge from silence and oppression into articulate strength and independence. And Suzanne Juhasz, focusing on *The Woman Warrior: Memoirs of a Girlhood among Ghosts* and *China Men*, examines Maxine Hong Kingston's deliberately female and male modes of storytelling that eventuate in her narrators' acquisition of a strong Chinese-American female identity.

Finally, the last two essays reveal how traditional narrative techniques can be employed to define and alter conventional female experience. Linda Wagner discusses Toni Morrison's use of traditional literary forms and devices to render firsthand impressions and accounts of female experience. Wagner shows how Morrison adapts to her feminist purposes the traditional *Bildungsroman*. Elaine Tuttle Hansen reveals how Marge Piercy's fiction, especially *Small Changes*, both uses and subverts the dominant discourse which serves the purposes and reflects the experience of a patriarchal society. Hansen shows how Piercy employs elements of the soap opera, "one of the oppressor's narrative modes," to "rewrite female experience."

We think that these ten essays provide in their diversity an overview of many of the aesthetic concerns with which American women writers are preoccupied today. No other volume exists that is focused on narrative technique in the works of such a wide variety of women writers. We hope the book will fill that gap and that it will also contribute to women's studies in general, to current scholarly dialogue on the question of women's literature and tradition, and to current discussion of the question of a female or feminist poetics. In addition to the essays, complete bibliographies of the works of each author appear in this volume. In many instances, these bibliographies are the first ever to be compiled; in others, they bring earlier bibliographies up to date. The bibliographies are as complete as we could make them. In some instances page numbers, month or season, or volume numbers are missing because, especially for a number of small and generally unknown literary magazines, we could not find the journal or any full reference to it in periodical indices. We include such incomplete references in the expectation that subsequent bibliographers may be able to finish the entries only partially listed here. Whenever we were able, we noted changes in the title of an item when it was reprinted by the author. In the entries for reviews by the authors, we included, whenever possible, the titles and authors of the books treated; in some instances, however, we had only the title of the review itself, and again subsequent bibliographers may be able to annotate these entries. We hope that the bibliographical data we have provided will encourage and facilitate future scholarship concerning the writings of the ten contemporary women authors whose works are analyzed in this volume.

NOTES

1. Hester Eisenstein's *Contemporary Feminist Thought* (Boston: G.K. Hall, 1983) provides an excellent analytical overview of the various "waves" of American feminism.

2. See for example Shulamith Firestone, *The Dialectic of Sex: The Case for Feminist Revolution* (New York: Bantam Books, 1970); Mary Daly, *Beyond God the Father: Toward a Philosophy of Women's Liberation* (Boston: Beacon Press, 1973). See also works by Nancy Chodorow and Adrienne Rich that appeared in the early seventies.

ANN BEATTIE

The Art of the Missing

Carolyn Porter

Ann Beattie is known for a certain kind of story. It is, notably, a *New Yorker* story, one marked by understatement, caustic dialogue, and an unsentimental view of social relations. These relations are found, or more often fail to be found, among members of the baby-boom generation, now in their twenties and early thirties. If they have children, they are necessarily unsentimental creatures, already wise in the ways of a world in which their parents are alienated, their homes unsettled, their futures unsure. The stereotype can be further refined. There are a dog, for example, indoor plants, and a lot of snow; the first two absorb an inordinate amount of the characters' emotional energy, and the last encloses them as if they were trapped inside one of those glass balls in which the snow flies when the ball is shaken or turned over.

While this stereotype is by no means inaccurate, it can easily blind us to the variety and the experimental energy of Beattie's work. Her characters, for example, are not exclusively young to middle-aged. "Victor Blue" is focused on one week in the life of an aged couple, the last week, as it turns out, for one of them. "Imagined Scenes" and "Marshall's Dog" include old people as crucial, if not central, characters in the picture being drawn. More important than the range of characters in her work, from babies to the dying generations, is a set of narrative techniques whose developing suppleness reflects an intense narrative imagination, one always at work at the task of finding the means to write the novel of manners in a period during which manners have lost the ground charted for them by even so recent an explorer as John Updike. If we look beneath the stereotype at a few of Beattie's narrative techniques, perhaps we can begin to account for the peculiar quality of her fictive, yet familiar world—the sense that something has been lost, although no one can quite remember what.

But first, let me clear the ground a little. It is fashionable these days, especially perhaps on the West Coast, to express a superior disdain for Beattie. Of the several people to whom I mentioned that I was writing this essay, not one expressed admiration for her work. They disliked her perspective, her style, her characters, or what they seemed collectively to regard as her snobbery. I confess to having shared this attitude, if in a milder version; I did not like the world she portrayed, but I could never manage to stop reading her. Rereading the five volumes of hers that have been published, I find that every one of these denigrators, myself included, could figure as a character in one of her books. Such an ironic tribute may mean nothing, or it may mean that Beattie has caught us out, revealed us in a light that is not merely unflattering, but disturbing—much as an old photograph of a group of friends can, in retrospect, disturb us by uncannily exposing the concealed facts, such as who loved whom, who was deceiving or being deceived by whom, even who was doomed.

The analogy with photography is apt in more ways than one, but it is most obviously apt for what the photograph leaves out—*why* X is deceiving Y, for example, or *why* Z is doomed. Beattie's recent stories are beginning to address the why, but in her first collection, *Distortions*, the characters and their relations are exposed without being explained. In effect, the hidden is revealed but not redeemed from what Henry James called life's "splendid waste."[1] Indeed, it is often the waste itself that is portrayed. A reader may complain that the picture lacks depth, but it remains disturbing. Further, if Beattie's techniques worked initially to represent the surfaces of a world perceived as surface, as I think they did, they have now begun to serve as a ground on which to build a more complex narrative.

A more formidable complaint is that such pictures lack breadth. Needless to say, the colleagues to whom I have referred as possible characters in Beattie's stories all come from and inhabit the same social stratum on which Beattie focuses her lens—the white, upper middle class. Here James's example is congruent, and one of his critical principles is apt: the author must be granted her subject. What does not figure in Beattie's fictive world would, and does, fill many people's lives—poverty, say, or hunger, or discrimination, to mention only the bluntest abstractions for all that remains unrepresented. James's point, of course, was to insist upon measuring a writer's worth, not by her subject, but by what she does with it. On the face of it a conservative principle, this rule applies as well from a certain time-honored perspective of the left. That is, if, as Lukacs argued, the artist's subject and perspective are dictated by her historical period and class, and if, as Sartre insisted, an individual's project is to make something of what time and place have made her, then a writer's subject is circumscribed by socially and historically determined conditions, and the great writer is the one whose art makes the most of those conditions by representing them accurately.[2] There are some problems with this line of reasoning, of course, not least of which is that it minimizes the question of an author's choice of subject. But this is not a troublesome issue for the kind of leftist to whom these remarks are addressed in order to remind him or her that the white upper middle-class world of Beattie's stories and novels is theoretically capable of displaying social truth.

Finally, in regard to the question of breadth, it is worth recalling the doubtful ground on which critics once compared Jane Austen's miniature art invidiously with Tolstoy's panorama. Fortunately the sexist bias that informs such views has in recent years given way, at least partially, in the face of feminist readings of Austen and other writers whose "merely" domestic or gothic or popular art has begun to reveal the narrative wealth that such labels served to repress. James's principle may have emerged from the most haut bourgeois critical mind in English letters, but it remains in force for any critic who values his or her own integrity.

This said, we can proceed to the integrity of Beattie's art, specifically to the narrative techniques she has developed toward a contemporary novel of manners. I should emphasize *toward*, since Beattie's two novels, *Chilly Scenes of Winter* and *Falling in Place*, are not altogether successful as novels. In what follows, I will focus on her first short-story collection, *Distortions*, then on her more recent one, *The Burning House*, because in these works we can see Beattie's techniques take shape and develop. It is not only, however, that her techniques are more clearly visible in the stories, but also that they work more effectively in this short form, which leads me to concentrate on these volumes and to claim that they are superior to Beattie's novels. It remains to be seen whether Beattie can write a fully successful novel, but it is already clear that her mastery of the short story derives from the sensibility of a novelist of manners. Nor do I think such mastery worth any less than that of the novelist. The short-story collection in the modern era has roots in a tradition that goes back to *Dubliners* and *Winesburg, Ohio*, a tradition that has come to fulfill many of the same functions as the novel of manners. While none of Beattie's collections is unified around a town or a central character, each is focused—as the stereotype indicates—on certain social groups and on the present, the tense used by Beattie in almost all her stories and even in her first novel. Further, one of the social marks of the generation and the period she is primarily concerned with portraying is its mobility. These people's lives do not adhere to a city or town. Instead, they are attached to cars, plants, dogs—that is, not only to objects, but to transitory ones. In short, the narrative means of capturing the manners of contemporary life are not easy to come by, and the short-story collection may well have some advantages over the novel. It may also be meeting the demands of a reading public not only dwindling in size, but one becoming more responsive to synecdoche. That is, just as cartoons have been simplified, reduced from detailed visual plenitude to spare line drawings as we have become attuned to the comic strip, perhaps readers—at least readers of the *New Yorker*—have grown accustomed to an analogous economy of exposition in narration, an economy of which Beattie's stories are exemplary.

Having hovered over the affective fallacy, I now return to hover again over the mimetic one by claiming that Beattie's techniques, even while producing results that often seem highly artificial, are informed by a clean aim at the real, the here and now, and that those techniques, so far, have worked better at portraying contemporary life in her short stories than in her novels. The central reason for this is that Beattie's most marked talent is for eliminating discrete chunks of exposition, that laying out of background information which the short story must find a way of minimizing. One way of occulting exposition and at the same time exploiting the limits of the short story is to develop a symbolic context and meaning for the events being portrayed, as both Joyce and Anderson did. Beattie's solution is strikingly different. By using the present tense, she not only removes any temptation to lapse into straight exposition, forcing it to emerge either through a character's consciousness or through dialogue, but also limits the consciousness in question severely. At the same time, she refuses the rewards of the symbolic; that is, her narratives are supported, not by metaphor, but by metonymy. Not all this is necessarily apparent in any one story, but it becomes clear in the course of *Distortions* as a whole.

The simplest of Beattie's stories in this volume are those that are focused on a single character whose experience is represented in a series of frames, as in a cartoon strip. "The Parking Lot," for example, follows an unnamed woman through a week in which she begins an affair. The affair itself is not represented, but the parking lot is. It serves not merely as visual background but as thematic center. The routine of her life is punctuated by her departure from the parking lot each day, the only time she seems to become conscious of herself or of her surroundings. The parking lot serves, not as symbol, but merely as link—virtually the only link in the woman's life. The story represents the cognitive dissonance endemic to the clerical worker's life, in which the cycle of work, exhaustion, eating, and sleeping repeats itself until "she finds herself in the parking lot, a whole day gone," wondering "what happened in the period between sitting at the dining table and now when she is walking across the parking lot?"[3]

Despite the enlightened arrangement by which she and her husband work alternate years, her life is utterly conventional, as are her attitudes. She cannot see why other people's marriages fail, why they too cannot make arrangements. Despite the fact that she is treated with a sustained, if muted irony, this woman's story is curiously humorless. She would be an easy target for satire, if it were not for the pity her case evokes. By staying just inside the rim of her consciousness, the narrative voice never allows us the distance necessary for satire, but by clinging to that rim, the voice prohibits any view of a genuine interior and indeed suggests that there is no such interior. What is missing is any self-consciousness, any awareness of the dissatisfactions that lead her to start the affair.

Not all these stories are so humorless or so affectless, however. "Wolf Dreams," like "The Parking Lot," portrays a woman lost to herself, but its heroine, Cynthia, is painfully conscious of her own unhappiness, though just as painfully unable to understand it. Cynthia's life is a caricature of a story from *Bride* magazine. She marries Ewell W.G. Peterson at seventeen, then Lincoln Divine at twenty-nine, and is now planning to marry Charlie Pinehurst as soon as she loses twenty pounds and her hair has grown long enough for her to have curls falling to her shoulders on her wedding day. She has a recurring nightmare in which she is standing at the altar with Charlie in a wedding dress not quite long enough to hide the fact that she is standing on a scale. It may be no wonder to us that she finally rejects Charlie—and his rejection of her—but it remains a wonder to her.

While "The Parking Lot" is one monotonous series of days fused by a seamless present tense, "Wolf Dreams" almost produces a plot, a developing sequence of events ending in Cynthia's rejection by Charlie. Like Lily Bart in Edith Wharton's *House of Mirth*, when she inexplicably fails to show up in time for church with Percy Gryce,

Cynthia strikes up a drunken conversation with a stranger on the train while Charlie has gone to the bar, as a result of which Charlie refuses to accompany her when they reach her home town and her waiting parents. Whereas the roots of Lily's ambivalence are not only revealed, but are made to serve as the basis of a social critique, Cynthia's ambivalence remains a mystery to herself and little more than a caricature of confusion to the reader. While she is a step ahead of the wife in "The Parking Lot" in the path toward self-consciousness, Cynthia will clearly never arrive even at the point reached by Jake Barnes in *The Sun Also Rises* when he says, "I did not care what it was all about. All I wanted to know was how to live in it."[4] Such a statement draws its force from the very possibility of meaning it denies, just as Hemingway's understated prose is fueled by the energy required to repress all those romantic desires to which it ironically refers, even clings. In the world of *Distortions*, however, the possibility of meaning is not even there to be denied. At the end of "Wolf Dreams," Cynthia sits alone at her parents' kitchen table and asks herself, "What am I trying to think about?" When she closes her eyes, all she can see is a picture of a "high white mountain. She isn't on it, or in the picture at all" (*D*, 167).

In the end, neither of these characters amounts to much more than a sketched figure that provides a focal point on which what might be called the idiocy of married life comes into view, in one as lived, in the other as both desired and spurned. Beattie's method here resembles that of the boy Bryce in the later story "Desire," when he cuts out a picture from a coloring book: "Bryce wasn't interested in coloring; he just wanted to cut out pictures so he could see what they looked like outside the book."[5] Like Bryce, whose efforts may well represent Beattie parodying herself, Beattie is here trying out oblique methods for gaining narrative access to lives that seem already flattened out, unreal. They remained flattened, but in "Marshall's Dog," she can be seen putting the cut-out pictures together in ways that begin to make them seem real.

"Marshall's Dog" is built out of segments arranged without apparent regard for chronology, plot sequence, or thematic development. The story opens with a segment describing Marshall's eighty-two-year-old mother. This is followed by a scene at Sam's cafe, where some teenage girls are being teased by a couple of boys. It turns out that one of them, Mary, is Marshall's niece. Marshall and his sister Edna live with their mother. Their brother, George, is Mary's father. George has had an affair with Beverly, a waitress in Sam's cafe.

Marshall and Edna drive a snowmobile. Marshall's dog shows up occasionally at the cafe.

As these facts emerge, we get a peculiar family portrait, peculiar because of the way the portrait is composed. One segment is often linked to the next by the most arbitrary verbal association. At the end of one section, Mary's mother offers to drive Mary to school and "looks at the car through the frosty window." The next section opens, "It is cold in the house," but this is Marshall's house, and this segment deals with Marshall's mother (D, 82). Or again, this segment ends with "the dog is barking. The soup is boiling over," a statement that seems, but actually is not, continuous with the opening line of the next segment, "What a mess" (D, 83). This "mess," it turns out, refers to the pizza smeared on Mary's shirt at Sam's cafe one summer when Mary is fifteen. Such metonymic associations serve not only to connect segments, but also to generate them. The opening segment, for example, begins:

> She was eighty-two when she died. She had the usual old-lady fears—Democratic Presidents, broken bones. When the spaghetti was snapped in half and dropped into the boiling water she heard the sound of her own bones cracking. She loved spaghetti. They had to eat so much spaghetti. She wouldn't eat the sauce. She had butter with her spaghetti. She used to knit for her son, Marshall. She loved her son, she knitted all the time. Once she knitted him a bathrobe and he broke out in a rash all over, an allergy to wool. [D, 78]

Even when metaphors appear, they refuse to function normally—that is, to create and develop symbolic meanings. Instead, they act as metonymy does in Roman Jakobson's theory, returning to the relations of contiguity which generate narrative movement.[6] Here, "old-lady fears" lead to "broken bones." "Broken bones" are like "spaghetti . . . snapped in half," but rather than building on this metaphor, the narrator goes on to what accompanies the spaghetti—sauce or butter. Spaghetti is, again, like yarn. But no sooner is that similarity functioning than it collapses once more into metonymic roaming until it reaches its end in the memory of Marshall's rash.

In a sense, the whole of "Marshall's Dog" is generated by this metonymic association, as if Beattie simply picked up one thread and then another in a piece of fabric, pulling each until it would not give any more, but meanwhile gathering the cloth into a pattern that highlights its textures. The technique resembles smocking. Such a conceit, however, fails to capture what is most elusive and disturbing about Beattie's metonymic method here—its capacity to substitute for the closure of a conventional plot development, a closure that feels like the expiration of a breath or of a life. The story opens with an announcement of the old lady's death but ends with the death of Marshall's dog, which serves as the referent for the title. But these deaths do not stand in any resonant symbolic relation to each other. Rather, when Marshall's dog is run over in the snow, it is simply that all the metonymic lines have been played out. They do not meet on some symbolic note; there is no epiphany, either about dogs or death. They simply exhaust themselves. Such a technique has the curious effect of making the arbitrary seem real, or perhaps of revealing how arbitrary is the real.

If, however, this world is real in some sense, it remains off balance, leaving us hoping that we have missed something. The title of the story underscores this quality. Marshall's dog is given pride of place even though its death evokes no great pathos. Unlike some of Beattie's dogs, it is genuinely peripheral to the lives of the characters. The dog is not there, throughout, and at the end it is not there for good. Perhaps, after all, it is the missing center, what is not there, that throws the metonymic engine into gear.

A similar technique is used to comic effect in "It's Just Another Day in Big Bear City, California." This story opens with a paragraph worth quoting in full:

Spaceship, flying saucer, an hallucination . . . they don't know yet. They don't even notice it until it is almost over their car. Estelle, who has recently gone back to college, is studying Mortuary Science. Her husband, Alvin William "Big Bear" Benton, is so drunk from the party they have just left that he wouldn't notice if it were Estelle, risen from the passenger seat, up in the sky. Maybe that's where she'd like to be—floating in the sky. Or in the morgue with bodies. Big Bear Benton thinks she is completely nuts, and people who are nuts can do anything. *Will* do anything. Will go back to school after ten years and study Mortuary Science. It's enough to make him get drunk at parties. They used to ask his wife about the children at these parties, but now they ask, subtly, about the bodies. They are more interested in dead bodies than his two children. So is Estelle. He is not interested in anything, according to his wife, except going to parties and getting drunk. [D, 232]

Like the opening of "Marshall's Dog," this paragraph moves from one idea to another along a metonymic axis, but instead of repeatedly running down, the chain circles back on itself, and the next paragraph starts over from the same point: "Spaceship, flying saucer, an hallucination. . . ."

At the center of this paragraph is the logical circularity: Estelle is studying mortuary science and therefore she is "nuts"; Estelle is "nuts" and therefore she is studying mortuary science. This, we learn, is why Big Bear gets drunk at parties, although it is also clear from the final sentence that it is because Big Bear is not interested in anything except going to parties and getting drunk that Estelle has gone back to school. One is reminded of R.D. Laing's knots. Big Bear and Estelle constitute a double bind, both sides of which the story proceeds to elaborate. Beattie builds the story out of segments, pieces of dialogue, and narration that represent both the past (this party, other parties, Estelle's brother's death in Vietnam) and the future (Estelle's and Big Bear's interaction with the spacemen, Donald, Fred, and Bobby). The illusion of moving forward in time, however, is undermined, not only by the use of the present tense, but also by the fact that the development of the story is actually organized around the drive to expand the implications of the opening paragraph metonymically.

Thus, for example, because Big Bear's son learns that there is a Big Bear City in California, we are eventually shown a scene in Big Bear City in which a child and his mother try to get a soft drink out of a broken dispensing machine in a gas station. Because Estelle lets the spaceman Bobby take a picture of her "mooning," Bobby is later depicted showing the picture to his friend on Mars. Because Estelle and Big Bear drive her dead brother's Peugeot, Estelle's brother is seen dying on a field in Vietnam, wondering "what will happen to his Peugeot" (*D*, 244). The story expands across space and time as if it were pursuing its associative links at random, until it can find a reasonable place to stop. Like "Marshall's Dog," though even more pointedly, the story comes to rest on a purely arbitrary close, ending with the line that becomes its title, "It's just another day in Big Bear City, California."

Unlike "Marshall's Dog," however, this story is propelled by metonymic associations that are fueled by an impulse we can see at work in other Beattie stories, such as "Imagined Scenes" or "Fancy Flights"—the desire for a fantasy that will prove different, better, richer than the reality in which the characters are caught. If you began with a hallucination that proved to be real, you would expect this desire to be fulfilled. Yet the scenes on Mars are virtually indistinguishable from those on earth. Little boys want goldfish or soft drinks; the goldfish die and the machines fail to deliver. Mothers are frustrated. Estelle's "hands roam around in dead bodies the way coyotes roam around the desert," Big Bear thinks, "just for something to do" (*D*, 232). In many of the segments, moreover, the same circular dialogue repeats itself, not only between Big Bear and Estelle, but also between the card saleswoman and her husband and between the spaceman Bobby and his son.[7] As the fantasy expands, it not only repeats itself in different settings, but also grows more familiar, more real. It's just another day in Big Bear City, California. It is as if something like free association led in a circle back to the quotidian.

Whether comic or somber, these early stories produce a vision of a world in a state of lack. Henry James would have called Beattie's a scenic method, and would have been right up to the point at which he would have despaired at the lack of a center. But it is that lack of a center which distinguishes Beattie's narrative method. Beginning with a set of characters in situation and bringing them into focus only gradually—and then obliquely—Beattie exposes and develops them as if they were a piece of film. This is both the virtue and the defect of her early work, and it is signaled, I think, by the title she gave her first collection. For *Distortions* refers not only to the distorted forms of human life portrayed in the stories, but also to the distortion implicit in her method of representation. Beattie's various means of telling-it-slant tell a certain truth, perhaps, but a limited one.

As I have indicated, the most significant advantage of Beattie's method is the remakable economy that it facilitates. Exposition is always deftly woven into narration. Sometimes this technique leaves the reader in doubt about the relations that the narration develops. "Victor Blue," for instance, obscures the gender of the narrative voice, destabilizing the reader's perspective for much of the story. Here, the lack of discrete exposition is exploited to provoke sudden, retrospective enlightenment; the narrator is not, we discover, a sister or companion to Ms. Edway, but is *Mr.* Edway. More often, however, the exposition spun out along with the narration has no such dramatic function, but serves rather to represent characters as fused with their contexts—geographical, familial, social—from the outset. While the result is striking in its capacity to encompass character and background in one narrative motion, the price paid for such economy is high. Characters so fused to their contexts cannot stand out from them, much less alter them. This sense of characters fused to a frame, of course, is most marked in such stories as "The Parking Lot," but even in "Marshall's Dog" or "Big Bear" it is less the development of characters than the deft manipulation of the frames by which the illusion of motion and change is created. The metonymic associations expand the frame, elaborating a larger picture, but the characters remain fixed within it.

It would be possible to argue, of course, that such limits are built into the genre of the short story itself, the art of which is that of revelation rather than of complex development. But the advance marked by *The Burning House* suggests that Beattie is more than capable of expanding these limits. (I pass over *Secrets and Surprises*, Beattie's intervening and transitional volume of stories, for the sake of economy.) The same techniques we have seen her use in *Distortions* are recognizable in *The Burning House*—story construction by segment, simultaneous narration and exposition, reliance on metonymy and the present tense—but here they produce a far more resonant result.

The economy mastered in *Distortions*, for example, is now put to more ambitious uses. In "Learning to Fall," Beattie tells one story, at the same time using it to tell another. One story is Ruth's. Ruth is the mother of Andrew, an eight-year-old who has suffered slight brain damage and facial paralysis as a result of a mangled forceps delivery. Andrew's father left Ruth six months before Andrew was born. Ruth teaches at a community college, where she earns hardly any money. Once or twice a month, her lover, Brandon, comes to spend the day with her. "Like many people," Brandon envies Ruth. "He would like to be her, but he does not want to take her on. Or Andrew" (*BH*, 9). When Brandon visits Ruth, Andrew goes to the city with Ruth's friend, who tells the story and whose own story eventually emerges in the course of her narration. She is married to one man, Arthur, and in love with another, Ray. Although she has broken up with Ray, she meets him in the city when she takes Andrew there. Indeed, it was when she quit being Ray's lover that she began taking Andrew to the city. By the third page her story begins to creep out around the edges of Ruth's and eventually encircles it. In effect, one narrative serves as exposition for the other, and then they change places, Ruth's story providing context for the narrator's.

By the end of the day in New York, where events form the actual narrative line, the unnamed narrator has given up trying to resist loving Ray. Taking her cue from Ruth, whose dance instructor has been teaching her to fall and is her model of valor in the face of an unjust fate, the narrator recognizes "what Ruth has known all along: what will happen can't be stopped. Aim for grace" (*BH*, 14). Here the associations by which the story unfolds are far more controlled than those in *Distortions*. One source of control is Beattie's use of a first-person narrator, a choice she makes far more often in *The Burning House* than in *Distortions*. As a consequence, what the narrator sees and does is circumscribed and guided by her own preoccupations. Further, while they seem to unroll metonymically as before, the associations turn out to be partially metaphorical, to build a loose structure of meaning. The pool of blue water at the bottom of the Guggenheim is related to Hall's Pond, where Ruth swam the day before Andrew was born; it is related in terms made explicit by the narrator when she hears herself admonishing Andrew not to drop pennies into the pool from the walkway because he might hurt somebody. Realizing the irony of protecting others from a child himself mangled at birth by an impatient doctor, she feels guilty, a feeling later made specific by her recognition that she has been using Andrew as an excuse to meet Ray. Meanwhile, Hall's Pond, introduced in the preceding segment in a scene remembered merely because it preceded Andrew's birth, has begun to function as the basis for a set of images in which birth, pain, pools, and drowning prefigure the narrator's own fears of letting go, losing control. Consequently, when the story lands on the line "Aim for grace," its almost onomatopoeic resonance derives from a whole train of moments of which this line is the echo and the culmination.

If such a reading seems strained, it is—at least in the sense that such images are never allowed by Beattie to sit around festering with symbolic meaning in the way such a reading might imply. The story unfolds with an easy grace, moving from one scene to the next until the day's end, and it does so by means of the techniques that I have described—apparently random associations recorded in the present tense, incorporating exposition seamlessly along the way. What is new here is that when the reader reaches the end, something has changed. The narrator has reached a turning point toward which the story has been driving all along. She has learned to fall, a phrase whose verbal origin may seem arbitrary, but whose meaning is enriched by its appropriateness to Ruth's entire life.

Beattie's stories now end, then, with more than arbitrary closes because their associations are no longer purely arbitrary. And whether it is cause or effect of Beattie's technical control in *The Burning House,* her characters have also changed. They are more likable, and their relationships with each other are stronger, whether for good or bad. The women, particularly, move out of their frames and come alive, whether with love and envy, as in "Playback," or with lonely terror, as in "Waiting." There is the same sense of something lost, something missing, but Beattie is now zeroing in on it, sometimes even naming it. In the title story, "The Burning House," a woman wonders why, though she has "known everybody in the house for years," she knows them "all less and less" as time goes by, and then she finds out. "Your whole life you've made one mistake," her husband tells her at the end, "you've surrounded yourself with men." He continues: "Let me tell you something. All men—if they're crazy, like Tucker, if they're gay as the Queen of the May, like Reddy Fox, even if they're just six years old—I'm going to tell you something about them. Men think they're Spider-Man and Buck Rogers and Superman. You know what we all feel inside that you don't feel? That we're going to the stars" (*BH*, 241). A comic epiphany, this, but with a punch, since it accounts perfectly for the behavior of every man in the story.

The power of Beattie's endings is even more evident in "Running Dreams." Here again, the first person enables Beattie to exploit old techniques to a more ambitious end. A series of discontinuous scenes delivered in the present tense portrays two couples, both estranged, but for different reasons, spending a weekend together and just barely keeping their building anger, fear, and hostility from exploding. This is a common enough situation for Beattie, but here the peripheral, dissociated qualities of these people's lives, emblematized by the David Hockney drawing they discuss at one point, is both set in relief and blown away—almost literally—by the final paragraph, in which the narrator, Lynn, recounts a memory of her dying father:

I didn't know my father was dying. I knew that something was wrong, but I didn't know what dying was. I've always known simple things: how to read the letter a stranger hands me and nod, how to do someone a favor when they don't have my strength. I remember that my father was bending over—stooped with pain, I now realize—and that he was winter-pale, though he died before cold weather came. I remember standing with him in a room that seemed immense to me at the time, in sunlight as intense as the explosion from a flashbulb. If someone had taken that photograph, it would have been a picture of a little girl and her father about to go on a walk. I held my hands out to him, and he pushed the fingers of the gloves tightly down each of my fingers, patiently, pretending to have all the time in the world, saying, "This is the way we get ready for winter." [*BH*, 197]

This description does more than reveal why Lynn is the strongest person in the group, although that is one of its purposes. By placing the present in context with the past, it shakes the present to its roots, exposing its emotional poverty when seen in relation to a scene of poignant plenitude. Finally, it is noteworthy that Beattie uses the photograph as an image here. The "picture of a little girl" imagined would resemble a host of pictures drawn from Beattie's earlier stories. It is as if she were placing an example of her earlier work into a new context, where it comes alive.

In *Distortions*, Beattie was spinning a net of words with which to catch life in motion almost at random. Her means were often extravagant, and extravagantly displayed, as in "Big Bear City" or in other stories such as "Wally Whistles Dixie," a parody of J.D. Salinger. In *The Burning House*, no such display is made of the artist's artistry, and there is nothing random about her aim. Yet the techniques developed in *Distortions* clearly served as necessary apprentice work for the lucid perfection of many of the stories in *The Burning House.* "Winter: 1978," the most ambitious story in the volume and arguably the finest piece of work Beattie has done so far, presupposes stories such as "Marshall's Dog" but leaves them far behind in its mastery of a similar subject—a group of people whose relations are captured in an emotional nexus in time.

The advance marked by "Winter: 1978" seems partly the result of a technique of juxtaposition. Just as in "Learning to Fall" two narrative planes operate in relation to each other and in "Running Dreams" the past suddenly stands over against the present, in "Winter: 1978" two settings, California and Connecticut, serve to enforce the story's move from a hollowed-out now to a then that proves almost as empty. Like many of the characters in *The Burning House,* Nick and Benton in "Winter: 1978" are the now successful members of the baby-boom generation. Benton's art sells well in L.A., through the agency of one Allen Tompkins, whose library in Beverly Hills is "illuminated by lamps with bases in the shape of upright fish that supported huge Plexiglass conch shell globes in their mouths" (*BH,* 79). Nick has made money in the record industry and spends his time making sure that such bands as "Barometric Pressure" are provided with chicken tacos. Both Nick and Benton come from wealthy families, but their own successes are personal, although accidental. Benton's work was discovered by Tompkins one night in the framing shop where Benton worked. Nick's entrance into the record industry is the result of his getting a job in exchange for making a dope connection with the former supplier of a philosophy professor's daughter.

"Winter: 1978" portrays these characters as they confront death, specifically the death of Benton's younger brother, Wesley, and generally the death of their youth. The story is constructed, as usual, out of segments, but because the past tense is used, the segments are ordered almost conventionally. They depict events that proceed chronologically in a single sequence, beginning in Los Angeles, where Nick lives and where Benton has come with his girl friend, Olivia, to sell his latest pictures to Tompkins, and ending in Connecticut, where Wesley has drowned and has been buried before Benton could be reached. That Nick should accompany Benton and Olivia back to Connecticut almost as if he were along for the ride is made entirely plausible by the portrait of life in L.A. with which the story opens. Once in Connecticut, however, Nick serves as a center of consciousness, sufficiently out of the picture to see it whole, yet sufficiently involved by his own common history with Wesley and Benton to take it personally.

For Nick, the East is home. As soon as he is headed there, he remembers "what Thanksgiving used to be like, and the good feeling he got as a child when the holidays came and it snowed" (BH, 86). He wishes for snow throughout his visit. In a passage that echoes Nick Carraway's famous description of his Midwest, Nick drives past "houses that stood close to the road. There was nothing in California that corresponded to the lights burning in big old New England houses at night" (BH, 105). Nick's sentimental longing for the New England winters of his youth, is undercut by the scene he confronts in Connecticut. Wesley's mother, Ena, presides over a parody of the "big old New England houses" of Nick's memories. She has assembled the fragments of her family at Wesley's house as a "tribute to Wesley—no matter that in the six months he'd lived there he never invited the family to his house" (BH, 90). She relentlessly invokes a rural New England tradition, ordering wood, for instance, from Hanley Paulson whom she seems to regard as a trusted servant of the gentry. It is not Paulson, however, who shows up with the wood, but his son, who steals all Wesley's pumpkins. The entire scene at Wesley's house testifies to the gap between Nick's sentimental image of New England and the reality of a world all too reminiscent of California. Uncle Cal, for example, has recently moved to East Hampton and hired a vegetarian decorator named Morris, "who paints the walls the color of carrots and turnips" (BH, 101).

Similarly, Nick's romantic memories of his own youth are undercut once his discrete images come unraveled. A snowy Christmas scene turns into a revelation of family disorder when Nick recalls his father's drunken impersonation of William Tell. The image of a large red stocking his uncle had hung for him during another Christmas turns into another scene of conflict between his uncle and his father. The only images that resist such disintegration are those Wesley saw and photographed.

Wesley's photographs—of wind chimes hanging on a broomstick in a graveyard, of a "tombstone with a larger-than-life dog stretched on top" (BH, 92), of Nick's hands folded on top of the New York Times—provide the only clues to a puzzle that no one save Nick is really concerned to solve: who Wesley was. Recalling Wesley's photographs becomes for Nick a means of mourning, although primarily a mourning for the loss of his own youth. Looking at his hands, Nick realizes that "what Wesley had seen about them had never come true" (*BH*, 105). Wesley himself remains an enigma whose death is appropriately imagined in the form of a photograph of two bright orange life vests floating beside a boat in water "gray and deep," a photograph Nick captions "Lake Champlain: 1978" (*BH*, 93). Such captions suggest why these images retain their force. As Nick remarks, "Photographer gets a shot of a dwarf running out of a burning hotel and it's labeled 'New York: 1968'" (*BH*, 92). The caption refuses to refer to the people or events photographed. It refers only to when and where the photographer was when he took the picture. This, the caption suggests, is what he saw at that time and in that place. No comment. No explanation. Even to inquire how the effect of a picture was achieved is a vain endeavor. When Nick asks Wesley how he got the "softness" in the picture of his hands, Wesley replies, "I developed it in acufine" (*BH*, 93).

Such photographs resemble Beattie's earlier stories in their insistence on simply portraying a scene without comment or interpretation. What and where take such precedence over why as almost to annihilate it. But here, such photographic images serve a larger narrative interest. "Lake Champlain: 1978" cannot be explicated. It cannot be read as a symbolic construct. But because it is situated within a narrative about time and loss, it can function not merely as an image, but as an experience of time and loss, as it manifestly does for Nick: "He had to catch his breath when the image formed. He was as shocked as if he had been there when they recovered the body" (*BH*, 93). The imagined photograph becomes an event in the story, specifically the event of Wesley's death as witnessed by Nick, and the story, in turn, becomes "Winter: 1978" because it recounts an equally resonant moment. On the one hand, Nick's images of New England unravel, as Connecticut and the past are exposed as the same world as California and the present, a world in which parents try to get rid of their children only to pretend to themselves later that they always cared. But his is not merely the ironic loss of something that never existed, for on the other hand, he experiences a real loss, one described perfectly in Benton's closing speech to his son, Jason: "Benton told him this fact of evolution: that one day dinosaurs shook off their scales and sucked in their breath until they became much smaller. This caused the dinosaurs' brains to pop through their skulls. The brains were called antlers, and the dinosaurs deer. That was why deer had such sad eyes, Benton told Jason—because they were once something else" (*BH*, 113). The cryptic copyright notice in *The Burning House*, "Irony & Pity, Inc.," is ironic in its self-reflectiveness, but it speaks as well to Beattie's larger capacity for pity.

If, as I have argued, Beattie's narrative method works by a metonymic unraveling, a movement from one detail to the next, her advances in *The Burning House* derive from a new focus on and control of that method. Her more frequent use of the first person, her willingness to let metaphors grow from and give resonance to the train of associations on which her stories ride, her use of the past tense—all these are marks of an author still experimenting, but with tools now refined and proven. The distance she has crossed could also be measured by comparing *Chilly Scenes of Winter* with *Falling in Place*, but her second novel fails, in my judgment, to live up to the promise of "Winter: 1978." It remains to be seen whether Beattie's techniques can be made to work for the novel, but they have already made something new of the short story, enabling it to cut into contemporary life where it hurts.

NOTES

1. Henry James, *The Art of the Novel: Critical Prefaces*, ed. R.P. Blackmur (New York: Charles Scribner's Sons, 1934), 120.

2. See George Lukacs, *Studies in European Realism* (New York: Grosset & Dunlap, 1964), and Jean Paul Sartre, *Search for a Method*, trans. Hazel E. Barnes (New York: Vintage Books, 1968).

3. Ann Beattie, *Distortions* (Garden City, N.Y.: Doubleday, 1976), 189; hereafter cited in the text as *D*.

4. Ernest Hemingway, *The Sun Also Rises* (New York: Scribner's, 1926), 148.

5. Ann Beattie, *The Burning House* (New York: Random House, 1982), 137; hereafter cited in the text as *BH*.

6. I am using metonymy here in a loose sense, although one that I believe remains rooted in Jakobson's theory. See his "Two Aspects of Language and Two Types of Linguistic Disturbances," in Roman Jakobson and Morris Hale, *Fundamentals of Language* (The Hague: Mouton, 1956), 58. For a discussion of metaphor and metonymy in modern literature, see David Lodge, *The Modes of Modern Writing: Metaphor, Metonymy, and the Typology of Modern Literature* (Ithaca, N.Y.: Cornell Univ. Press, 1977).

7. See *Distortions*, 242-43, 247, 248.

A Bibliography of Writings by

ANN BEATTIE

Carolyn Porter

BOOKS

Chilly Scenes of Winter. New York: Doubleday, 1976.
Distortions. New York: Doubleday, 1976.
Secrets and Surprises. New York: Random House, 1979.
Falling in Place. New York: Random House, 1980.
Jacklighting. Worcester, Mass.: Metacom Press, 1981.
The Burning House. New York: Random House, 1982.
Love Always. New York: Random House, 1985.

SHORT STORIES

"Victor Blue." *Atlantic* 232 (December 1973): 112-14. [Reprinted in *Distortions.*]

"A Platonic Relationship." *New Yorker* 50 (8 April 1974): 42-46. [Reprinted in *Distortions.*]

"Imagined Scenes." *Texas Quarterly* 17 (Summer 1974): 52-60. [Reprinted in *Distortions.*]

"Fancy Flights." *New Yorker* 50 (21 October 1974): 40-46. [Reprinted in *Distortions.*]

"Wolf Dreams." *New Yorker* 50 (11 November 1974): 45-51. [Reprinted in *Distortions.*]

"Dwarf House." *New Yorker* 50 (20 January 1975): 34-83. [Reprinted in *Distortions.*]

"Snakes' Shoes." *New Yorker* 51 (3 March 1975): 36-40. [Reprinted in *Distortions.*]

"Vermont." *New Yorker* 51 (21 April 1975): 36-44. [Reprinted in *Distortions.*]

"Downhill." *New Yorker* 51 (18 August 1975): 26-29. [Reprinted in *Distortions;* in *In the Looking Glass,* ed. Nancy Dean and Myra Stark (1977).]

"Wanda's." *New Yorker* 51 (6 October 1975): 37-44. [Reprinted in *Distortions.*]

"Colorado." *New Yorker* 52 (15 March 1976): 36-44. [Reprinted in *Secrets and Surprises.*]

"The Lawn Party." *New Yorker* 52 (5 July 1976): 26-32. [Reprinted in *Secrets and Surprises.*]

"Eric Clapton's Lover." *Virginia Quarterly Review* 52 (Summer 1976): 486-94. [Reprinted in *Distortions.*]

"Secrets and Surprises." *New Yorker* 52 (25 October 1976): 40-46. [Reprinted in *Secrets and Surprises.*]

"Weekend." *New Yorker* 52 (15 November 1976): 46-54. [Reprinted in *Secrets and Surprises.*]

"Tuesday Night." *New Yorker* 52 (2 January 1977): 29-31. [Reprinted in *Solo: Women on Woman Alone*, ed. Linda and Leo Hamalian (1977); in *Secrets and Surprises.*]

"Shifting." *New Yorker* 53 (21 February 1977): 38-44. [Reprinted in *Secrets and Surprises.*]

"Distant Music." *New Yorker* 53 (4 July 1977): 27-32. [Reprinted in *Secrets and Surprises.*]

"A Vintage Thunderbird." *New Yorker* 54 (27 February 1978): 32-40. [Reprinted in *Secrets and Surprises.*]

"The Cinderella Waltz." *New Yorker* 54 (29 January 1979): 28-36. [Reprinted in *Prize Stories, 1980: The O'Henry Awards*, ed. William Abrahams (1980); in *The Burning House.*]

"The Burning House." *New Yorker* 55 (11 June 1979: 34-40. [Reprinted in *The Burning House.*]

"Greenwich Time." *New Yorker* 55 (29 October 1979): 36-41. [Reprinted in *The Burning House.*]

"Waiting." *New Yorker* 55 (20 August 1979): 24-28. [Reprinted in *The Burning House.*]

"Learning to Fall." *Ms.* 8 (January 1980): 54. [Reprinted in *The Burning House.*]

"Gravity." *New Yorker* 56 (2 June 1980): 40-42. [Reprinted in *The Burning House.*]

"About Love, Guilt, Infidelity on a New York Summer Night." *Vogue* 170 (July 1980): 148.

"Running Dreams." *New Yorker* 56 (16 February 1981): 36-40. [Reprinted in *The Burning House.*]

"Playback." *Vogue* 171 (February 1981): 152. [Reprinted in *The Burning House.*]

"Afloat." *New Yorker* 57 (21 September 1981): 38-40. [Reprinted in *The Burning House.*]

"Girl Talk." *New Yorker* 57 (7 December 1981): 46-49. [Reprinted in *The Burning House.*]

"Mr. B and the Miraculous Christmas Tree." *House and Garden* 153 (December 1981): 78.

"A Reasonable Man." In *The Treasury of American Short Stories*, ed. Nancy S. Sullivan. New York: Doubleday, 1981.

"Winter: 1978." In *Best American Short Stories, 1981*, ed. Hortense Calisher and Shannon Ravenel. New York: Houghton-Mifflin, 1981. [Reprinted in *The Burning House.*]

"Sunshine and Shadow." *Atlantic* 249 (January 1982): 42-45. [Reprinted in *The Burning House.*]

"Like Glass." *New Yorker* 58 (22 February 1982): 40-42. [Reprinted in *The Burning House.*]

"Blue . . . A Short Story." *Vogue* 172 (April 1982): 376-77.

"Desire." *New Yorker* 58 (14 June 1982): 34-39. [Reprinted in *The Burning House.*]

"Moving Water." *New Yorker* 58 (8 November 1982): 38-42.

"Coney Island." *New Yorker* 58 (24 January 1983): 34-37.

"Television." *New Yorker* 59 (28 March 1983): 32-34.

"Lofty." *New Yorker* 59 (8 August 1983): 30-31.

"One Day." *New Yorker* 59 (29 August 1983): 28-31.

"Heaven on a Summer Night." *New Yorker* 59 (28 November 1983): 52-55.

"Times." *New Yorker* 59 (26 December 1983): 36-39.

"In the White Night." *New Yorker* 60 (4 June 1984): 42-43.

"Summer People." *New Yorker* 60 (24 September 1984): 46-53.

"Janus." *New Yorker* 61 (27 May 1985): 33-35.

ARTICLE

"Journals." *Film Comment* 17 (September/October 1981): 2.

GRACE PALEY

Chaste Compactness

Ronald Schleifer

Life is a newborn who bears, who plays.

—Heraclitus[1]

Enclosed in this "elsewhere," an "enceinte" woman loses communital
meaning, which suddenly appears to her as worthless, absurd, or at best,
comic—a surface agitation severed from its impossible foundations.
. . . Here, alterity becomes nuance, contradiction becomes a variant,
tension becomes passage, and discharge becomes peace.

—Julia Kristeva[2]

In a recent interview Grace Paley discussed the relation between her
storytelling and the fact that she is a woman. "For a long time," she
said, "I thought women's lives . . . I didn't really think I was shit, but I
really thought my life as a woman was shit. Who could be interested
in this crap? I was very interested in it, but I didn't have enough social
ego to put it down. . . . Women who have thought their lives were
boring have found they're interesting to one another."[3] Paley is speaking of the difficult discovery of what Jonathan Culler, following
Elaine Showalter, has recently called the possibility of "reading as a
woman,"[4] the discovery, that is, that the *position* of a woman—what
Culler calls "the experience of being watched, seen as a 'girl,' re-
stricted, marginalized" and what Paley calls simply the experience of
the ordinary boredom of a woman's life—can offer articulations of
experience that can "show," as Paley goes on to say, "how mysterious
ordinary life is."[5] Reading as a woman, then, is not only reading from
the margin—what Gayatri Spivak calls a "feminization" of reading
that problematizes the subject of discourse[6]—but also a reading that
articulates another version of experience altogether. It is, as Peggy

Photo by Diana Davies

Kamuf has written, to read a text as if it were written by a woman: "reading it *as if* it had no (determined) father, *as if,* in other words, it were illegitimate, recognized by its mother who can only give it a borrowed name."[7] Reading as a woman transforms the form and authority of fiction so that the boring quotidian concerns Paley could not imagine as the legitimate subject of art are transformed into concern for the ordinary ongoingness of the surface of things—not only their comic agitations, but, as I will argue, their chaste compactness without depths—that characterizes Paley's short stories.

Paley has also said that the subject of her writing—"life, death, desertion, loss, divorce, failure, love"—is "daily life. I wouldn't call it ordinary, just daily life. . . . And I'm very anti-symbolical. . . . I don't write anything but what I'm writing about. I'm not writing about meaning beyond meaning."[8] Paley uses her situation as a woman, and especially her situation as a mother, to eschew the appropriation and totalization of "meaning"—its authority and form—for a more spacious conception of life. The appropriation of meaning is a species of will to power; it is an attempt, as Kamuf says, to "contain an unlimited textual system, install a measure of protection between this boundlessness and one's own power to know, to be this power and to know that one is this power."[9] In contrast to a plural voice, the appropriating voice is what Mary Jacobus calls "the unified 'I' which falls as a dominating phallic shadow across the male page, like Casaubon's monumental egotism."[10]

Against this power of subject and form Julia Kristeva posits the spaciousness Paley attempts to narrate as "a nexus of life and language (of species and society)—the child." In the writings of Rousseau and Freud, Kristeva explains,

it was as if Reason were suddenly neither satisfied simply to test its restraining bond by confronting texts, nor to strain meaning by writing the speaking being's identity as fiction; it was forced, instead, to face reproduction of the species (the boundary between "nature" and "culture") and the varied attitudes toward it. Reason was thus transcended by a *heterogeneous element* (biology: life) and by a *third party* (I/you communication is displaced by *it*: the child). These challenge the speaker with the fact that he is not whole, but they do so in a manner altogether different from that in which the obsessed person's wretched consciousness ceaselessly signifies his bondage to death. For if death is the Other, life is a third party; and as this signification, asserted by the child, is disquieting, it might well unsettle the speaker's paranoid enclosure.[11]

The position between species and society, nature and culture, transforms the Other of death into the "third party" of life: an other figured by Kristeva as a child. This, she argues, is best comprehended from the *position* of woman, and thus she sees the artist as someone who "gives birth," just as Paley describes the subject of her art simply as "daily life." In this situation, "sublation here is both eroticizing without residue and a disappearance of eroticism as it returns to its source." "The speaker reaches this limit," Kristeva continues, "this requisite of sociality, only by virtue of a particular, discursive practice called "art." A woman also attains it (and in our society, *especially*) through the strange form of split symbolization (threshold of language and instinctual drive, of the "symbolic" and the "semiotic") of which the act of giving birth consists. [12]

This is the *position* of a woman that Paley articulates in her stories. Paley's woman is marginalized without "interest," excluded from power, illegitimate. She is the mother who recognizes a world of life beyond herself in her children; an artist who recognizes voices besides her own in her "work"; and a citizen who recognizes a world—"tornadoes," "flood," "catastrophes of God"—beyond her own concerns. As she says, her stories deal with ordinary relations between men and women—life, death, desertion, loss, divorce, failure, love—and her stories aim, as I shall argue, at reconceiving the form of storytelling by reconceiving their endings and at discovering a different authority of telling by articulating a new sense of their subject's relation to voice. At her best, Paley achieves the chaste compact spaciousness of short stories in which authority does not come from deathbed pronouncements and summings up, but can best be figured in terms of birthbeds, listening, and calling forth voices.

Storytelling: The Play of Endings

> There is nothing that commends a story to memory more effectively than the chaste compactness which precludes psychological analysis. And the more natural the process by which the storyteller forgoes psychological shading, the greater becomes the story's claim to a place in the memory of the listener, the more completely is it integrated into his own experience, the greater will be his inclination to repeat it to someone else someday, sooner or later.
>
> —Walter Benjamin [13]

The goal of Paley's storytelling can be seen in one of her best early stories, "The Pale Pink Roast," in *The Little Disturbances of Man*. Anna and her daughter accidentally meet Peter, Anna's former husband and Judy's father, as they walk through the park. They have not seen each other in several years, and when Peter learns that Anna is moving back to New York, he finds a sitter for Judy and goes to help

Anna move in. In her new and expensive apartment "Peter put up the Venetian blinds, followed by the curtains. He distributed books among the available bookcases. He glued the second drawer of Judy's bureau. . . . He whistled while he worked."[14] Afterwards, they kiss: "She was faint and leaden, a sure sign in Anna, if he remembered correctly, of passion. 'Shall we dance?' he asked softly, a family joke. With great care, a patient lover, he undid the sixteen tiny buttons of her pretty dress and in Judy's room on Judy's bed he took her at once without a word. Afterwards, having established tenancy, he rewarded her with kisses. He dressed quickly because he was obliged by the stories of his life to remind her of transience" (LD, 50).

Over coffee in the next room, Peter asks Anna how she can afford her new apartment, and she answers that her new husband, who will be following her from Rochester in a few days, is quite successful in business. Peter is dumbfounded: "You're great, Anna. Man, you're great. You wiggle your ass. You make a donkey out of me and him both. You could've said no. . . . Why'd you do it? Revenge? Meanness? Why?" "Wait a minute, Peter," she says; "Honest to God, listen to me, I did it for love" (LD 51). In this interchange, virtually at the end of the story, Paley offers a sense of their whole married life together: how Peter is not able to notice what is happening right before him, but seeks instead to find the meaning and explanation of his experience. There is no symbolic significance in this ordinary conversation after lovemaking—Paley offers us no psychological analysis—the conversation is simply there, calling for interpretation rather than providing explanation.

Such a call is intrinsic in all stories, according to Paley: a story is embedded in life. A story does not show life from the vantage point of the ending. A story eschews the egotism of meaning—Peter's understanding of Anna's behavior solely as a *symbolic* gesture in relation to himself—in favor (like life, like children) of possibilities. A story, for Paley, in Walter Benjamin's expression, is an "exchange of experiences"; its value lies in the possible readings it provokes, the necessity of its repetition, and in the fact that, as Benjamin continues, it "sinks the thing into the life of the storyteller, in order to bring it out of him again. Thus traces of the storyteller cling to the story the way the handprints of the potter cling to the clay vessel."[15]

Here we can see why many reviewers of Paley's work have noted the extraordinary power of her stories to articulate different voices, and we can see why she herself emphasizes storytelling as a form of listening.

Speaking of her first stories, Paley has said, "And before I wrote those stories, I was just stuck in my own voice. Until I was able to use other people's voices, that I'd been hearing all my life, you know, I was just talking me-me-me. While I was doing that, I couldn't write these stories. And when I was able to get into other voices consciously, or use what I was hearing, and become the story hearer—when I could do that, I just suddenly wrote them. It was a true breakthrough." What Peter cannot do is tell the story in Anna's voice; he cannot see her love when it is right before him. Other characters in Paley also cannot listen and retell stories: Mrs. Raftery has only her own voice, "distanced" from others, while the narrator of "A Conversation with My Father," in *Enormous Changes at the Last Minute*, has learned the patience to wait and listen. "Well," she tells her father, "you just have to let the story lie around till some agreement can be reached between you and the stubborn hero." "Aren't you talking silly, now?" her father answers.[17]

Her father thinks she is talking silly because, like Peter, he wants to discover the meaning of her stories: he wants her characters to have backgrounds, stock, character, direction, truth, meaning ("Tragedy! Plain tragedy! Historical tragedy! No hope. The end" [*EC*, 167]). That is, he wants a plot like a line—in his dying he *sees* that plot is inexorably like a line. Against this notion the daughter says, it is "plot, the absolute line between two points, which I've always despised. Not for literary reasons, but because it takes all hope away. Everyone, real or invented, deserves the open destiny of life" (*EC*, 162).

What the daughter is interested in—what the story embedded in "A Conversation with My Father" offers—is a sense of the surface of things, the ordinary disturbances of everyday life, not their depths. As John tells Ginny in "An Interest in Life," her list of troubles would never get her on "Strike It Rich": " 'No question in my mind at all,' said John. 'Have you ever seen that program? I mean, in addition to all of this—the little disturbances of man'—he waved a scornful hand at my list—'they *suffer*. They live in the forefront of tornadoes, their lives are washed off by flood—catastrophes of God. Oh, Virginia' " (*LD*, 99). What Ginny hopes for—what, after all, "Strike It Rich" or "Queen for a Day" offers—is enormous changes at the last minute. These changes, embodied in the titles of Paley's books, are part of her project as a storyteller: "Everyone would sit out on boxes and folding chairs and talk," Paley remembers of her childhood, "about in-laws, children, husbands, wives, what it was all about. That's what you listen for and expect when you're a kid: the next conversation will tell you what it's all about, if you only listen to it." Telling stories means listening to the real life of people—"everyone can tell one"[18]—articulating and discovering the possibility of change and freedom in the end.

As a woman, Paley is in a position to make such discoveries in stories. In Benjamin's study, entitled "The Storyteller," of the works of Nikolai Leskov, Benjamin argues that the story, as opposed to the novel, focuses on the most *ordinary* of things. While the novel, like Peter in "The Pale Pink Roast," attempts to fathom the "meaning of life," stories are both focused and based upon the ordinary: the ability to exchange experiences, the reality of boredom, and both the usualness and the authority of death. "There used to be no house," Benjamin writes,

hardly a room, in which someone had not once died. . . . Today people live in rooms that have never been touched by death. . . . It is, however, characteristic that not only a man's knowledge or wisdom, but above all his real life—and this is the stuff stories are made of—first assumes transmissible form at the moment of his death. . . . Suddenly in his expressions and looks the unforgettable emerges and imparts to everything that concerned him that authority which even the poorest wretch in dying possessses for the living around him. This authority is the very source of the story.[19]

What Benjamin leaves out in defining the authority of the story is the fact that people used to be born as well as die in those houses and rooms—a fact that the position and experience of being a woman makes more readily discernible. For Paley, stories concern themselves with real life and with things as ordinary (and as powerful and mysterious in their ordinariness) as birth and death. The concern for ordinary relations—transmissions—is central to Benjamin, yet he focuses on the authority of possession—*his* knowledge, *his* wisdom, the traces of the storyteller—rather than on that other authority of beginnings that Paley offers. Ongoingness is important to Benjamin—"actually," he says, "there is no story for which the questions as to how it continued could not be legitimate. The novelist, on the other hand, cannot take the smallest step beyond that limit at which he invites the reader to a divinatory realization of the meaning of life by writing 'Finis.'"[20] But ongoingness is accomplished in bequeathing possessions, not in the strange and complicated relations between generations living together.

Thus Benjamin's emphasis on possibility does not imply the resources of articulation that Paley, as a mother as well as a storyteller, possesses. At the end of "The Long-Distance Runner"—also the end of *Enormous Changes at the Last Minute*—Faith tells her story to her family:

I repeated the story. They all said, what?

Because it isn't usually so simple. Have you known it to happen much nowadays? A woman inside the steamy energy of middle age runs and runs. She finds the houses and streets where her childhood happened. She lives in them. She learns as though she was still a child what in the world is coming next. [*EC*, 198]

At the end of her collection Paley presents a story that combines beginning and ending, the imagined child as well as the middle-aged woman. Such a combination defines her storytelling, in which both the ordinary pain of a fact as commonplace as time making a monkey of us all and the possibility of some hoped-for change can be heard. That is, stories possess the authority of a living voice—even the disturbing authority of the last words of the suffering of living—yet they also possess that other authority (this is what makes them living) of transmission without possession; such transmission creates at least the illusion of enormous changes and new beginnings. Both kinds of authority are clearly seen in "A Conversation with My Father," where approaching death makes the father want to hear only his own story, a story that ends, and where also sympathy and love make the narrator conceive of her other story, which depicts an enormous change at the last minute for the addict, as a narrative of new beginnings.

This combination defines the characteristic endings of Paley's stories. Both little disturbances and enormous changes are brought together at the close of her stories to create a sense of ordinary ongoingness that eschews that melodrama of closure. Instead of articulating the meaning of life, her stories attempt to address ongoing life, to illuminate the play of closure and openness in "lives that haven't been seen."[21] At the end of "Wants" the heroine articulates her desire for both ending and not ending—"I want, for instance, to be a different person"; "I wanted to have been married forever to one person, my ex-husband or my present one" (*EC*, 5). Mrs. Raftery ends "Distance" by asking "What the devil is it all about, the noisiness and the speediness, when it's no distance at all? How come John had to put all the courtesy calls in to [his wife] Margaret on his lifelong trip to Ginny?" (*EC*, 26). "An Interest in Life" ends with John and Ginny on the kitchen floor making love, "and the truth is, we were so happy, we forgot the precautions" (*LD*, 101); "Living" ends with the placement of dying amid all the ordinary hubbub of life (*EC*, 61); and as we have seen, "The Pale Pink Roast" ends with the ordinary articulation of love. All Paley's endings are marked by a sense that life goes on.

But perhaps the most enormous of changes is the death of Samuel at the end of his story—a death Paley portrays, without melodrama, in the ordinariness of ongoing life: "Oh, oh, she hopelessly cried. She did not know how she could ever find another boy like that one. However, she was a young woman and she became pregnant. Then for a few months she was hopeful. The child born to her was a boy. They brought him to be seen and nursed. She smiled. But immediately she saw that this baby wasn't Samuel. She and her husband together have had other children, but never again will a boy exactly like Samuel be known" (EC, 106). Faced with the enormity of the changes she portrays, Paley eschews melodrama for the quotidian, the articulation of the ordinary. Rather than the melodrama of conclusion—whether it is the "Finis" of the novel or Peter's authoritative interpretation—she presents endings that project ongoing love, the authority of possibilities.

Thus the love articulated at the end of "The Pale Pink Roast" plays on the surface of life, a kind of fiction, an exchange of experience, a signifier of desire (which is also a surface experience). And even the title of this story suggests that experience can play rather than signify—so that alterity becomes nuance, contradiction a variant, tension a passage—and that experience can be valued in its activity, on the surface, rather than in its meaning:

"Peter, you're the one who really looks wonderful. You look just—well—healthy."

"I take care of myself, Anna. That's why. . . ."

"You always did take care of yourself, Peter."

"No, Anna, this is different." He stopped and settled on a box of curtains. "I mean it's not egocentric and selfish, the way I used to be. Now it has a real philosophical basis. Don't mix me up with biology. Look at me, what do you see?"

Anna had read that cannibals, tasting man, saw him thereafter as the great pig, the pale pink roast.

"Peter, Peter, pumpkin eater," Anna said. [LD, 47-48]

The title of the story does not suggest (if we use the terms of Peter Brooks) a "metaphorical and expressionistic quest," but a kind of metonymy, a "true mannerism, a love of surfaces for their own sake."[22] Anna recognizes Peter in his otherness and so, unlike Peter in his need to understand and explain her, she does not have to refer all his actions symbolically back to herself. Peter learned to take care of himself, he tells Anna, when he asked his grandfather—"that old jerk, the one that was so mad, he didn't want to die"—if he had any "real hot tips" about life:

"He came up with an answer right away. 'Peter,' he said, 'I'd go to a gym every goddamn day of my life; the hell with the job, the hell with the women. Peter, I'd build my body up till God hisself wouldn't know how to tear it apart. . . . This structure, this . . . thing'—he pinched himself across his stomach and his knees— 'this me'—he cracked himself sidewise across his jaw—'this is got to be maintained. The reason is, Peter, *It is the dwelling place of the soul.*' In the end, long life is the reward, strength, and beauty." [*LD*, 48]

For Peter, his body represents himself—metaphorically it is his dwelling place, its condition a kind of reward—whereas for Anna, no such signification exists.

Here, just as Benjamin suggests, it is a story of dying that occasions another story—Peter's story about his grandfather. The story is as authoritative as any Peter tells. It certainly carries more authority than Peter's assertion that he is no longer egocentric and selfish, yet it still betrays his repeated gesture to *explain* things. So, of his grandfather, Peter finally says, "Bad or good, Anna, he got his time in, he lived long enough to teach the next generation" (*LD*, 49). Peter understands his grandfather's story as an explanation, nothing more; he dismisses his grandfather in the same way he dismisses Anna when he learns she is married. Peter reads to get the point—a point that always refers back to himself—and once he thinks that he gets the point, the subject of discourse is no longer of any interest—good, bad, or peculiar—to him.

When I spoke of the "The Pale Pink Roast" earlier, I said that the interchange between Anna and Peter came virtually at the end of the story. In fact, there is a little more, as if Paley legitimately wanted to question the continuation of the story, to know "what's gonna happen next."

Anna was crying. "I really mean it, Peter, I did it for love."
    "Love?" he asked. "Really?" He smiled. He was embarrassed but happy. . . .
    In no time at all his cheerful face appeared at the door of the spring dusk. In the street among peaceable strangers he did a handstand. Then easy and impervious, in full control, he cartwheeled eastward into the source of night. [*LD*, 51-52]

At the end Peter regains control and dances off. Paley, then, combines endings: Peter's understanding that he is loved, that love itself is a commodity, a thing to be possessed, and that he will continue to be sure and full of himself; and a second ending showing us—asking us to hear—the marriage of Anna and Peter, the play of love between people, the possibility of happiness beyond the comedy of social relations. Anna did indeed give him a gift of love, one that is repeated throughout Paley's stories; yet it is a gift that Peter, full of himself, cannot see as something other than what he is to himself, a sign for his meaning. Lacking the generosity of spirit most of Paley's women exhibit, Peter cannot see that love is an exchange of experiences.

Maieutic Discourse: The Play of Voices

> Every animal, including *la bête philosophe*, strives instinctively for the optimum conditions under which it may release its powers. Every animal, instinctively, and with a subtle flair that leaves reason far behind, abhors all interference that might conceivably block its path to that optimum. (The path I am speaking of does not lead to "happiness" but to power, to the most energetic activity, and in a majority of cases to actual unhappiness.) Thus the philospher abhors marriage and all that would persuade him to marriage, for he sees the married state as an obstacle to fulfillment. What great philosopher has ever been married?
>
> —Friedrich Nietzsche[23]
>
> All that is really necessary for the survival of the fittest, it seems, is an interest in life, good, bad, or peculiar.
>
> —Grace Paley (*LD*, 98)

If, as I have been arguing, Paley describes a source of authority in her authorship, her storytelling, that is different from the authority of dying described by Benjamin, then some important questions still remain: What difference does this make for her narratives? How does this difference arise? What—to ask the novelist's question—does it mean? Benjamin begins his essay by lamenting the fact that "the art of storytelling is coming to an end":

Less and less frequently do we encounter people with the ability to tell a tale properly. More and more often there is embarrassment all around when the wish to hear a story is expressed. It is as if something that seemed inalienable to us, the securest among our possessions, were taken from us: the ability to exchange experiences.

One reason for this phenomenon is obvious: experience has fallen in value. And it looks as if it is continuing to fall into bottomlessness.[24]

For Benjamin the loss of the value of experience is directly related to the need to explain experience that I have already discussed. Although Benjamin does not say so, this loss is directly related to the will to power articulated by Nietzsche in the epigraph to this section. Paley is trying to achieve something other than power and explanation; she is "trying," as she says, "to show how mysterious ordinary life is."[25] To this end her stories have to reconceive experience beyond (or before) a sense of power and closure. They are her attempt, in a way richer than Benjamin's deathbed scene suggests, to exchange experiences.

For Paley such exchanges are ongoing—stories go on and it is legitimate to ask how they continue. Thus "An Interest in Life"— told in Ginny's voice—is repeated in the voice of Mrs. Raftery in a later story, "Distance." In the earlier story Ginny's husband has left her with three children and she begins to have an affair, as we have seen, with Mrs. Raftery's married son, John. At one point, speaking of her husband, she articulates the problem we are addressing here, the problem of the ordinary, the difference between the experience of men and women:

But for his own comfort, he should have done better lifewise and moneywise. I was happy, but I am now in possession of knowledge that this is wrong. Happiness isn't so bad for a woman. She gets fatter, she gets older, she could lie down, nuzzling a regiment of men and little kids, she could just die of the pleasure. But men are different, they have to own money, or they have to be famous, or everybody on the block has to look up to them from the cellar stairs.

A woman counts her children and acts snotty, like she invented life, but men *must* do well in the world. I know that men are not fooled by being happy. [*LD*, 94]

Articulating the ordinary is altogether different from explaining the world; it is a way, if it is possible, of articulating happiness. Such happiness, as Ginny expresses it, has to do with *others*—with men and kids here—and the recognition that they are, in fact, here. Rather than the egotism of being looked up to—and the supreme egotism of meaning and truth—there is something else; nuzzling, pleasure, the invention of life.

Yet why should woman be distinguished from man in relation to happiness? The difference, as I have suggested, has to do with the recognition of others. Anna and Ginny *recognize* the existence of others in ways that Peter, Mrs. Raftery, and Benjamin's novelists do not. They recognize that their experience is not necessarily *all* experience, that the "truth" cannot be *one*. Pertinently, of Nietzsche's misogyny and his whole seeming occultation and "symbolization" of women, Jacques Derrida, glossing Nietzsche's assertion that "life is a woman!", has written:

the credulous and dogmatic philosopher who *believes* in the truth that is woman, who believes in truth just as he believes in woman, this philosopher has understood nothing. He has understood nothing of truth, nor anything of woman. Because, indeed, if woman *is* truth, *she* at least knows there is no truth, that truth has no place here and that no one has a place for truth. And she is woman precisely because she herself does not believe in truth itself, because she does not believe in what she is, in what she is believed to be, in what she thus is not.[26]

Here Derrida plays with both truth and woman, plays to articulate, I believe, a kind of happiness outside the will to power, a vertigo that occasions will to power: happiness in the fact that things go on.[27] Derrida's point is that the other—whether it be woman or the world or simply the otherness of children—cannot mean anything; they can only be an occasion for articulation, engagement, recognition. They are only surfaces, which, like the many references to Paley's stories I have made throughout this essay, can be cited and exchanged but not forced to give up meanings; they do not force meaning upon us.[28] When asked whether writing is aggressive, Paley said that telling a story is "bringing lives together and speaking for groups of people, not for one person. . . . But mostly, when you're doing something worthwhile . . . you're really illuminating a dark object, or person, or fact."[29] Illumination rather than explanation is her aim, and it produces a kind of invention of life.

This invention is not possession. After John fails to visit, Ginny thinks, "I had to give him up after two weeks' absence and no word. I didn't know how to tell the children; something about right and wrong, goodness and meanness, men and women. I had it all at my finger tips, ready to hand over. But I didn't think I ought to take mistakes and truth away from them. Who knows? They might make a truer friend in this world somewhere than I have ever made. So I just put them to bed and sat in the kitchen and cried" (LD, 97–98). Ginny can explain her experience, but she knows, or hopes, that there are other explanations, different experiences. That is, she hopes for the play of voices, for the possibility—fulfilled in "An Interest in Life"—of an enormous change.

The play of voices in Paley's stories offers what could be called, following Socrates and Kierkegaard, the maieutic function of discourse, the role of the midwife in the dialectic of (in Paley's words) "two events or two characters or two winds or two different weathers or two ideas or whatever bumping into each other" in stories.[30] Such a maieutic function has the authority of transmission, but its aim, as Kierkegaard says, is ("*without authority* to call attention") to be an occasion for "upbringing and development."[31] Such storytelling radically depends on the listener. "I think what you're forgetting," Paley answered William Gass,

what you're underestimating, are the readers. It's true to write one part of that town but they bring something to it and they hear and they understand and they make that whole town and that's what happens when you write. . . .

GASS: What I mean by this is that I don't want the reader filling in anything behind the language.

PALEY: Right, that's what's wrong with you. You don't leave him enough space to move around.32

It is room that Ginny wants for her children, room for play, for happiness beyond (or within) the plottedness of the world; she prefers a sense of time—pleasure, nuzzling, happiness, or simply interest—as a kind of radiation outside of plottedness. She is fooled by an interest in the surface of life because she recognizes others, because, perhaps, she possesses that authority (which Benjamin overlooks) inherent in giving birth. Pertinently, Jane Gallop has recently written of "the mother's dilemma": "the experience of an internal hetero-geneity which she cannot command." "The experience of moth-erhood," Gallop continues, "is not the phallic experience that the child supposes it to be. Rather it is an experience of vulnerability—'in a body there is grafted, unmasterable, an other.' . . . 'In a body' that the woman is accustomed to think of as her own, there is an other which cannot be hers. The mother calls herself as totality, as self, into question because within 'her' is something she does not encompass, that goes beyond her, is other. This experience, Kristeva thinks, might prepare her for a general, 'permanent calling into question.'"33

This embedded otherness, this calling into question, is achieved in Paley's storytelling through its ability to be retold again and again and repeatedly made meaningful for both its teller and its future teller, its listener. Ginny does not want to explain the world to her children because hers might not be the only world, and to explain it is to close "the open destiny of life" (*EC*, 162). In retelling the same story, Mrs. Raftery is faced with things—the noisiness of love, the speediness of life—that she cannot explain.

Such a conception of storytelling necessarily involves a reconcep-tion of narrative economy and narrative temporality. As Kathleen Hulley has written of Paley's stories,

Now, there are a number of interesting technical strategies occurring here: If on the surface her text seems ordinary, unthreatening, untheoretical, it is nevertheless true that she "leaves everything out." The world evoked is so fully conceived, so solidly physical that we hardly notice that the text is without narrative center, that time and space float to us not from hidden depths, but upon surfaces which disturb our conventions of solidity and reflection. . . .

By leaving no behind or underneath to her telling, Paley performs the scene of writing. Truth is not veiled, yet it is a woman.[34]

What Paley leaves out is the symbolical self-reference of the novelist, the psychological analysis that is precluded by the chaste compactness of storytelling. In its stead is the surface of the world, the play of happiness. Consider Nietzsche's remark that "all people who have depth find happiness in being for once like flying fish, playing on the peaks of waves; what they consider best in things is that they have surface: their skin-coveredness."[35] The world is solid because it is "other"—because Ginny can conceive of another, because beneath her skin has been another. The people of Paley's fiction are born into a world separate from themselves, even when, like Mrs. Raftery or Peter, they take themselves as the sole measure of their experience.

And more importantly, they are born into time. Time is not a line, as the father in "A Conversation with My Father" wants; it is not a thing to be manipulated, or saved, or, as Peter suggests, "rewarded." Rather, time, like happiness, is lived, as Ginny says, "good, bad or peculiar" (LD, 98) by a particular individual and contains a particular value. "I tend not to look at things psychologically, but historically," Paley has said, and by this she means she has eschewed the symbol for the surface relationships, the meaning for the person.[36] The time of her stories is the time of voices—digressive, nonlinear, recognizing a listener as an other as well as evaluating time. Pertinently, Kierkegaard too attempts to conceive of time, not as a "spatializing model" that reifies and commodifies time, but in a sense of "lived-time." This spatialized model "allows for the 'placing' of events in spatial relation but does not allow for judgment of their value":

Kierkegaard hopes to defend or restore time's value by giving priority to "lived-time," an alternative concept of the relation of meaning and event; of past, present, and future. Kierkegaard's metaphor of lived-time reflects his desire to restore value to time as an ideological location for common action, for reestablishing the specific histories of individuals and groups by revealing the coherence of their past, present, and future. This is precisely the coherence spatialized time denies for a more abstract, general "history." . . . "Knowledge" becomes in [Kierkegaard's] culture the "objectification" of history in space that separates the lived symbolic value of events from their intellectually produced meaning in a reflected image.[37]

To follow a linear plot is to assume that all time is equal—points on a line in the "spatialized" model. It assumes the necessity of putting "Finis," or the "The End," of which the narrator's father so approves in "A Conversation with My Father," in a narrative because no ongoing authority marks the ending.

Because Paley attempts to narrate lived-time, because in her stories she attempts to exchange experiences, she marks their endings, as we have seen, with little disturbances that are also enormous changes, both of which catch in her throat. Both can register in a voice because her time is the lived coherence of past, present, and future— of generations—rather than the plotted differences of homogenized time. Thus "Enormous Changes at the Last Minute," a story that places Alexandra between her dying father and her young, hippy lover, ends with the birth of Alexandra's illegitimate son and her lover's song of praise that "was responsible for a statistical increase in visitors to old-age homes by the apprehensive middle-aged and the astonished young" (*EC*, 136). This story brings the times of these generations together with a sleight of hand that saves Alexandra's father from a "novelistic" ruination of "his interesting life at the very end of it when ruin is absolutely retroactive" (*EC*, 33). Paley saves the situation and at the same time narrates the kind of lived-time of which Kierkegaard speaks by substituting a birth for the dying implied by the temporal logic of the story. In doing so she also defines, I think, the kind of "happiness" that Ginny describes: "Alexandra's father's life was not ruined, nor did he have to die. Shortly before the baby's birth, he fell hard on the bathroom tiles, cracked his skull, dipped the wires of his brain into his heart's blood. Short circuit! He lost twenty, thirty years in the flood, the faces of nephews, in-laws, the names of two Presidents, and a war. His eyes were rounder, he was often awestruck, but he was smart as ever, and able to begin again with fewer scruples to notice and appreciate" (*EC*, 134-35).

When Mrs. Raftery notices how much younger than she Ginny is, she thinks "all of a sudden they look at you, and then it comes to them, young people, they are bound to outlast you, so they temper up their icy steel and stare into about an inch away from you a lot" (*EC*, 23). Here Mrs. Raftery's conception of time is the same as that of Peter, for whom the crises of linear time—marriage, divorce, remarriage—define and explain experience, even love. In the end Alexandra's father's accident short-circuits the linear circuit of time and allows him to understand and live—in a way Mrs. Raftery cannot— the coherence of generations; he seems a newborn playing and bearing children. The accident allows him to realize that real life is transmissible in a way different from Benjamin's notion of bequeathment. If deathbeds provide the authoritative legacies that are sources of stories, real life also provides the different authority of that other ordinary, yet mysterious event of giving birth to and conceiving—and conceiving of—another, which Paley recovers and articulates in her work. The generosity of Paley's storytelling goes further than the legacy of wisdom and knowledge of Benjamin describes by transforming the authority and form of stories and offering possibilities—articulations—of change and love and happiness in the ordinary goings-on of life.

NOTES

1. Fragment 52, cited in Julia Kristeva, *Desire in Language*, trans. Thomas Gora, Alice Jardine, and Leon S. Roudiez (New York: Columbia Univ. Press, 1980), 292, n.9.

2. "Motherhood according to Bellini," in *Desire in Language*, 240.

3. Kathleen Hulley, "Interview with Grace Paley," *Delta* 14 (1982): 27.

4. Jonathan Culler, *On Deconstruction* (Ithaca: Cornell Univ. Press, 1983), 43-64; see also Elaine Showalter, "Toward a Feminist Poetics," in *Women Writing and Writing about Women*, ed. Mary Jacobus (New York: Barnes & Noble, 1979), 22-41.

5. Hulley, "Interview," 35.

6. Gayatri Spivak, "Displacement and the Discourse of Woman," in *Displacement: Derrida and After*, ed. Mark Krupnick (Bloomington: Indiana Univ. Press, 1983), 173.

7. Peggy Kamuf, "Writing like a Woman," in *Women and Language in Literature and Society*, ed. Sally McConnell-Ginet, Ruth Borker, and Nelly Furman (New York: Praeger Publishers, 1980), 298.

8. Hulley, "Interview," 34.

9. Kamuf, "Writing like a Woman," 297.

10. Mary Jacobus, "The Difference of View," in *Women Writing and Writing about Women*, 19. Although Spivak takes exception to Kristeva's "masculist celebration of motherhood," she aptly describes male power (p. 169) and argues for deconstruction as a " 'feminist' practice" (p. 184). Peggy Kamuf also warns that the assumption of "a clear distinction between masculine and feminine discourse runs the risk of merely corroborating the father's position in the end" (p. 285). While I would not want to argue this distinction, I would argue that the "situations" and "positions" of men and women can suggest and articulate different experiences.

11. Kristeva, *Desire in Language*, 271.

12. Ibid., 240.

13. Walter Benjamin, "The Storyteller: Reflections on the Works of Nikolai Leskov," in *Illuminations*, ed. Hannah Arendt, trans. Harry Zohn (New York: Schocken Books, 1969), 91.

14. *The Little Disturbances of Man* (New York: Viking Press, 1956), 49; hereafter cited in the text as *LD*.

15. Benjamin "Storyteller," 83, 91-92.

16. Joan Lidoff, "Clearing Her Throat: An Interview with Grace Paley," *Shenandoah* 32 (1981): 7.

17. *Enormous Changes at the Last Minute* (New York: Farrar, Straus, Giroux, 1960), 164; hereafter cited in the text as *EC*.

18. Lidoff, "Clearing Her Throat," 5, 9.

19. Benjamin, "Storyteller," 94.

20. Ibid., 100.

21. Lidoff, "Clearing Her Throat," 23.

22. Peter Brooks, *The Melodramatic Imagination* (New Haven: Yale Univ. Press, 1976), 199.

23. Friedrich Nietzsche, *The Genealogy of Morals*, trans. Francis Golffing (New York: Anchor Books, 1956), 242.

24. Benjamin, "Storyteller," 83-84.

25. Hulley, "Interview," 35.

26. Jacques Derrida, *Spurs: Nietzsche's Styles*, trans. Barbara Harlow (Chicago: Univ. of Chicago Press, 1978), 53.

27. This, I think, is a motive for Nietzsche's metaphor of "eternal return." For a discussion of this and the authority of another marginal discourse, see Nancy Mergler and Ronald Schleifer, "The Plain Sense of Things: Violence and the Discourse of the Aged," *Semiotica*, forthcoming.

28. Marianne DeKovan also lets Paley speak for herself in numerous quotations; see "Mrs. Hegel-Schtein's Tears," *Partisan Review* 48 (1981): 217-23.

29. Lidoff, "Clearing Her Throat," 17.

30. Ibid.

31. Søren Kierkegaard, *My Activity as a Writer,* in *The Point of View for My Work as an Author,* trans. Walter Lowrie (New York: Harper Torchbooks, 1962), 151. For an extended discussion of this aspect of Kierkegaard's rhetoric, see Ronald Schleifer and Robert Markley, "Writing without Authority and the Reading of Kierkegaard," in *Kierkegaard and Literature: Irony, Repetition, and Criticism,* ed. Ronald Schleifer and Robert Markley (Norman: Univ. of Oklahoma Press, 1984), 3-22.

32. Donald Barthelme, William Gass, Grace Paley, and Walker Percy, "A Symposium on Fiction," *Shenandoah* 27 (Winter 1976); 7-8.

33. Jane Gallop, *The Daughter's Seduction* (Ithaca: Cornell Univ. Press, 1982), 116, 123.

34. Kathleen Hulley, "Grace Paley's Resistant Form," *Delta* 14 (May 1982): 10.

35. Friedrich Nietzche, *The Gay Science*, trans. Walter Kaufmann (New York: Viking Books, 1974), 217.

36. Lidoff, "Clearing Her Throat," 20. The question of psychological readings of Paley—especially the Lacanian readings offered throughout the special issue of *Delta*—14 (May 1982)—devoted to her work—is an important one. Brooks notes that psychoanalysis is "a systematic realization of the melodramatic aesthetic" (*Melodramatic Imagination*, 201). "When this abyss is located within the structure of mind by Freud," he writes, "it is as *das Unbewüsste*, the unconscious and the unknown, which yet must be

known through its effects. The signs of the world are symptoms, never interpretable in themselves, but only in terms of a behind" (p. 202).

Paley herself has spoken to this issue when asked about "the kind of theoretical speculations the French like": "I think a lot of that's interesting, but, see, first of all, for me the story exists really off the page in a way that for the, it's all lying around there on the. . . . I see it getting deeper and deeper into the page, until it disappears out the back end of the book. . . . It's not that I don't love the page. I mean I love the books. But . . . I'm really speaking about speaking the story, or being able to say it and to tell it and to talk it. . . . As for the story, it's not so much that you don't read it on the page, it's just that in the story itself there has to be some memory, some human memory of where it came from" (Lidoff, "Clearing Her Throat," 25-26). Still, I myself have proposed a kind of Lacanian understanding of time that comes close to what is suggested here in "The Space and Dialogue of Desire: Lacan, Greimas, and Narrative Temporality," *Modern Language Notes* 98 (1983): 871-90.

38. Paul Bove, "Søren Kierkegaard and the Penitentiary of Reflection," in *Kierkegaard and Literature*, 30, 31.

A Bibliography of Writings by

GRACE PALEY

Ronald Schleifer

BOOKS

The Little Disturbances of Man: Stories of Men and Women at Love. New York: New American Library, 1956.

Enormous Changes at the Last Minute. New York: Farrar, Straus & Giroux, 1960.

Later the Same Day. New York: Farrar, Straus, and Giroux, 1985.

UNCOLLECTED STORIES

"Somewhere Else." *New Yorker* 54 (23 October 1978): 34-37.

"Friends." *New Yorker* 55 (18 June 1979): 32-38.

"Love." *New Yorker* 55 (8 October 1979): 37.

"Dreamer in a Dead Language." *American Review, No. 26.* New York: Bantam Books, 1977, 391-411.

"At That Time; or, The History of a Joke." *Iowa Review* 12 (1981): 266-67.

"Lavinia." *Delta* 14 (May, 1982): 41-45. [This issue of *Delta*, edited by Kathleen Hulley, is devoted to Paley.]

ARTICLES

"Mom." *Esquire* 84 (December 1975): 85-86.

"Other People's Children: The Young Shoots of Vietnam." *Ms.* 4 (February 1976): 10ff.

"My Mother." *Ms.* 8 (May 1980): 100.

MISCELLANEOUS

Barton Midwood, "Short Visits with Five Writers and One Friend." *Esquire* 74 (November 1970): 150-53.

Donald Barthelme, William Gass, Grace Paley, Walker Percy. "A Symposium of Fiction," *Shenandoah* 27 (Winter 1976): 3-31.

Frieda Gardiner, "The Habit of Digression: An Interview with Grace Paley." *Wordsworth*, 28 October 1979, p. 127.

Leonard Michaels, "Conservation with Grace Paley." *Threepenny Review* 3 (1980): 4-6.

Joan Lidoff, "Clearing Her Throat: An Interview with Grace Paley." *Shenandoah* 32 (1981): 3-26.

Maya Friedman, "An Interview with Grace Paley." *Story Quarterly* 13 (1981): 32-39.

Kathleen Hulley, "Interview with Grace Paley." *Delta* 14 (May 1982): 19-40.

Ruth Pery, "Interview with Grace Paley." In *Women Writers Talking* (New York: Holmes & Meier, 1982).

ANNIE DILLARD

Narrative Fringe

William J. Scheick

We wake, if we ever wake at all, to mystery," says Annie Dillard at the beginning of *Pilgrim at Tinker Creek* (1974).[1] This remark is a thesis statement, not only for *Pilgrim at Tinker Creek* but also for Dillard's *Tickets for a Prayer Wheel* (1974), *Holy the Firm* (1977), and *Teaching a Stone to Talk* (1982). So inscrutable is this mystery of creation, Dillard explains, that the best one can do in life is to "discover at least *where* it is that we have been so startlingly set down, if we can't learn why" (*TC*, 12): "There is nothing to be done about it, but ignore it, or see" (*TC*, 270). Seeing is everything for Dillard: "All I want to do is stay awake, keep my head up, prop my eyes open, with toothpicks" (*TC*, 86). In her writings, her Thoreauvian "meteorological journal[s] of the mind" (*TC*, 11), Dillard seeks to awaken the reader to a new way of seeing,[2] to make the reader undergo a radical change of vision tantamount to a conversion experience; "I am not making chatter," Dillard warns, "I mean to change his life" (*TC*, 132).

This new perception in the reader is evoked by Dillard's language. Language, however, is an ambiguous instrument. On the one hand, "seeing is . . . very much a matter of verbalization" for Dillard, who says, "unless I call attention to what passes before my eyes, I simply won't see it" (*TC*, 30). On the other hand, she notes later in her first book, "the second I verbalize this awareness in my brain, I cease to see" (*TC*, 79). Reconciling these two remarks is not easy. In the latter comment Dillard stresses the paradox of language; language focuses on, and at the same time inadvertently veers away from, that which is seen. Language displaces the perceived object and in this sense con-

Photo by Renée DeKona

ceals what it tries to reveal: "In order to make a world in which their ideas might be discovered, writers embody those ideas in materials solid and opaque, and thus conceal them."[3] This ambiguous capacity of language to reveal and conceal mimics nature, which also, according to Dillard, "does reveal as well as conceal" some mystery (*TC*, 16). Especially the mystery of natural beauty appears to be a "language to which we have no key; it is the mute cipher, the cryptogram, the uncracked, unbroken code" (*TC*, 107).

For Dillard, language is important as language, however vexing its failure to signify things as they are. The mysterious matrix between seeing and not seeing that constitutes verbalization is, for Dillard, intrinsically artful. For her the matrix of language "is a selection and abstraction from unknowable flux"; "language is itself like a work of art" insofar as "it selects, abstracts, exaggerates, and orders" (*LF*, 70). Implicitly artful, language achieves its highest ends for Dillard when it is directed by a writer to function within a still more encompassing artful structure designed to awaken a reader to the mystery of natural beauty. "Art is the creation of coherent contexts," Dillard says in *Living by Fiction*: "The work of art may, like a magician's act, pretend to any degree of spontaneity, randomality, of whimsy, so long as the effect of the whole is calculated and unified" (*LF*, 32, 28). In other words, just as in nature "form follows function" (*TC*, 135), so too should form follow function in literary art, especially literary art concerning nature. Throughout her writings Dillard strives for a calculated and unified narrative manner that exemplifies the intrinsic artistry of language and of nature, a revealing and concealing manner designed to evoke in her readers a mode of seeing equivalent to her own experience of rapt concentration on the mysterious mute cipher of natural beauty (*TC*, 31-33).

Dillard's narrative manner creates a liminal space between verbalizing the seen (revealed surfaces) and seeing beyond what can be verbalized (concealed depths). For Dillard nature abounds with revealed surfaces and concealed depths: "nature is very much a now-you-see-it, now-you-don't affair" (*TC*, 16). Sometimes nature's opaque surfaces become translucent, when an influx of light can give the human perceiver a sense of the depth and continuity of nature. Dillard remarks one of these occasions near the conclusion of *Pilgrim at Tinker Creek*: "A kind of nothing is what I wish to accomplish, a single-minded trek toward that place where any shutter left open to the zenith at night will record the wheeling of all the sky's stars as a pattern of perfect concentric circles" (*TC*, 251). At such a time nature's light intimates some unifying order—the perfect concentric circles of the stars—some underlying continuity or code at the heart (depths) of the mute cipher that is natural beauty. For most of us such moments of "enlightenment" are rare, and Dillard's wish to "stay awake" derives from her aim to "change [her reader's] life," to make her reader—like camera film on which "the moment's light prints"—more sensitive to occasions when nature's opacity transforms into translucence.[4] Although as a part of creation we can never know the whole of which we are a part, during such moments of translucency we receive hints of an overall artistic design informing the mysterious language of natural beauty.[5] These moments of translucency reveal the liminal edge of the particular (the temporal, the opaque surface) where it touches the universal (the eternal, the transparent depth).[6] This liminal edge is most often detected at the margin of nature's particulars; the tops of mountains, for example, are "serrated edges . . . so thin they are translucent" and the breaking waves evince an edge of "live water and light" that is "translucent, laving, roiling with beauty" (TC, 92, 103).

Sometimes Dillard refers to this liminal edge as a *hemline* between eternity (spirit) and time (matter) in nature, "a fabric of spirit and sense so grand and subtle, so powerful in a new way, that we can only feel blindly of its hem" (TC, 7). Most often Dillard refers to this edge as a *fringe*—the fringe of a bird's wing or of a fish's fin, for example (TC, 11, 130). "Spirit and matter are a fringed matrix," Dillard explains;[7] "intricacy means that there is a fluted fringe to the something that exists over against nothing, a fringe that rises and spreads, burgeoning in detail" (TC, 131). This fringe demarcates where the terror (matter) and beauty (spirit) of life intersect, for "terror and a beauty insoluble are a ribband of blue woven into the fringes of garments of things both great and small" (TC, 24; cf. pp. 159-60).

The intersection of this terror and beauty is "God's Tooth" (HF, 51), where life is flayed and frayed. "All our intricate fringes, however beautiful, are really the striations of a universal and undeserved flaying" (TC, 134), Dillard observes, for "the world is actual and fringed, pierced here and there, and through and through, with the toothed conditions of time and the mysterious, coiled spring of death" (TC, 234): "we the living are nibbled and nibbling—not held aloft on a cloud in the air but bumbling pitted and scarred and broken through a frayed and beautiful land" (TC, 227).

For Dillard this frayed liminal edge raises as many doubts as it seems to provide affirmative answers about the meaning of life. The terror of the flaying of life seems balanced by the beauty of the fraying of life. Even if Dillard cannot confidently affirm that "the frayed and nibbled fringe of the world is a tallith, a prayer shawl" (*TC*, 242), she knows that "beauty is real" within "the intricate fringe of spirit's free incursions into time" (*TC*, 266); that is, given the reality of the intricate beauty of nature's cryptogram, Dillard accepts life's "undeserved flaying" as a mystery within an overall artistic design in nature, within a divine artistry providing—like literary art, in Dillard's opinion (*LF*, 28, 32)—a calculated, coherent, and unified context.

For Dillard all art, literary or natural, conveys this frayed liminal fringe. For her great art is "juncture itself, the socketing of eternity into time and energy into form" (*LF*, 164). Great art conveys "the rim of knowledge" (*LF*, 170), where beauty and terror intersect. In her own art Dillard tries to depict this frayed intersection of matter and spirit, of the temporal and the eternal, of opaque surfaces and translucent depths, of terror and beauty. In her art Dillard relies on a narrative fringe, a liminal edge where the reader glimpses the rim or hemline between time and eternity.

Holy the Firm is an excellent example of this narrative technique. Like *Pilgrim at Tinker Creek*, *Holy the Firm* cues the reader to its author's technique whenever it specifically refers to the "serrate margin of time," to "the fringey edge where elements meet and realms mingle, where time and eternity spatter each other with foam" (*HF*, 20, 21). *Holy the Firm* also emphasizes the figure of the artist as someone who encounters the "lunatic fringe" (*TC*, 144), someone who *sees* the intersection of matter and spirit in the world as well as in himself or herself. In Dillard's opinion, the artist spans "all the long gap with the length of his love, in flawed imitation of Christ on the cross stretched both ways unbroken and thorned. So must the work be also, in touch with, in touch with, in touch with; spanning the gap, from here to eternity" (*HF*, 72). In *Holy the Firm* Dillard achieves a narrative fringe suggesting this terrible and beautiful Christlike intersection of time and eternity.

Ostensibly *Holy the Firm* consists of a journal record of three days, 18-20 November, recording Dillard's thoughts about a seven-year-old girl named Julie Norwich, who on the 19th had her face severely burned and disfigured by an exploding airplane. At first the reader of *Holy the Firm* might anticipate a narrative governed by a linear, sequential sense of time. The narrative, however, consists of various fragments without evident transitions, a narrative collage, depriving the reader of a comfortable sense of continuity at the level of narrative surface.[8] At one point Dillard suddenly and without transition warns the reader, who has already been having trouble detecting a temporal narrative progression in the book, that "nothing is going to happen in this book. There is only a little violence here and there in the language, at the corner where eternity clips time" (*HF,* 24). Referring here to a correspondence between her narrative technique (her narrative fringe) and the liminal edges (the intersections of eternity and time) glimpsed in nature, Dillard suggests that for a sense of continuity in her book one must look not at the surface of temporal details, but into the depths of their eternal significance.

In fact *Holy the Firm* commences with an impressionistic account of the author awakening to exigent sunlight on the morning of November 18. This event is presented as an experience of a liminal edge in nature, when eternity and time intersect, "when holiness holds forth in time" (*HF,* 11). In lieu of temporal sequential narration as the sun rises there is rapture, and this rapture is epitomized by the waking author's only spoken word, an inarticulate but reverent "Oh" (*HF,* 12, 13). To her awakening senses, especially her sight, the day becomes ever more sharply focused until "the sky clicks securely in place over the mountains, locks around the islands, snaps slap on the bay" (*HF,* 12). This brief experience of translucence at the "serrate margin of time," of an illuminated depth intimating an underlying divinity—"I wake in a god" (*HF,* 11)—in nature, coalesces with the opaque particulars of mountains, islands, and bay clicking securely into place. Then the reader suddenly encounters without transition another narrative beginning, one of a conventional sort: "I live on northern Puget Sound, in Washington State, alone. I have a gold cat, who sleeps on my legs, named Small" (*HF,* 13). However much the reader might prefer this fulfillment of a conventional expectation of a narrative, he or she will not find sufficient continuity at the surface level of *Holy the Firm;* the absence of this continuity at the linear, temporal narrative level urges the reader to find it elsewhere in Dillard's book. In *Holy the Firm* continuity is intimated, just as in nature an underlying continuity is intimated. In Dillard's work this underlying continuity is suggested by her narrative fringe—moments when surface details in her account are brought to the edge of visibility, where momentarily they lose their revealed and verbalizable temporal surface opacity (their "thingness," their conventional meaning) and seem—to author and reader—to become translucent; in *Holy the Firm,* as in nature for Dillard, this translucency suggests a concealed and unverbalizable, eternal depth, where an artlike continuity and design can be faintly detected.

Consider, for instance, the islands Dillard sees from her home on

northern Puget Sound. These islands are first mentioned in the opening impressionistic account of morning sunlight, and in this account
the islands emerge as if from the dawn of creation: "Islands slip blue
from [the god-of-day's] shoulders and glide over the water . . . [as] the
sky clicks securely in place . . . [and] locks round" them (HF, 12). The
islands attain increasing temporal reality until they become "unima-
ginably solid islands" (HF, 21). Dillard tries to draw a key to the
islands seen from her window and she wishes to discover their
names. But the names vary from one source to another, and Dillard
eventually realizes the futility of her desire to fix each island tem-
porally with a name, as if a name could designate the essential definition of the chunk of land it apparently identifies.

The trouble is that these islands exist, from Dillard's perspective,
"at the world's rim" (HF, 23), and occasionally she receives hints that
something else, perhaps other islands, exist just beyond her usual
range of vision on the horizon. On November 18, for example, "a veil
of air" lifts, and Dillard sees "a new island . . . the deepening of
wonder, behind the blue translucence the sailor said was Salt Spring
Island," an island newly seen, the name of which she has "no way of
learning" (HF, 25–26). "The deepening of wonder": the newly seen
island signifies more than another temporal solidity; it becomes a
metaphoric index to a pervasive continuum within creation that
evokes wonder, a continuum that includes something spiritual
beyond the horizon of the phenomenological. On the horizon perceived by our reading mind's eye Dillard's image of islands transub-
stantiates into a metaphor for spiritual insight, even as on November
18 the actual islands before her eyes give a glimpse of their origins
from within the deep continuum of eternity and time. It is a matter of
seeing: "I see it! I see it all! Two islands, twelve islands, worlds, gather
substance, gather the blue contours of time, and array themselves
down distance, mute and hard" (HF, 28). As perceived from the
window of her room and—since "this room is a skull" (HF, 22)—from
the window of her eyes, these islands indicate for Dillard that sometimes nature's temporal solid surfaces can momentarily become
translucent; when this happens with the islands at the rim of the
world, she gets a glimpse of the "serrate margin of time" where
eternity and time intersect in a way intimating a continuity of an
artlike design or purpose within creation:

And now outside the window, deep on the horizon, a new thing appears, as if we
needed a new thing. It is a new land blue beyond islands, hitherto hidden by haze and now
revealed, and as dumb as the rest. I check my chart, my amateur penciled sketch of the

skyline. Yes, this land is new, this spread blue spark beyond yesterday's new wrinkled line, beyond the blue veil a sailor said was Salt Spring Island. How long can this go on? But let us by all means extend the scope of our charts.

I draw it as I seem to see it, a blue chunk fitted just so beyond islands, a wag of graphite rising just here above another anonymous line, and here meeting the slope of Salt Spring: though whether this be headland I see or heartland, or the distance-blurred bluffs of a hundred bays, I have no way of knowing, or if it be island or main. I call it Thule, O Julialand, Time's Bad News; I name it Terror, the Farthest Limb of the Day, God's Tooth. [*HF*, 50-51]

Just as the newly seen island gave Dillard a glimpse of the rim of the world, the "serrate margin of time," God's Tooth, where eternity and time interpenetrate, so too in the above passage does Dillard's prose, her narrative fringe, convey to the reader translucent hints of a transcendental significance to the temporal specificity of the islands she sees in Puget Sound.

When, in the foregoing long quotation, Dillard refers to the newly seen island as a "spread blue spark" she coalesces the image of the island and another image important in her management of narrative in *Holy the Firm:* the image of fire. Late in the book, in fact, she "sees" the "islands on fire," a "thousand new islands today, uncharted . . . on fire and dimming" (*HF*, 66, 68). In Dillard's mystical perception all of nature burns, as if, like the burning morning described at the opening of the account, everything in nature ceaselessly emanates from the dawn of creation at the margin of time. In *Holy the Firm* Dillard develops this image of fire in her remarks concerning the attraction of moths to flames. She describes in detail the fate of a golden female moth, with a two-inch wing span, that flew into the flame of Dillard's candle. Dillard describes in succession the burning of the moth's six legs, two antennae, and various mouth parts—each fact emphasizing the physical reality of the moth. Her final description reads, "And then this moth-essence, this spectacular skeleton, began to act as a wick. She kept burning. The wax rose in the moth's body from her soaking abdomen to her thorax to the jagged hole where her head should be, and widened into flame, a saffron-yellow flame that robed her to the ground like any immolating monk. That candle had two wicks, two flames of identical height, side by side. The moth's head was fire. She burned for two hours, until I blew her out" (*HF*, 17). This image of the moth with a head of fire surfaces from time to time in *Holy the Firm*, but the specificity and opacity of its phenomenological surface reality as described in Dillard's introduction of the image is transformed until the image becomes a translucent emblem signifying the artist.

Dillard subtly prepares the reader for this metamorphosis of the image of the burning moth by noting that at the time of the moth's immolation she was reading James Ramsey Ullman's *The Day on Fire* (*HF*, 15), a novel about Rimbaud, who, Dillard says, "burnt out his brains in a thousand poems" (*HF*, 17). Like the moth's head of flame, the artist's "face is flame . . . lighting the kingdom of God for the people to see; his life goes up in the works" (*HF*, 72). This remark, appearing late in the book, requires the reader to perceive a deeper meaning in the apparently mundane destruction of a moth by a candle flame; it also requires the reader to interpret differently the extraordinary accident that produced Julie Norwich's burned face. Julie, the reader is told at the end of the book, is "like the moth in wax, [her] life a wick, [her] head on fire with prayer, held utterly, outside and in" (*HF*, 76). Julie, who looks somewhat like Dillard (*HF*, 41), has come to know the experience of the artist, the experience of Rimbaud, with his burnt-out brains, and of Dillard: "I am moth; I am light" (*HF*, 65). By coalescing the images of the moth, Julie, herself, and the artist, Dillard creates a narrative fringe where specific concrete, ordinary particulars of life become translucent signifiers of continuity and design, depths of meaning below phenomenological surfaces.

Dillard's images of "islands on fire," a moth's "head on fire," and a child's face on fire coalesce with her images of seraphs, saints, and nuns in *Holy the Firm.* The artist's "face is flame like a seraph's" (*HF*, 72), and seraphs "are aflame with love of God"; "they can sing only the first 'Holy' before the intensity of their love ignites them again and dissolves them again, perpetually, into flames" (*HF*, 45). In Julie's tragic accident Dillard sees an emblem of the artist's face burning like that of a seraph. Just as the moth with the burning head looks "like a hollow saint, like a flame-faced virgin gone to God" (*HF*, 17), so too Julie, "like the moth . . . [with her] head on fire," becomes a nun in the service of the divinity behind nature: "You might as well be a nun" (*HF*, 74). A "nun lives in the fires of the spirit" (*HF*, 22), Dillard mentions early in the book; and such a nun is like an artist who—like the moth, Julie, and a seraph—has a face of flame, is like Dillard herself: "I'll be the nun for you. I am now" (*HF*, 76).

At first Dillard's image of the nun appears in a literal context. We are told that Julie once dressed Dillard's cat in a "curious habit" so that the cat "looked like a nun" (*HF*, 40, 41). We have no sense yet of how this episode foreshadows what will happen to Julie; nor do we anticipate that the violence of Julie's conversion of the cat into a nun—she rammed the cat into the dress and hit it on its face— adumbrates the violence—the exploding airplane—that will hit

Julie's face and convert her, metaphorically, into a nun. Later in the book these specific, opaque, temporal details become translucent when they intimate some "eternal" truth about the artist; then they intimate that some aesthetic continuity informs the design both of nature and of Dillard's work.

That Dillard's artistry reflects the underlying design of nature is also suggested by the imagery of the arch in *Holy the Firm*. In the impressionistic rendering of sunrise that commences the book we read that "today's god," objectified in the sun, "arches, cupping sky in his belly; he vaults, vaulting and spread, holding all" (*HF*, 12). Even at night Dillard senses this divine arch as she stands "under the ribs of Orion" (*HF*, 76). This macrocosmic arch is microcosmically reflected in every human being, who possesses within him or herself "buttressed vaults of . . . ribs" (*HF*, 65). Insects, too, exhibit this pattern when, for instance, dead moths become "arcing strips of chitin . . . like a jumble of buttresses for cathedral domes" (*HF*, 14). Within macrocosmic and microcosmic expressions of nature is manifested an arched place of worship.

The act of worship within vaulted and vaulting nature is itself an act of arching, of arced burning—"light arches" (*HF*, 72). This image of arching or arcing becomes translucent—suggestive of a deeper significance—when it coalesces with Dillard's fire and nun, or saint, imagery. In *Holy the Firm* all creation is depicted as immolated in a flaming service arching toward the divinity behind nature; all creation worships—that is, burns—in nature's church: the cathedrallike buttresses that are within each natural form besides being characteristic of nature generally. A moth with a head of fire, a little girl flamefaced, a seraph aflame with love of God—everything burns and arches as it "flutter[s] . . . in tiny arcs" (*HF*, 15). Even the exploding airplane, which snagged its wing on a tree, like a moth "fluttered in a tiny arc" (*HF*, 35). All nature arches, burns, or prays with love, "vaulting . . . [with] love . . . and arcing to the realm of spirit bare" (*HF*, 44).

Especially the nunlike artist burns, or prays; like the moth, like Julie, like the seraph, the artist has a head of arcing flame. The artist's work archlike "span[s] the gap, from here to eternity" (*HF*, 72). This mystical worship, or burning, of the artist through the arcing art work, however, remains earthbound; the artist's arc strives heavenward "till 'up' ends by curving back" (*HF*, 69): "Eternity sockets twice into time[,] and space curves" (*HF*, 71). Even the islands at the rim of creation, at "the fringey edges where . . . realms mingle," seem to burn, to arch, between two sockets of an eternity intimated by the blank spread of water and the spread of sky (*HF*, 29, 47). The coalescing of the image of arcing or arching with the images of island, fire, and nuns—artists—occurs in Dillard's narrative fringe, where the temporal opacity of these images seems to become translucent—where pushed to the edge of their conventional meanings they "enlighteningly" intimate some artlike divine pattern in the depths of creation.

The image of arcing or arching, moreover, informs the narrative structure of *Holy the Firm*, which comprises three essays that record Dillard's thoughts during three successive days in November. The first day, Wednesday, is a newborn and salted day socketed into eternity.[9] It is a day of intense worship, of prayerful arching, for the artist-nun who celebrates how the god of day "sockets into everything that is, and that right holy" (*HF*, 30).

On Thursday, in contrast, Julie Norwich has her face burned by an exploding airplane. Thursday, the date of the second essay of *Holy the Firm*, is characterized by a downward arc, the reverse of the upward thrust of the preceding day and of the first essay in the book. On this second day Dillard descends into the dark night of the soul, where she contemplates the fact of Julie's terrible suffering.[10] Nervous, rattled, Dillard sits by her window and chews the bones in her wrist (*HF*, 49). Since she and Julie look somewhat alike, Julie's fate seems to bear implications concerning Dillard's own fate—a bleak prospect as Dillard stares out the window at "no wind, and no hope of heaven . . . since the meanest of people show more mercy than hounding and terrorist gods" (*HF*, 36). Dillard confronts the "evidence of things seen: one Julie, one sorrow, one sensation bewildering the heart, and enraging the mind, and causing [Dillard] to look at the world stuff appalled (*HF*, 46). Little wonder that she chews the bones in her wrist as her doubts begin to border on severe skepticism:

> Has God a hand in this? Then it is a good hand. But has he a hand at all? Or is he a holy fire burning self-contained for power's sake alone? Then he knows himself blissfully as flame unconsuming, as all brilliance and beauty and power, and the rest of us can go hang. Then the accidental universe spins mute, obedient only to its own gross terms, meaningless, out of mind, and alone. The universe is neither contingent upon nor participant in the holy, in being itself, the real, the power play of fire. The universe is illusion merely, not one speck of it real, and we are not only its victims, falling always into or smashed by a planet slung by its sun—but also its captives, bound by the mineral-made ropes of our senses. [*HF*, 48]

Julie's tragedy and Dillard's dark night of the soul position them both at the Thule-like fringe of life and of its meaning—the fringe where they are torn by God's Tooth.

Friday, the third day, recorded in the third essay of the book, is marked by a slow but certain recovery from the near despair of the preceding day. Having kept awake in order to deal with sobering thoughts through the night and through the dark night of the soul, Dillard drinks boiled coffee as morning begins to arrive. With morning comes her acceptance of the fact "that we are created, *created*, sojurners in a land we did not make, a land with no meaning of itself and no meaning we can make for it alone. Who are we to demand explanations of God?" (*HF*, 61-62). Faith arcs within her as she reaffirms that a Christlike "spanning the gap, from here to eternity" is our destiny, especially evident in the burning worship of nun-artists such as Julie and Dillard. Dillard's arcing forth reaffirms the reality of a pattern within "the one glare of holiness": "the world in spectacle perishing ever, and ever renewed" (*HF*, 67). The perishing, or downward arc, of Thursday transforms into the renewal, or upward arc, of Friday, and the third essay in *Holy the Firm* appropriately concludes with a celebration of the arrival of morning that recalls the ecstatic celebration of morning at the start of the first essay: "Mornings, when light spreads over the pastures like wings, and fans a secret color into everything, and beats the trees senseless with beauty, so that you can't tell whether the beauty is *in* the trees—dazzling in cells like yellow sparks or green flashing waters—or *on* them—a transfiguring silver air charged with the wings' invisible motion; mornings, you won't be able to walk for the power of it: earth's too round" (*HF*, 75).

Just as the earth is round and the diurnal cycle comes round to morning, so moves the tripartite pattern of faith, doubt, and faith renewed. Faith and doubt compose a continuum similar to the juncture of eternity and time. The arcing affirmation of the opening and closing sections of *Holy the Firm* dramatizes how "eternity sockets twice into time[,] and space curves." The beginning and ending of *Holy the Firm* are socketed into eternity; they arc with faith upward into eternity. The downward curve—doubt—of the middle section of the book is merely the lower half of the mystical circle, or roundness, of creation. The uppermost arc of this circle, toward which the opening and closing passages of the book tend, remains veiled in mystery as are the spread sea and sky which surround the arc of each island Dillard tries to map. What is important is the fact that "space curves," that the very curve of either the upward arc of faith or the downward arc of doubt implies circular completion. This implied circular continuum is what nature at once reveals (in the arcs we perceive) and conceals (the completed circuits we cannot see but which we intuit). For Dillard, this circular continuum combining time (the seen) and eternity (the unseen) is the origin of art—"any work of art symbolizes juncture itself, the socketing of eternity into time and energy into form" (*LF*, 164); this circular continuum is also the foundation of hope, for our consideration of the "world as a text . . . as a work of art. . . . absolutely requires that we posit an author for it" (*LF*, 144).[11]

Where eternity and time are twice socketed in this circular reality is God's Tooth, where "holiness splinter[s] into a vessel" (*HF*, 64), where terror (splintering) and beauty (holiness) interface, where matter (vessel) and energy (holiness) intersect. Julie's story is an instance of "holiness splintered into a vessel" at the frayed fringe of creation. To tell Julie's story and her own story—for she and Julie are somewhat alike as nun-artists—Dillard manages a narrative structure and a narrative technique that convey a sense of this juncture of time and eternity by "expand[ing] the arc of the comprehended world" to "the rim of knowledge where language falters" (*LF*, 170). The narrative structure of *Holy the Firm* begins with an arc of affirmation, curves downward into doubt, and then with renewed faith arcs upward again. The total, circular configuration of this narrative structure suggests that the two upward arcs are veiled in mystery but nonetheless apparently meet in a divinity which gives meaning, purpose, and design to all of creation abiding in the lower half of this mystical circle. This narrative structure in *Holy the Firm* is reinforced by Dillard's technique of narrative fringe: moments when surface details, such as islands, flames, nuns, and arcs, in her account are brought to the edge of visibility at the rim of their conventional meaning, where momentarily they lose their revealed temporal surface opacity (their usual sense) and seem to become translucent— that is, they suggest a concealed "eternal" depth, or significance, where an artlike continuity and design in nature and in Dillard's book can be faintly detected.

Neither the structure of the book, with its seemingly contradictory variations in mood and its nonlinear progression of narrative, nor its style, with its many interfacing images, permits the reader any certain reliance on firmness of detail. The underlying firmness, or significance, of what is narrated in Dillard's book must be sought elsewhere by the reader; it must be sought in the hinted at holy depths beneath the opaque surface details made translucent in Dillard's narrative fringe. In these depths the reader glimpses "holy the firm"—an underlying continuity and design which is at once the revealed and concealed secret of nature and the revealed and concealed art of Dillard's book.

NOTES

1. *Pilgrim at Tinker Creek* (New York: Harper's Magazine Press, 1974), 2; hereafter cited in the text as *TC*.

2. In "The I in Nature," *American Notes and Queries* 16 (1977): 3-5, Margaret McFadden-Gerber notes the importance of seeing in *Pilgrim at Tinker Creek*. The importance of sight and light in this book is discussed in David L. Lavery's "Noticer: The Visionary Art of Annie Dillard," *Massachusetts Review* 21 (1980): 255-70. How a single vision resolves contradictions in the depiction of life in this book is emphasized by Margaret Loewen Reimer in "The Dialectical Vision of Annie Dillard's *Pilgrim at Tinker Creek*," *Critique* 24 (1983): 182-91. In "The Artist as Nun: Theme, Tone, and Vision in the Writings of Annie Dillard," *Studia Mystica* 1, no. 4 (1978): 17-31, Robert Paul Dunn discusses Dillard's management of her reader's response.

3. *Living by Fiction* (New York: Harper & Row, 1982), 156; hereafter cited in the text as *LF*.

4. "When I walk with a camera, I walk from shot to shot, reading the light on a calibrated meter. When I walk without a camera, my own shutter opens, and the moment's light prints on my own silver gut" (*TC*, 1).

5. *Holy the Firm* (New York: Harper & Row, 1977), 46; hereafter cited in the text as *HF*.

6. "The universal/loves the particular," *Tickets for a Prayer Wheel* (Columbia: Univ. of Missouri Press, 1974), 33.

7. *Teaching a Stone to Talk: Expeditions and Encounters* (New York: Harper & Row, 1982), 130; hereafter cited in the text as *TS*.

8. "The contemporary modernist fiction writer . . . flattens narrative space-time by breaking it into bits; he flattens his story by fragmenting its parts and juxtaposing disparate elements on the page. He writes in sections; he interrupts himself by a hundred devices" (*LF*, 48; cf. pp. 21-23).

9. Throughout *Holy the Firm* Dillard uses images of salting or baptism (*HF*, 24, 25, 29, 41, 62, 66, 68, 72, 73); these images coalesce with the other significant images discussed in this essay and are particularly suggestive of a baptism of fire.

10. Robert Paul Dunn notes that the three days roughly represent, respectively, the stages of illumination, purgation, and union that characterize the mystical way ("The Artist as Nun," 17-31). Dillard has equated the three days to Creation, the Fall, and Redemption: see Nancy Lucas, "Annie Dillard," *Dictionary of Literary Biography Yearbook: 1980* (Detroit: Gale Research Co., 1981), 187.

11. Although Dillard chooses to believe in the world as a divinely created

art work, she does admit that possibly human beings do not discover patterns of continuity, but might invent them (*LF*, 184-85; cf. *TS*, 152).

A Bibliography of Writings by

ANNIE DILLARD

William J. Scheick

BOOKS

Tickets for a Prayer Wheel [Poems]. Columbia: Univ. of Missouri Press, 1974.
Pilgrim at Tinker Creek. New York: Harper's Magazine Press, 1974.
Holy the Firm. New York: Harper & Row, 1977.
Living by Fiction. New York: Harper & Row, 1982.
Teaching a Stone to Talk. New York: Harper & Row, 1982.
Encounters with Chinese Writers. Middletown, Conn.: Wesleyan Univ. Press, 1984.

SHORT STORIES

"Life Class." *Carolina Quarterly* 24, no. 2 (1972): 23-27. [Reprinted in *Antaeus* 36 (1980): 52-54.]
"Ethiopian Monastery." *Hollins Critic* 10, no. 4 (August 1973): 12.
"Five Sketches." *North American Review* 260, no. 2 (Summer 1975): 30-31.
"Some Easy Pieces." *Antioch Review* 33 (1975).
"The Stone." *Chicago Review* 26, no. 4 (1975): 152-53.
"Doughnut." *Antioch Review* 34 (1975-76): 22-25.
"A Christmas Story." *Harper's Magazine* 252 (January 1976): 58.
"Stone Doctor." *Epoch* 26 (Fall 1976): 63.
"Utah." *Tri-Quarterly* 35 (Spring 1976): 96-98.
"At Home with Gastropods." *North American Review* 263 (Spring 1978): 50.
"The Living." *Harper's Magazine* 257 (November 1978): 45-64.

POEMS

"Dominion of Trees." *Carolina Quarterly* 23, no. 3 (1971): 76-77. [Reprinted in *Tickets for a Prayer Wheel*.]
"After Noon." *Carolina Quarterly* 25, no. 3 (1973): 60. [Reprinted in *Tickets for a Prayer Wheel*.]
"Feast Days: Christmas." *Atlantic Monthly* 232 (December 1973): 67. [Reprinted in *Tickets for a Prayer Wheel*.]
"The Man Who Wishes to Feed on Mahogany." *American Scholar* 42 (Spring 1973): 279-80. [Reprinted in *Tickets for a Prayer Wheel*.]
"The Heart." *Poetry* 125 (February 1975): 260.

"A Natural History of Getting through the Year." *Poetry* 125 (February 1975): 261.

"Quatrain of the Body's Sleep." *Poetry* 125 (February 1975): 262.

"Monarchs in the Field." *Harper's Magazine* 253 (October 1976): 104.

"Metaphysical Model with Feathers." *Atlantic Monthly* 242 (October 1978): 82.

"Soft Coral." *Antigonish Review* 48 (Winter 1982): 5.

ARTICLES

"Monster in a Mason Jar." *Harper's Magazine* 247 (August 1973): 61-67. [Reprinted in *Pilgrim at Tinker Creek*.]

"Heaven and Earth in Jest." *Harper's Magazine* 247 (October 1973): 73-76.

"Sojourner." *Living Wilderness* 37 (Autumn 1973): 2-3; 37 (Winter 1973): 2-3; 38 (Spring 1974): 2-3. [Reprinted in *Pilgrim at Tinker Creek*.]

"The Force That Drives the Flower." *Atlantic Monthly* 232 (November 1973): 69.

"Footfalls in a Blue Ridge Winter." *Sports Illustrated* 40 (February 1974): 72-76. [Reprinted in *Pilgrim at Tinker Creek*.]

"Sight into Insight." *Harper's Magazine* 248 (February 1974): 39-46. [Reprinted in *Pilgrim at Tinker Creek*.]

"Artists of Beauty." *Living Wilderness* 38 (Winter 1974): 62-63. [Reprinted in *Teaching a Stone to Talk*.]

[Article] *Prose*, Spring 1974. [Reprinted in *Pilgrim at Tinker Creek*.]

"Nature's Parasites: Survivors in a Fallen World." *Cosmopolitan* 176 (June 1974): 214. [Reprinted in *Pilgrim at Tinker Creek*.]

[Article] *Living Wilderness* 38 (Summer 1974): 2-3.

"Thinking about Language." *Living Wilderness* 38 (Autumn 1974): 2-3. [Reprinted in *Teaching a Stone to Talk*.]

"The Shape of Change: Idea in Theodore Roethke's Love Poetry." *Mill Mountain Review* 2 (1975): 125.

"The Deer at Providencia." *Living Wilderness* 39 (Spring 1975): 46-47.

"Innocence in the Galapagos." *Harper's Magazine* 250 (May 1975): 74-82. [Reprinted in *Teaching a Stone to Talk*.]

"Jungle Peace." *Holiday* 56 (September 1975): 24-27.

"On a Hill Far Away." *Harper's Magazine* 251 (October 1975): 22-25. [Reprinted in *Teaching a Stone to Talk*.]

[Article] *Potomac*, 21 December 1975. [Reprinted in *Teaching a Stone to Talk*.]

"The Death of a Moth." *Harper's Magazine* 252 (May 1976): 26-27. [Reprinted in *Holy the Firm*.]

"Mirages." *Harper's Magazine* 255 (December 1977): 84-85. [Reprinted in *Teaching a Stone to Talk*.]

"Some Notes on the Uncertainty Principle." *New Lazarus Review* 1 (1978): 49.

"A Field of Silence." *Atlantic Monthly* 241 (February 1978): 74-76. [Reprinted in *Teaching a Stone to Talk*.]
"A Speech on Socks." *New York Times*, 12 December 1978, Sec. A., 23.
"A Note on Process." *Jeopardy* 15 (1979): 8.
"Learning to Chop Wood." *Christian Science Monitor*, 24 January 1979, 2.
"A Note on Process." *Christian Science Monitor*, 30 April 1979, 25.
"Is There Really Such a Thing as Talent?" *Seventeen* 38 (June 1979): 86.
"Is Art All There Is?" *Harper's Magazine* 261 (August 1980): 61-66. [Reprinted in *Living by Fiction*.]
"Contemporary Prose Styles." *Twentieth Century Literature* 27 (1981): 207-22. [Reprinted in *Living by Fiction*.]
"Teaching a Stone to Talk." *Atlantic Monthly* 247 (February 1981): 36-39.
"Island Reflections." *Science 81* 2 (April 1981): 62.
"The State of the Art: Fiction and Its Audience." *Massachusetts Review* 23 (Spring 1982): 85-96.
"Total Eclipse." *Antaeus* 45/46 (Spring-Summer 1982): 43-55. [Reprinted in *Teaching a Stone to Talk*.]
"Wish I Had Pie." *Black Warrior Review* 8 (1982): 75.
"A Watcher of Things." *Christian Science Monitor*, 8 April 1982, 20.
"The Joys of Reading." *New York Times Magazine*, 16 May 1982, 47.
"Expedition to the Pole." *Yale Literary Magazine* 150 (June 1982). [Reprinted in *Teaching a Stone to Talk*.]
"The Bats." *Hollins Critic* 32, no. 6 (Spring 1982): 11.

REVIEWS

"Winter Melons" [*Notes from a Bottle Found on the Beach at Carmel* and *Points for a Compass*, both by Evan S. Connell]. *Harper's Magazine* 248 (January 1974): 87-90.
"Tales of Grandeur, Tales of Risk" [*Ishi in Two Worlds* by Theodora Koreber; *People of the Deer*, by Farley Mowat; *The Harmless People*, by Elizabeth Thomas; *Books of Eskimos*, by Peter Frenchen; *The Forest People*, by Colin M. Turnbull; *The Mountain People*, by Colin M. Turnbull]. *Harper's Magazine* 249 (November 1974): 122.
"Critics' Christmas Choices" [*The Ballad of T. Rantula*, by Kit Reed; *The Better Part*, by Kit Reed; *Tender Memories*, by Rosellen Brown; *Cora Fry*, by Rosellen Brown; *Black Tickets*, by Jayne Anne Phillips; *Final Payments*, by Mary Gordon; *Blood Mountain*, by John Engels; *Hymn for Drum*, by Rosanne Coggeshall; *River*, by Fred Chappell; *Bloodfire*, by Fred Chappell; *Wind Mountain*, by Fred Chappell; *Permission to Speak*, by Steve Orlen; *Available Light*, by Phillip Booth; *Kicking the Leaves*, by Donald Hall; *New Words*, by Coleman Barks; *The Zimmer Poems*, by Paul Zimmer; *The Alphabet of Grace*, by Frederick Beuchner; *Memory and Mind*, by Norman Malcolm; *Snake River of Hells Canyon*, by Johnny Carey; *The Decipherment of Linear B*, by John Chadwick; *Natural Symbols*, by Mary Douglas; *Purity and Danger*, by Mary Douglas; *Sher-*

pas through Their Rituals, by Sherry B. Ortner; *The Emergence of Man,* by John Pfeiffer; *Art and Illusion,* by E. H. Gombrich; *Abstract Art,* by Dora Vallier; *The Unknown Shore,* by Dore Ashton; *Structuralism in Literature,* by Robert Scholes; *Samuel Johnson,* by Walter Jackson Bate; *John Keats,* by Walter Jackson Bate; *Woman of Letters,* by Phyllis Rose]. *Commonweal* 106 (1979): 693-94.

MISCELLANEOUS

"A Face Aflame: Interview." Edited by P. Yancey. *Christianity Today* 22 (1978): 958-63.

"An Interview with Annie Dillard." Edited by Michael Burnett. *Fairhaven Review* (1978).

"Introduction." *Moments of Light,* by Fred Chappell. Newport Beach, Calif: New South Press, 1980.

"Introduction." *Wind on the Sand,* by Pinions. Pinions, N.Y.: Paulist Press, 1981.

ANNE REDMON

The Fugal Procedure of *Music and Silence*

Catherine Rainwater

Discussing in an interview the genesis of *Music and Silence* (1979), Anne Redmon recalls that she spent many hours listening to the music of J.S. Bach that her protagonist, Maud Eustace, plays on the cello. A reader of Redmon's elaborately orchestrated text is probably not surprised to learn that this author "love[s] very complicated, layered" musical forms such as "preludes and fugues."[1] Indeed, though Redmon claims no extensive knowledge of music, she apparently learned much from listening, and applied this knowledge in the construction of her novel.[2] In its narrative management, *Music and Silence* verbally approximates fugue, a musical genre that doubtless appeals to Redmon because of the complex vision it affords. Much like Redmon's novel, fugue is both a quest for unity and order and a concession to chaos and disorder. This paradoxical nature of fugue is apparent even in the etymology of the word: *fugue* derives from two Italian terms, *fugere* (to pursue) and *fugare* (to flee).[3] Accordingly, a fugue is always simultaneously in pursuit of, and in flight from, the principles of unity that govern it. As will be seen, Redmon's narrative management in *Music and Silence* closely resembles the composer's management of voices in fugue.

Briefly and simply, a fugue is an imitative, contrapuntal arrangement of choral or instrumental voices. The word *counterpoint* denotes a combination of independent but harmonic melodies while *imitation* refers to the ways in which a musical theme or subject is

Photo by Peter O'Rourke

first stated in one voice, then reiterated successively in other voices. A round, for example, is the simplest kind of imitation. A fugue can have almost any number of voices, but the first states the subject alone. This first voice usually continues to be heard throughout the fugue in accompaniment to successive voices' statements of theme; sometimes the accompaniment itself emerges distinctly as a countersubject. All developments of the subject are called *exposition,* and other passages, derived from but not directly stating the subject, are called *episode,* the entire fugue consisting of exposition and episode in alternation.

In general, such is the pattern taken by the fugue. The pattern is flexible, however; composers have rarely conformed to the prescriptive rules of the "academic fugue" of musical theory.[4] A composer may, for example, employ any number of voices, or invent a double, triple, or even quadruple subject. In short, a fugue is "contrapuntal texture . . . [contained] in . . . formal design."[5] It presents to the ear a surface chaos (increasing with number of voices, subjects, and tonal answers), but this chaos is controlled by the formal relations between voices that must be maintained. As one musicologist has said, "In no other form is the relationship of the parts so completely evident."[6] Thus paradoxically a formal exercise in free invention, fugue "pursues" unity in its adherence to a basic pattern and subject, and "flees" unity in its insistence upon surface disorder, invention and episodic elaboration. Developed primarily through theory rather than practice, moreover, fugue is probably one of the most self-reflexive of musical genres.[7] As Patricia Carpenter explains, fugue self-consciously imposes a prescribed order upon disorder; it constitutes a response to a chaotic universe that celebrates the very chaos it organizes.[8] Consequently—and much like the novel—the fugue is often defined more by its procedure than by its formal traits.[9] Within a broadly defined framework, it explores compositional possibilities rather freely.

To discover the fugal procedure of *Music and Silence* is not merely to discover an arbitrary mode of construction. Redmon's narrative, like fugue, embodies a particular world view and a distinctive response to human and artistic experience. Despite her lack of formal musical training, Redmon seems intuitively to sense how fugue is a vehicle well suited to express the tumultuous concerns of the "contrapuntal twentieth century."[10] Indeed, throughout history, fugue has emerged as a predominant style of musical composition in times of social, religious, and scientific revolution—in the late seventeenth, early eighteenth, and twentieth centuries. The fugue arose out of various polyphonic genres reflecting the increasingly intricate, often self-reflexive vision of the sixteenth and seventeenth centuries; it reached its height of development in the works of J.S. Bach during the first half of the eighteenth century. Bach's church music incorporates many of the polyphonic techniques which, before his time, characterized secular music rather than sacred. His liturgical compositions reflect the gradual displacement of the comparatively simple, medieval cosmology, suggested in monophonic choral music, by the far more complex, post-Copernican world view, a displacement that occurred as the church adapted to increasing secular influences.[11] Bach's fugues, then, both contribute to and are the result of the perceived complexities of a developing modern cosmology. Not surprisingly, the post-Einsteinian twentieth century has witnessed a revival of interest in fugue.[12] In this century, the principles of uncertainty, relativity, randomness, and entropy find maximum expression in works such as Paul Hindemith's *Ludus Tonalis* (1943).[13] The adoption of the term *fugue* in modern psychiatry, moreover,—to describe schizophrenic periods of flight from reality—even further implies that fugue is a form germane to the twentieth-century vision.[14]

Fugue contemplates disorder, arbitrarily imposes order, and thus suggests, like much of twentieth-century art, that pattern and meaning might be the products of human invention rather than empirical traits of experience. The emphasis in the preceding statement must fall on the word *might,* however, for in the development of variation, contrapuntal relations, and episodic development, the fugue appears to discover pattern and form as much as it follows any outwardly imposed structure. Indeed, one of the polyphonic genres from which fugue developed is the *ricercare,* a term which means "to search out" and thus implies discovery as well as invention.[15]

Through the managed relations among voices, Anne Redmon's *Music and Silence* organizes the chaotic "textures" of human experience fugally into an aesthetic unity; such unity is either imposed or discovered by the "sacred consciousness" of the individual, particularly the artist.[16] Like fugue, *Music and Silence,* through its alternating narrative voices, both pursues and flees this ordering impulse that governs the text overall. Furthermore, Redmon's text is emphatically a searching out: not only do the characters themselves search out the patterns of their fate (cosmological formal design) or willed freedom (individual free-form variation), the narrative also develops a momentum of gradual discovery. Employing silence as well as statement, the narrative seems engaged in a process of searching out some immanent pattern and meaning in and between the voices. Such a discovery is not made completely by any one of the characters, or even by the omniscient narrator. As will be seen, despite its omniscience, this third-person narrative voice is also a searcher, not in complete possession of any final truth but subject to changes introduced by Maud's exploring, inventing voice in flight from the narrator's more unified, deterministic vision. The fullest discovery becomes available perhaps only to the reader, to whom alone are available all the voices of the text as well as the interstices between the voices—the silences between the music. The narrative procedure of *Music and Silence* thus leads ultimately to the reader's heightened awareness of immanent meaning arising from the "music" (mere human communication or an aesthetic vehicle) and the silence uniquely shaped by such music.

Just as the first voice in a fugue establishes the theme or subject, the first voice in *Music and Silence* establishes in chapter one the general configuration of the novel. The first voice we hear belongs to the omniscient narrator, who, partially from the point of view of Beatrice Pazzi, quickly focuses the narrative on Maud Eustace. This narrator possesses a comprehensive, godlike view of events and through devices such as foreshadowing implies total knowledge of past and future. Early in the first chapter, for example, Beatrice hears a scream in the stairwell that foreshadows her own scream near the end of the novel. Running up the stairs toward the sound, she encounters the crazed Arthur Marsdan: "In a reflex beyond her control she crosses herself as the faithful in last moments do. . . . She thought, 'This can't be so, this can't be so, he's going to kill me.' "[17] This time, he "hurtle[s] right past her," but at the end of the book when her own scream sounds in the stairwell, he does kill her.

Thus through the narrator's omniscience the reader receives early an impression that the lives of characters such as Beatrice are predetermined. In fact, in Beatrice's case, the narrator's omniscience reflects the divine omniscience that curtails the free will she exercises as a Roman Catholic. The preordained nature of her life is further suggested when, as in the passage quoted earlier, she experiences "reflex[es] beyond her control." Despite her exaggerated self-discipline, moreover, Beatrice has to a great extent been controlled by the demands of others throughout her life as the "family saint" (*MS*, 42). Her death as sacrificial martyr at the hands of Arthur Marsdan likewise seems compelled by a variety of the same exterior, inexorable force that drives him to Maud's door. A character even more predestined than Beatrice, mad Arthur has not even a limited free will, for he has jettisoned it to become the wrathful instrument, sometimes of a Calvinistic God, sometimes of manipulative pagan gods of destruction. We learn about Arthur also primarily through the omniscient narrator, who knows his past and his future unfolded and unfolding from "the regular tick-tock of [his] life" (*MS,* 57).

Chapter one establishes the general configuration of *Music and Silence* by introducing through a controlled, remote omniscient voice, the possibility of determinism and by focusing the narrative on Maud's life, which eventually suggests the contrapuntal possibility of free will. Although the omniscient narrator continues throughout chapters three, five, seven, ten, fourteen, and sixteen to accompany the first-person voice of Maud, chapter one fixes the religious, philosophical, and psychological context within which Maud's more freely inventive voice searches out her destiny. As the second voice to enter, Maud pursues and flees the conditions of existence implied by the first voice in chapter one as well as in subsequent omnisciently narrated chapters that elaborate upon lives which develop as countersubjects to Maud's.

One such life developed as a countersubject to Maud's is that of Beatrice. As the novel progresses, the careful reader hears many echoes of the same concerns in the two women's personalities and histories. Such echoes, suggested rather than overtly declared, contribute to the thematic relations of the human melodies or narrative voices in this fugal novel. And even more significant, these echoes reinforce the tension between what appears preordained in the lives of characters narrated by the omniscient voice and what seems yet open-ended in Maud's life, worked out in the larger, more deterministic context of the omnisciently developed sections. Mutual traits of Maud and Beatrice—and as will be seen later, of Maud and Arthur—emphasize the more freely inventive quality of Maud's existence.

Both Maud and Beatrice have grown up wealthy, under "the mantle of what was ladylike" (*MS,* 9). Both lived through troublesome, deprived relationships with their mothers, who for different reasons could not give as much love as they took. Beatrice's mother, a pampered, Old World aristocrat, required excessive self-sacrifice from her female children, especially Beatrice. Consequently, until middle age, Beatrice has been controlled by "Mama's" demands. Maud's mother, after years of emotional unavailability to her daughters, hanged herself before a window observed by Maud from the garden below. Perhaps as a result of starvation for maternal care, both Beatrice and Maud suffer from varieties of unrequited love; both try to escape their pain through forms of willed emotional anesthesia. When Maud's dream of a "purely" spiritual love affair with Thomas Alba fails, she seeks release from pain in "willed *hopelessness*" (*MS*, 20). Like Maud, Beatrice suffers from unrequited love, but her love has no specific object. She longs for human "contact" (*MS*, 18), but simultaneously recoils from it in fear of pain. As a physician she uses anesthetic drugs to relieve the pain of cancer patients, and she induces emotional anesthesia in herself to avoid the intimate contact with such people that, ironically, "she sought—oh, sought" (*MS*, 18). In their misery, both Beatrice and Maud seek saviors: Beatrice lives within the comforting but unearthly spirituality of Catholicism, with Christ as her savior; Maud looks for more secular saviors, usually in the form of idealized, unattainable men such as Alba. Like many people who look for saviors, both women wish to escape the conditions of their existences: Maud notices how Beatrice "longs to die" (*MS*, 22), and Maud herself eagerly surrenders control of her life to whoever seems stronger—to a series of lovers such as Martin and Maurice and then to Alba. Finally, both women in their emotional difficulties find personal expression nearly impossible. Beatrice cannot speak: "If only she could talk! What were words? Why couldn't she use them? How often she had struggled out towards people she'd wanted to love and been cut down, stopped still at the point of contact. . . . Who'd stopped her tongue? Why was she dumb?" And Maud cannot play music anymore: " 'I am no longer able to play,' she said. 'I have been so upset . . . that my hands shake too much and I can't—so much as play the C-major scale' " (*MS*, 17).

Another character whose life, narrated by the omniscient voice, develops as a countersubject to Maud's is Arthur Marsdan. In common with her—and with Beatrice—he shares a childhood dominated by an emotionally disturbed, overdependent mother; she was "a model of maternal rectitude. . . . She and he had done everything together. . . . There was no chance of being out of her sight for a moment. . . . He wander[ed] to her bedroom in the night where she made him lie on the end of her bed always inviting him closer into it, always denying him access with her jumpy moods. . . . She was . . . omniscient, omnipresent, and omnipotent" (*MS*, 58). Like Maud—and Beatrice—Arthur also suffers from unrequited love. His deranged love for a terrible God and for Maud becomes obsessive. Just as Maud worshipfully sees those she loves as "Prince Charming" (Alba) and "fairy godmother" (Aunt Aileen), Arthur sees Maud as "his love goddess from the pit" (*MS*, 75). "She had become his mantra" (*MS*, 73). Incorporating Beatrice into his bizarre mythology, he sees her as

"Maud's devil, Maud's angel. . . . 'The Angel of Death' came closer and lodged home. . . . She fortified the stairs. The eyes . . . ate into his purpose, drained him of his intention to exorcise Maud. 'If you think I have a devil cast it out' was sonorous to his inner ear—indeed fugal the way it fractured into myriad little tongues of flame that sang it" (MS, 75-76). Sexually and emotionally repressed, he lives most of his years in an uncommunicative, anesthetized condition. Then, after "twenty years' strapped-in emotions" (MS, 69) he gains focus and language to become a fanatical mouthpiece of the Bible: "He had gone so far beyond the convention of explaining himself to himself or to others that he never even shrugged" (MS, 69). Finally, just as Maud at first seeks refuge in superstition, Arthur denies free will and sees himself as the instrument of fierce preternatural forces.

In the lives of Maud, Beatrice, and Arthur the reader hears varieties of the same melody. These separate but harmonious strains in *Music and Silence* are "indeed fugal"; the stated thematic content of Maud's life is "fractured into myriad little tongues of flame that [sing] it." Still, each life maintains its own unique texture, for Maud is finally not like Beatrice or Arthur; neither is Beatrice finally like Arthur, although she "[feels] a fundamental sympathy for the man" (MS, 15) because she understands the ineffable aspect of his religious faith. Like the melodies in fugue, the human lives in Redmon's novel are distinctive parts of an ostensibly chaotic phenomenal composition. As parts of this apocryphal human composition the characters seek the origins of being—"the foot of the Cross"—and the meaning possibly arising from the seemingly arbitrary juxtaposition of their lives. In its insistence upon the need for human communion, Redmon's text suggests that beneath the surface chaos of daily life, human beings are related in subtly evident and inevitable ways that recall the separate, formally related melodic voices in a fugue: as Maud says in the concluding chapter, Beatrice "did what she did for me, for herself—because it was the thing she had to do. . . . It simply *is* a progression of tones. Beatrice simply was—or is—a mathematical fact" (MS, 273).

An essential part of the reader's aesthetic experience of *Music and Silence* involves the ability to discern this relatedness of voices that exists beneath the textured verbal surface. This surface seems deliberately crafted to approximate the circular, repetitive, random, and halting quality of daily existence. The alternating narrative voices begin to tell a story, suddenly stop, and later resume in a slightly different place so that the reader must work to discover the continuity. Neither voice speaks a chronological, linear sequence, but proceeds at intervals broken by pensive silence. In any fugal composition, the listener must develop a sensitive ear to hear how the voices both pursue and depart from the subject that unites them. In *Music and Silence,* the reader becomes such a listener, who discovers the contrapuntal relation between the controlled, omniscient voice and the more inventive, tentative voice of Maud that occupies the uncertain, unformulated present moment.

Although Maud's life constitutes the unified subject or narrative center of the novel, her voice becomes the foremost pattern-breaking, disunifying force in Redmon's work. She alters the course suggested for her by the omniscient voice through narration of lives parallel (or countersubject) to Maud's—but, as will be seen, this omniscient voice is limited after all, and never actually knows the overall shape of Maud's existence. In contrast to the detached, deterministic first voice, Maud's is immediate, confused, and improvisational. Maud discovers through her journal—an improvisational genre—the ostensibly fixed patterns of her life and simultaneously changes these patterns and invents new ones. Her pursuit of herself through the journal results in a flight from fixity toward personal power.

Maud's private writings are a record of all her pursuits and flights—toward and away from her mother, her father, Thomas and Ilse Alba, Arthur, Beatrice, and herself. The journal originates with Beatrice's challenge to her when, because of depression, Maud can no longer play the cello: " 'If you can't play, why don't you write?' " (*MS,* 18). Maud accepts the challenge, and substituting language for music—"wordless language"—she begins to "search out" the themes and patterns of her life. This search becomes a discovery, a breaking and a making of patterns. Self-defining and self-liberating, Maud's journal explores and revises the universe spoken into existence by the godlike omniscient voice.

Maud's voice is characterized by uncertainty, limited vision, and ambivalence. Whereas the lives of characters such as Beatrice and Arthur seem already determined, Maud records in her journal a life in which she makes forays in many directions. By chapter seventeen, the open-ended final chapter, which Maud narrates, her life has assumed a more definite shape, which illustrates the power to change.

Such power eventuates, paradoxically, from her early inability to control her life as well as from her increasing self-direction. Throughout most of her existence and unlike Beatrice and Arthur, Maud has never adhered to any governing philosophy or religion. Instead, she has been inconsistent and eclectic in her explanations of existence and has believed at once in magic and fairy tales, in "destiny" (*MS*, 19), and at times in nothing at all. Ironically, this lack of direction renders her available for exploration and open to hope—both avenues of release from fixed patterns. Maud looks at life from a variety of perspectives: as a Christian, when she tries to understand Beatrice and Arthur and to locate "the foot of the Cross"; as a believer in magic, when she contemplates Aunt Aileen and the Albas; as an atheist, when she rejects Beatrice as some type of "religious" person; and, most profoundly, as an artist, when she plays music, writes, and otherwise invents her life. The melody of Maud's voice thus reveals many variations.

While for religious persons such as Arthur and Beatrice release can apparently come about only through death, for Maud release comes about through art: "my very act of sitting here, letting one word flow after another prises me at least from *willed* hopelessness. If, in writing, I say I have no hope, I cannot be telling the truth. The mere attempt to sort things out is an investment in the future" (*MS*, 20). Music functions in the same contrapuntal fashion with hopelessness for Maud: "I stroked a key and sound leapt up and kissed my ear . . . until a whole alphabet of keys spilled out spelling nothing but giving hope of meaning" (*MS*, 25). The contrast between the artistic Maud and the religious Beatrice and Arthur corroborates the statement of another artist in the novel, Ilse Alba: "both [art and religion] pursue truth, but art gets it right. Religion makes limitations on experience" (*MS*, 187). Certainly those in the novel who are primarily religious appear more limited than the artists. For Maud, art becomes synonymous with self-liberating hope. Art and hope are allied through the improvisational voice of Maud in counterpoint with the omniscient voice, through which are allied religion and various degrees of predestination.

Maud's lack of a formulated system of beliefs places her in an oddly fortunate state of ignorance in counterpoint with the omniscience of the first voice. She does not know the answers to questions she poses, and she is usually wrong when she does venture an answer. She believes, for example, that she is "going to end on the end of that man's knife. . . . The dice are loaded before I even roll them" (*MS*, 20). Indeed, Maud prefers to believe in such predestination because it absolves her from responsibility for herself. Through art, however, she gradually comes to accept incompleteness, uncertainty, and the possibility that she resembles Ilse Alba in possessing the power to "ma[ke] a pattern" (*MS*, 277), instead of merely to follow one.

In fact, together with Thomas Alba and Aunt Aileen, Ilse becomes one of the characters whose lives develop in episodic relation to Maud's. Through her journal Maud investigates and, to some extent, invents the stories of these people; and just as a fugal subject gives rise to episodic elaborations, which are derived from but never directly state the subject, Maud's story gives rise to the stories of significant others, related to her yet ultimately offering contrasting human examples.

Aunt Aileen, for instance, provides a strain of joy and optimism within the dirge of Maud's youth. Aileen visits "Castle Gloom" as a "fairy godmother." She "swanned [in] . . . and lit us up" (*MS*, 28). Maud's tendency to fictionalize, in fairy-tale style, the lives of desirable others extends also to the Albas. Thomas as "Prince Charming" and Ilse as "the fairy princess," later to become the powerful witch, "lived . . . under fluttering pennants near the clouds" (*MS*, 49). As readers, we have almost no objective access to the lives of these characters that people Maud's journal; we hear of them filtered through Maud's consciousness and language. Her episodic inventions of the lives of such persons empower her. In strong contrast to her own life, the lives of the characters she contemplates allow her to hear more clearly the "progression of tones" that compose the unique texture of her own existence and to hear the possible variations she might introduce into the melody of her life as she self-consciously considers these people as parts of the composition. Her fairy-tale vision has an important function in this empowering process, for the genre has its origins in the human magical transformation of self—through fiction making—from powerless to powerful.[18] Indeed, toward the end of the journal, the reader begins to hear the modulations in Maud's melody that are the result of her imaginative examination of the lives of these important other people. Within the overall fugal procedure of *Music and Silence* Maud's journal might be said to develop as *fantasia,* a musical form generically comparable to the fairy tale. Just as *fantasia* explores several highly imaginative variations upon a theme, Maud's journal imaginatively explores possible variations upon the theme of her own existence.

Maud's acquisition of power appears most emphatically in the concluding chapter, which she narrates. Fugally, the novel returns to a final statement of the subject, Maud's life, but in a new key, so to speak. Presented at last with the same human problems that she faced in the beginning, Maud now confronts life from a new perspective; to some extent she speaks in a new voice that eventuates from communion with significant others and, through writing, with an implied audience. Maud's gradual attainment of personal power substantially mitigates the deterministic views presented through the omniscient voice, which consequently begins to seem more limited than a reader might at first have assumed. Indeed, the careful reader sees that the omniscient voice has had no access to Maud's life in its totality. Maud lies outside the scope of the first voice's omniscience, particularly after she gains control of her own life. Unlike the more predictable Beatrice and Arthur, she does not live within the bounds of a religion or a philosophy that "makes limitations on experience." Instead, she represents the freely inventive forces of art that can alter the fixed forms and patterns that seem to dictate human destiny. Thus, within the orderly, fated, or predestined universe implied by the omniscient narrator, Maud develops as a disunifying agent of change. Still, her life is not only a flight from such order; she also defines herself as well as liberates herself and therefore also pursues pattern, order, and meaning. In chapter seventeen, a thoroughly transformed but recognizable subject—Maud—emerges.

As a fugal exercise, *Music and Silence* consists of voices arranged contrapuntally to explore a variety of existential possibilities. In fugue or, indeed, in any musical composition, moreover, the management of silence becomes as important as the management of sound. In *Music and Silence,* as the title suggests, management of silence is a component of narrative technique.

Redmon's novel develops a great variety of silences—the anesthetized silence of Beatrice's self-imposed loneliness; Arthur's dangerous, inarticulate silence preceding his religious "conversion"; Maud's depressive silences; the sacred silence of worship; and, finally, the profound silence of being that galvanizes pursuit of human communion and spurs flight from painful contact. Even more important, however, Redmon employs in her novel a variety of narrative silences. Such silences contribute to the overall fugal nature of the novel and emphasize the fugal qualities of human experience in general.

Redmon's alternating third-person omniscient narrator and first-person limited voice begin and suspend their narratives in a manner resembling the discontinuous entrances and exits of fugal voices. Almost inevitably, the voices in the text arbitrarily stop and later resume their stories in a different place from where they left off in preceding chapters. Consequently, the novel consists of seventeen fragmented sections that evince continuities which are neither chronologically nor logically linear. Instead, as I have shown, important continuities accrue through thematic and imagistic echoes, overlappings, and associations. Elaborate motifs involving spiders, hands, blindness, gardens, and rivers further strengthen the connections between characters and chapters. This manner of development demands much of the reader, who, like the audience of a fugue, must develop an ear sensitive to the unity that prevails within a composition that inherently resists unity.

Furthermore, like many contemporary musical compositions, especially fugues, Redmon's novel consists of passages in which patterns are introduced, then left incomplete, to be completed by the reader or listener in the silences between the sections. Perhaps the best example of this demand on the reader involves the many references to the death of Maud's mother and Maud's subsequent conceptions of art. For Maud art, suffering, and death become associated psychologically as year after year she observes her mother finding release from pain in playing the piano; finally, her mother hangs herself, framing a macabre scene in the window that is visible to young Maud below. Throughout the text, death and art consequently appear to Maud as synonymous modes of release from consciousness. At a crucial moment, she wants to "kill the cello" itself. Then, she thinks, "All would be well" (MS, 37). Redmon's text often introduces just enough of such information to set the mind in search of the completed pattern, just as composers of fugue often introduce a melodic fragment that suggests but does not state its completion. Such completions necessarily take place in the listener's contemplative silence.

Owing to Redmon's deliberately discontinuous narrative management, each of the chapters of her text is surrounded by silence, giving the reader the opportunity to make completions. A chapter does not conclude so much as it merely halts, its message or some variation of it to be taken up again later in one voice or another. Even the final chapter is not a conclusion but a resting place in Maud's turbulent life, where she begins to heal—her "severed nerves reconnecting themselves slowly" (MS, 274). Here, too, the reader must actively complete the text—the remainder of Maud's life, like the rest of a song partly sung, is "inly heard" (MS, 5). Redmon's narrative silences suggest the existential silences in which characters and reader are isolated and emphasize the fugal nature of human interaction. Voices reach out of silence in hope of communion and connection with others. These voices contribute to the surface chaos of experience; yet, Redmon's novel insists, in their hopeful search for communion and meaning these voices "ma[ke] a pattern." Redmon's voices surrounded by silence approximate actual human voices as they rise—declaring, questioning, fragmented, and searching—out of the silence of the isolated self and fall back into it. In these silences patterns are completed. This fundamental silence exists before and after speech or song and, in fugal art, assumes an importance equal to that of sound.

The many narrative silences in Redmon's novel force the reader to consider them as integral parts of the total orchestration of the text. Such consideration leads to the discovery of essentially two kinds of silence. On the one hand, the novel posits silence as the chaotic ground of being—the "foot of the Cross"—the unfathomable origin of all voices. Again and again, the omniscient narrative voice rises, godlike and mysterious, out of the silence and bears apocryphal knowledge. Maud's more tentative voice originates in the silence of her own depression. As an artist, she writes and plays music in order to give meaning and shape to an otherwise tormenting inner silence. Also as an artist, she ponders the origins of art itself. Maud the child is awestruck by the magic of the piano and "for a long time . . . sat on the stool before it, wondering if it would animate itself and play without [her] having to touch it" (*MS*, 25). As an adult she plays the cello, which "speak[s] to [her] like an oracle" and which also seems supernaturally animated: "I gave it form and gave the breath to what was already in it" (*MS*, 25).

In Redmon's novel the origins of art and, indeed, of all human meaning remain deliberately vague because they are rooted in this ineffable center of being. Even though *Music and Silence* to some extent endorses Beatrice Pazzi's Roman Catholicism as a desirable mode of being, it also acknowledges the universe as an apocryphal creation of a God—or gods—who remains thoroughly hidden. Beatrice and Arthur sustain themselves through—quite different—varieties of blind faith, and Maud gropes as blindly through a more secular array of existential possibilities. One kind of silence, then, is that which precedes speech, song, or communication and which is thus painful.

If origins remain vague in *Music and Silence,* destinations emerge much more clearly, and these destinations imply a second kind of silence—that which follows community. Individual voices aim toward contact, connection, and communion. Above all endorsing the value of human communion, Redmon's polyphonic text aims toward the silence of the reader's isolated consciousness, just as each of her characters seeks admittance to another's consciousness. The ideal reader of the text could be said to resemble Beatrice Pazzi when she discovers Maud, the cellist, living in the apartment below. The music enters her contemplative silence and seems " 'very beautiful—like a meditation.' " With this remark "Beatrice had clearly struck. Maud instantly softened. . . . 'I'm glad you heard it that way,' she said. They were silent" (*MS*, 17). Just as Maud demands a special type of listening on the part of Beatrice, Redmon's text demands a particular way of reading on the part of the reader, who must perceive the unity beneath the surface chaos, make the connections between the fragmentary chapters, and hear the harmony within the dissonance. To a high degree the reader of *Music and Silence*, like a listener to a fugue, must learn how to make completions within the text which, much like Maud's music rising through Beatrice's floor, consists of "stops and starts" (*MS*, 3). Maud's "softened" response to Beatrice when the older woman reveals aesthetic sensitivity suggests that for Redmon art very much functions as a point of human contact. Art originates in a lonely, chaotic, and unformed silence but aims toward a more profound, shared silence—shaped, patterned, and significant. Overall, Redmon's fugal novel corroborates a statement made by Roland Barthes: "a text's unity lies not in its origin but in its destination"—the reader.[19] Though they do not share a common poetics, Barthes and Redmon might agree that the reader plays an active role in relation to the text. For Redmon, at least, the reader becomes another "sacred consciousness" who must, like the musician, learn how to listen.

NOTES

1. See Catherine Rainwater and William J. Scheick, "An Interview with Anne Redmon," *Three Contemporary Women Novelists: Hazzard, Ozick, and Redmon* (Austin: University of Texas Press, 1983), 331. Published as a special issue of *Texas Studies in Literature and Language* 25 (Summer 1983).

2. Ibid.

3. Most dictionaries explain that the word *fugue* is derived from the Latin *fuga*—meaning "flight." A more careful analysis of the origin of the word, however, appears in Alfred Mann, *The Study of Fugue* (New York: W.W. Norton, rev. ed. 1965) and in Andre Hodeir, *The Forms of Music*, trans. Noel Burch (New York: Walker, 1966).

4. See *New Grove Dictionary of Music and Musicians* (1980), s.v. "fugue."

5. See *Columbia Encyclopedia*, 4th ed. (1975), s.v. "fugue."

6. Mann, *Study of Fugue*, 49.

7. See Mann, *Study of Fugue;* see also *New Grove Dictionary.*

8. Patricia Carpenter, "The Janus Aspect of Fugue: An Essay in the Phenomenology of Musical Form" (Ph.D. dissertation, Columbia Univ., 1971).

9. See *New Grove Dictionary*, s.v. "fugue"; on the novel as "procedure,"

see especially those critics such as Georges Poulet in the phenomenological tradition. In Poulet's "Phenomenology of Reading," for example, *New Literary History: A Journal of Theory and Interpretation* 1 (Fall 1969): 53-68, the literary text is discussed as the locus of some type of mental activity not captured in the text itself but existing as a part of the procedure of reading. Attempts to define the novel are far too numerous and diverse to be enumerated here, but in general it has been those twentieth-century theorists responding in various ways to the phenomenological tradition who have spoken of the processes involved in the novel rather than of any clearly defined formal elements. For valuable discussion of the history of such theoretical questions see, for example, Hazard Adams, *The Interests of Criticism: An Introduction to Literary Theory* (New York: Harcourt, Brace and World, 1969); and *Critical Theory since Plato* (New York: Harcourt Brace Jovanovich, 1971).

10. *New Grove Dictionary*, s.v. "fugue," 17.

11. See Mann, *Study of Fugue*; see also Karl Gustav Fellerer, *The History of Catholic Church Music*, trans. Francis Brunner (Baltimore: Helicon Press, 1961).

12. *New Grove Dictionary*, "fugue," 17.

13. For a study of Hindemith's modernity, see Ian Kemp, *Hindemith* (London: Oxford University Press, 1970).

14. Another contemporary Roman Catholic novelist, Walker Percy, employs fugal elements in his novel *The Last Gentleman* (1966). His main character also suffers from schizophrenic dissociation called "fugue" by psychiatrists.

15. See *Columbia Encyclopedia*, 4th ed., s.v. "ricercare"; see also Mann, *Study of Fugue*.

16. See Rainwater and Scheick, " 'Some Godlike Grammar': An Introduction to the Writings of Hazzard, Ozick, and Redmon," *Texas Studies in Literature and Language* 25 (Summer 1983): 193-97, for a discussion of the significance of consciousness in Redmon's fiction. See also Flannery O'Connor's discussion of consciousness in the novels of Roman Catholic writers, "Novelist and Believer," in *Mystery and Manners*, ed. Sally and Robert Fitzgerald (New York: Farrar, Straus & Giroux, 1969), 158-67; O'Connor's view parallels Redmon's implied view in a number of ways.

17. Anne Redmon, *Music and Silence* (New York: Penguin Books, 1980), 6; henceforth cited in the text as *MS*.

18. See Bruno Bettelheim's study of the fairy tale, *The Uses of Enchantment: The Meaning and Importance of Fairy Tales* (New York: Vintage Books, 1977).

19. Barthes, "The Death of the Author," in *Image, Music, Text*, trans. Stephen Heath (New York: Hill and Wang, 1977), 148.

A Bibliography of Writings by

ANNE REDMON

Catherine Rainwater

BOOKS

Emily Stone. London: Secker and Warburg, 1974.

Music and Silence. London: Secker and Warburg, 1979; New York: Holt, Rinehart and Winston, 1979.

SHORT STORY

"Bat Time." *Bananas* (London) 8 (Summer 1977): 8-12.

REVIEWS

"The Resistible Rise of the Lady Killers" [*Deliver Us from Love,* by Suzanne Brogger]. *Sunday Times* (London), 6 March 1977, 41.

"All You Lack Is Love" [*Living Like I Do,* by Nell Dunn]. *Sunday Times* (London), 15 May 1977, 40.

"The Private Face of War" [*The Danger Tree,* by Olivia Manning; *The Lover Next Door* by Keith Alldritt; *The Bottom of the Bottle,* by Georges Simenon; *Even Cowgirls Get the Blues,* by Tom Robbins; *The Book of Muntu Dixon,* by Norma Meacock]. *Sunday Times* (London), 14 August 1977, 35.

"The High Price of Morality" [*The Ice Age* by Margaret Drabble; *Ends and Means,* by Stanley Middleton; *A Victim of the Aurora,* by Thomas Keneally]. *Sunday Times* (London), 4 September 1977, 39.

"Adam's Black Vision of the Universe" [*The Plague Dogs,* by Richard Adams; *The French Consul,* by Lucien Bodard; *Lorenzino,* by Arvin Upton; *Great Granny Webster,* by Caroline Blackwood]. *Sunday Times* (London), 25 September 1977, 39.

"Lancelot, Ladies, and Lust" [*Lancelot,* by Walker Percy; *Childwold,* by Joyce Carol Oates; *Tell Me Now, and Again,* by Richard Llewellyn; *The Maiden Voyage,* by Joan Biggar]. *Sunday Times* (London), 16 October 1977, 41.

"Women Stripped Naked" [*Little Tales of Misogyny,* by Patricia Highsmith; *The Farewell Party,* by Milan Kundera; *The Dark Lady,* by Louis Auchincloss; *Attachments,* by Judith Rossner]. *Sunday Times* (London), 6 November 1977, 41.

"A Tall Story with the Ring of Confidence" [*Imperial 109,* by Richard Doyle; *The Dark Pageant,* by Edward Lucie-Smith; *Leaving Standing Still,* by Pierre Marsay]. *Sunday Times* (London), 27 November 1977, 40.

"Through the Good Taste Barrier" [*Brothers of the Head,* by Brian Aldiss; *A Pebble from Rome,* by R.T. Plumb; *The Crucified Fool,* by Peter Munk;

Double Decker, by Eva Jones]. *Sunday Times* (London), 15 January 1978, 41.

"The Prince of Darkness" [*Blind Date*, by Jerzy Kosinski; *Ladybird in a Loony Bin*, by Ian Cochrane; *Preservation Hall*, by Scott Spencer; *Under the Rainbow*, by Miranda Heyman]. *Sunday Times* (London), 5 February 1978, 41.

"Tales of Women in Love" [*Little Sisters*, by Fey Weldon; *Everything in the Garden*, by Elizabeth North; *The Girl with a Squint*, by Georges Simenon; *Monday Lunch in Fairyland*, by Angela Huth]. *Sunday Times* (London), 26 February 1978, 41.

"In the Footsteps of a Visionary" [*The Tree of the Sun*, by Wilson Harris; *No Mama No*, by Verity Bargate; *Harvest Home*, by David Toulmin; *Blood Relations*, by Eilis Dillon]. *Sunday Times* (London), 19 March 1978, 41.

"The Pleasure of the Pain Principle" [*Mrs. Reinhardt and Other Stories*, by Edna O'Brien; *Mother's Footsteps*, by Harriet Waugh; *Don Q*, by José Lopez Portillo; *Altered States*, by Paddy Chayevsky]. *Sunday Times* (London), 21 May 1978, 41.

"Love in a Cold Climate" [*Laughable Loves*, by Milan Kundera; *Enemies of the System*, by Brian Aldiss; *On Margarita's Sands*, by Bernard Kops]. *Sunday Times* (London), 11 June 1978, 41.

"The Heart of Darkness" [People in the Crowd, by Pat McGrath; *The Reservation*, by Ward Ruyslinck; *Men on White Horses*, by Pamela Haines; *Climbers on a Stair*, by Elspeth Davie]. *Sunday Times* (London), 2 July 1978, 41.

"A Fate Worse Than Death" [*A Heavy Feather*, by A.L. Barker; *The Bad Sister*, by Emma Tennant; *Kassandra and the Wolf*, by Margarita Karapanow; *The Monkey King*, by Timothy Mo]. *Sunday Times* (London), 23 July 1978, 41.

"William Trevor's Muted Music" [*Lovers of Their Time*, by William Trevor; *The Shadow Master*, by Elaine Feinstein; *Natural Shocks*, by Richard Stern; *The Action*, by Francis King]. *Sunday Times* (London), 24 September 1978, 41.

"This Story of Yours" [*The Pardoner's Tale*, by John Wain; *Teach Us to Outgrow Our Madness*, by Kenzaburo Oe; *The Cutting Edge* by Penelope Gilliat; *The Clique*, by Ferdinand Mount]. *Sunday Times* (London), 15 October 1978, 40.

"Do Novels Need a Sex Change?" [*A Piece of Night*, by Michele Roberts; *Love Comes in Buckets*, by Katharina Havekamp; *Here Goes Kitten*, by Robert Gover]. *Sunday Times* (London), 5 November 1978, 41.

"Dickens: A Cast of Thousands" [*The Mutual Friend*, by Frederick Busch; *The Opportunity of a Lifetime*, by Emma Smith; *The Bookshop*, by Penelope Fitzgerald; *Office Life*, by Keith Waterhouse]. *Sunday Times* (London), 26 November 1978, 40.

"The Ardent Heroine" [*A Woman*, by Sibilla Aleramo; *Neglected Lives*, by Stephen Alter]. *Books and Bookmen* 24 (April 1979): 46-47.

"Birth and Rebirth" [*Surfacing,* by Margaret Atwood; *The Coelacanth,* by Rosalind Brackenburg]. *Books and Bookmen* 24 (May 1979), 47.

"Faulkner's Southern Comfort" [*Uncollected Stories of William Faulkner,* ed. Joseph Blotner; *William Faulkner: His Life and Works,* by David Minter]. *Sunday Times* (London), 8 February 1981, 43.

CYNTHIA OZICK

Invention & Orthodoxy

Ellen Pifer

> He rejects the carven images which his ancestors made, the images of
> gold and silver, ivory and marble. But he worships the *ideal* image without
> seeing that it is an image. And it came to pass that after him even those
> men who knew the message brought down from Sinai did not perceive
> that an image formed of ideas as little resembles God as an image formed
> of any coarse physical matter.
>
> —**Lev Shestov,** *In Job's Balances*

The narrative features of Cynthia Ozick's fiction, her use of self-referential devices and fantastic events, clearly place it within the development of postmodernist or antirealist literature. The philosophical and technical self-consciousness of postmodernism—the way it calls attention to the process and problems of its own narration, for example—has made contemporary fiction a predominantly ironic and parodistic literary mode. What sets Ozick's work apart from that of her postmodernist contemporaries is the orthodox vision conveyed through her sophisticated and playful narrative techniques: a vision of moral and spiritual truth rooted in the Old Testament and its Ten Commandments. Inspired by the ancient wisdom of Mosaic law, Ozick's consciousness as a writer has been forged by the history and traditions, as well as by the suffering, of the Jewish people. Far from creating orthodox or didactic effects, however, her fiction is often irreverent, startling, even grotesque. Subject to unexpected twists and sudden disasters, the universe of Ozick's two novels, various novellas, and numerous short stories is frequently visited by magic and the demonic. Irradiating the quotidian landscape, elements of the fantastic cast a symbolic light on local characters and conditions. Drawing upon the traditions and lore of Judaism, Ozick

Photo by Ricki Rosen

conjures her Jewish magic to illuminate the moral dimensions of both fiction and contemporary reality.

Two recent and related works by Ozick brilliantly reveal the paradoxical originality and orthodoxy of her fiction: the short story, "Puttermesser: Her Work History, Her Ancestry, Her Afterlife," and the subsequent novella, "Puttermesser and Xanthippe."[1] Their eponymous heroine, Ruth Puttermesser, is a New York City lawyer struggling against the forces of discrimination and corruption in this world while dreaming of a better one to come. As her author demonstrates, Puttermesser's eventual attempt to institute a reign of reason in her city does even greater violence to the human condition than does the villainy ravaging it from within. To explore the implications of this paradox, Ozick employs a self-conscious narrative persona who alternately serves as guide, watchdog, and goad to her unwary readers. Calling attention to the literary status of the text, the narrating persona deliberately reveals Puttermesser's author to be a fallible mortal, not an omniscient god. By qualifying even the author's power to create images, Ozick's self-conscious narrative techniques illuminate and underscore her central theme: the dangers of idolatry.

A characteristic example of narrative reflexivity occurs midway through the short story when the narrating persona pauses to address the reader in a few short paragraphs that signal a fork in the road of Puttermesser's biography: "Now if this were an optimistic portrait," she says, "exactly here is where Puttermesser's emotional life would begin to grind itself into evidence." Ozick's readers must not expect such conventional satisfactions, however; a romantic denouement "is not to be." The narrator declares that Ruth Puttermesser, already past thirty, "will not marry," though she may involve herself in "a long-term affair"—though again, "perhaps not" (P, 31). By drawing attention to Puttermesser's fate, the narrator warns us that certain tried and true narrative conventions—the assurance of a "happy ending," for example—have no place in this story. And while the author's intentions appear to be clear—for she has "authority" over the fiction—some of the doubt riddling problematic human existence is also reflected in the text. Certain details of Puttermesser's existence, such as a possible long-term affair, have yet to be determined; the narrator, and perhaps even the author, is privileged but hardly omnipotent.

Shortly after the passage cited above, there follows an extended account of Puttermesser's visit to her Uncle Zindel, who appears to live among the "Spanish-speaking blacks" of New York City and to teach his niece Hebrew twice a week. Initially Puttermesser's visit, and the loving instruction in the mysteries of the Hebrew alphabet that she receives from her uncle, are vividly rendered. But just as Puttermesser, with bent head, begins to trace "the bellies of the holy letters," the narrator calls a halt to the proceedings. "Stop, stop!" she cries, rhetorically waving an invisible hand at the author. "Disengage, please. Though it is true that biographies are invented, not recorded, here you invent too much. A symbol is allowed, but not a whole scene: do not accommodate too obsequiously to Puttermesser's romance. . . . Uncle Zindel lies under the earth of Staten Island. Puttermesser has never had a conversation with him; he died four years after her birth" (P, 35-36). By admonishing Puttermesser's author-"biographer" in front of the reader, as it were, the narrator succeeds in demoting the authorial presence from remote god to simple human being. Puttermesser's "biographer" is, by virtue of being a mere mortal, an impressionable author in danger of indulging her own, as well as her protagonist's, romantic longings. Though the powers of creation may bestow apparently godlike authority on an author or biographer, each is only human. This truth, as we shall see, has the gravest implications for Puttermesser herself; in the subsequent novella, "Puttermesser and Xanthippe," she will assume, with disastrous consequences, some godlike powers of her own.

When the narrrator beseeches Puttermesser's author to "disengage, please," she is diplomatically, if somewhat stagily, suggesting that the reader perform a similar mental operation. To disengage may also mean, in the business of reading, to engage more closely with the text at hand. One might even take time to leaf back to the page on which the scene with Uncle Zindel began—the scene, that is, which did not actually occur. There the reader notes with reawakened attention the deceptively innocent phrase, enclosed in parentheses, that might have been overlooked initially: "Twice a week, at night (it seemed), she went to Uncle Zindel for a lesson" (P, 33). *Seeming* belongs, of course, to the world of appearances. This innocent phrase, tucked within parentheses, opens a chink in the surface of reality and alerts us to the ironies that lie coiled beneath like springs—or, to borrow a later metaphor, like a snake. Early in Puttermesser's "life history," Ozick warns her readers to approach this story with a certain wariness. Both reader and author, after all, are fallible mortals subject to the tendency to identify with and therefore to indulge the desires of a fictional character. As Ozick later makes clear, self-indulgence puts us in danger of complying with Puttermesser's own folly—her belief in "the uses of fantasy" and the idolatrous practices to which such faith inevitably leads (PX, 91). Lest we unwittingly succumb to idolatry—by exalting our own powers of creation—Ozick delineates the moral limits to which even poetic license is subject. Hence the narrator admonishes us, along with the author-biographer, not to "invent too much": "do not accommodate too obsequiously to Puttermesser's romance." According to Ozick's moral vision, fiction has as deep an obligation to truth-telling as any work of history—though it must be admitted that invention inheres in both forms of narrative.

Her skillful handling of the narrating persona allows Ozick to draw attention to the presence of symbol and invention in her narrative while simultaneously invoking its claims to truth. She manages this effect primarily by suggesting that all biographers are authors of fiction, the case of Puttermesser's "biographer" being a pointed example. While Puttermesser's "biography" has, therefore, the truth of history about it—being the record, after all, of a life—every biography, no matter the subject, is "invented, not recorded." Both the biographer and the storyteller bestow shape, definition, and meaning on their subject by employing the patterns of art and imaginative invention. Elsewhere, in a published essay, Ozick elaborates upon this analogy: "A good biography," she says, "is itself a kind of novel. Like the classic novel, a biography believes in the notion of 'a life'—a life as a triumphal or tragic story with a shape, a story that begins at birth, moves on to a middle part, and ends with the death of the protagonist."[2] It is the shape and notion of "a life" that this miniature "biography" of Puttermesser—spanning her "ancestry," "work history," and "afterlife"—both invokes and parodies. From the title's peculiar suggestion of an afterlife to the narrator's stagy interruptions, this biography playfully exposes its inherent contradictions. Ozick's narrative techniques are not the product of mere aesthetic gamesmanship, however. Puttermesser's life history is a parody, first and foremost, because she has no history. Though she longs to "claim an ancestor," her only meeting with Uncle Zindel is a fantasy. "She demands connection—surely a Jew must own a past. Poor Puttermesser has found herself in the world without a past" (*P,* 36).

The playful sabotage of Uncle Zindel's existence within the narrative is only one example of the way in which Ozick uses parody to expose a profoundly serious, if not tragic, historical dilemma that permeates her fiction: the destruction of Jewish identity by the forces of deracination, from the obliterating horrors of the Holocaust to the less obvious perils of contemporary assimilation. Unmoored in the New World from Judaic tradition and fidelity to Mosaic law, Ruth

Puttermesser, the descendant of immigrants, can in effect claim neither a Yankee nor a Jewish heritage. Her dispossession is satirically underscored by the narrator's description of Puttermesser's immigrant "grandfather in his captain's hat." This forefather, whom Puttermesser knows only by his photograph, was merely a counterfeit captain—his hat a replica of the ones he sold as "a hat-and-neckwear peddler to Yankees." Pointing up the irony of the grandfather's Yankee pose, Ozick's narrator informs us that Puttermesser's grandfather "gave up peddling to captain a dry-goods store in Providence, Rhode Island" (P, 26, 36). In this wry sentence, the reappearance of the captain's hat in verbal form suggests that Puttermesser's grandfather clung to his Yankee guise even after he had peddled his last hat. Puttermesser's father, the son of this counterfeit captain, evidently furthered the process of cultural dispossession. His daughter Ruth, we are told, "began life as the child of an anti-Semite. Her father would not eat kosher meat—it was, he said, too tough. He had no superstitions" (P, 37). And while great-uncle Zindel is her mother's relative, "Puttermesser's mother does not remember him." He is only "a name in the dead grandmother's mouth." To his name and legend, nonetheless, "Puttermesser clings. America is a blank, and Uncle Zindel is all her ancestry" (P, 36).

History, as the protagonist of another Ozick story says, has become "a vacuum."[3] New York City teems with the uprooted offspring of mutually hostile races and forgotten cultures. The dream of a regenerated New World lies in ruins—the wilderness of a hundred clashing "life-styles" replacing memory in "America's blank." Symptomatic of this dispossession, Puttermesser's younger sister has married "a Parsee chemist" and gone to live with her Indian husband in Calcutta: "Already the sister had four children and seven saris of various fabrics" (P, 22). Here Ozick's laconic syntax satirically equates the children with the saris, as bizarre manifestations of cultural rootlessness. Within two generations the Yankee captain's hat has been replaced by seven saris; the ease with which cultures are abandoned and adopted suggests not tolerance among peoples but their mutual deprivation.

Like "America's blank," Puttermesser's "work history" invokes its opposite: discontinuity rather than progression. In recognition of this discontinuity, Ozick's narrator interjects further apparently casual remarks that satirically expose the social injustice that operates in an alleged democratic society. Once again she employs deliberately reductive syntax to underscore the dehumanizing forces against which Puttermesser struggles. Despite her academic honors, her position as editor of the *Yale Law Review* and her "standardized" English pronunciation—drilled into her by fanatical teachers, elocutionary missionaries hired out of the Midwest by Puttermesser's prize high school—Puttermesser's work history is a story of defeat. True assimilation into the cultural mainstream proves impossible. Immediately upon graduation from law school she is hired, "for her brains and ingratiating (read: immigrant-like) industry," by "a blueblood Wall Street firm" (*P,* 24-25). Here the narrator's apparently casual comment, enclosed within another set of parentheses, suggests the disconcerting reality behind the mask of social propriety. The dedicated industry by which Puttermesser hopes to gain a foothold in the social establishment only confirms, to her blueblood employers, her essential identity as a futilely aspiring immigrant. This sense of futility is reaffirmed in a later sentence, informing us that routinely "three Jews a year joined the back precincts" of "Midland, Reid & Cockleberry" and "three Jews a year left—not the same three," however (*P,* 25). By syntactically reducing them to interchangeable entities, Ozick suggests that these young Jews, while certainly usable to the elite Wall Street firm, are as expendable, culturally speaking, as the seven saris of Puttermesser's sister or her grandfather's Yankee captain's hat.

Weary of being patronized, Puttermesser eventually finds a new job in the city Department of Receipts and Disbursements, where she is "not even a curiosity." Here those who share her title of assistant corporation counsel are mostly "Italians and Jews"—though, again, Puttermesser bears the distinction of being the only woman. The department soon emerges as a microcosm of the chaotic, anonymous, and brutal world of the urban melting pot. Here there are "no ceremonies and no manners," only "gross shouts, ignorant clerks, slovenliness, [and] litter on the floor." The ladies' room reeks of urine, the departments of corruption. Heads of departments are "all political appointees—scavengers after spoils" (*P,* 28). Puttermesser, the highly motivated, scholastically brilliant granddaughter of an immigrant peddler, has climbed the American ladder of success only to discover the ignominy of existence among scavengers and thieves. Her response to this ignominy is, once again, to indulge in fantasy, as evinced by her nightmarish vision of the Municipal Building where she works: "It was a monstrous place, gray everywhere, abundantly tunneled, with multitudes of corridors and stairs and shafts, a kind of swollen doom through which the bickering of small-voiced officials whinnied" (*P,* 28). The building is likened at once to an underground maze for rats and to a permanent psychotic condition—where oppression and doom swell to organic life, crushing all that is human. In Puttermesser's mind, the American dream has become a Kafkaesque nightmare. And from this hellish nightmare of the present the dreamer seeks escape, through "the uses of fantasy," to a better "World to Come." As though compensating for her failure to recover her lost ancestry as a Jew, Puttermesser drifts into daydreams of a future paradise.

The "dream of *gan eydn*—a term and notion handed on from her great-uncle Zindel"—is what links Puttermesser's unrequited longing for a past, or ancestry, to her utopian fantasies of a "World to Come." To "postulate an afterlife" is, like the fantasized visit to Uncle Zindel, "a game in the head not unlike melting a fudge cube held against the upper palate" (*P,* 31-32). This implied comparison between Puttermesser's delectable fantasies of heaven and the rich pleasures of eating chocolate fudge is sustained by other images throughout the narrative. Derived from both Hebraic Eden and the pagan world of nature, Puttermesser's dream of paradise is also an intellectual's garden of rational delights. For Puttermesser, it is in "the green air of heaven [that] Kant and Nietzsche together fall into crystal splinters" like some radiant philosophical manna (*P,* 32-33). Her Eden, summoned in the language of "old green book[s]," is both a philosopher's and a child's paradise, offering "perfection of desire upon perfection of contemplation" along with an unstinting supply of delicious fudge. Conveniently enough, and in keeping with the nature of romantic fantasy, "in Eden there was no tooth decay" (*PX,* 155; *P,* 32). Fed by the radiant waters of "Intellect and Knowledge," Puttermesser's "luxuriant dream" betrays an escapist's indulgence (*PX,* 117). Like her weakness for fudge, her dream expresses a naive longing for the sweet life (*P,* 32).

By carefully arranging the elements of her narrative, Ozick creates the startling suggestion that Puttermesser's dream of paradise is allied to her nightmarish fantasies of hell. Not coincidentally, Puttermesser's luxuriant dream of a new Garden of Eden—where it is "green, green, green everywhere, green above and green below"— suggests the same verdant growth as the Municipal Building's monstrous "vegetable organism." In Puttermesser's view, this "building and its workers were together some inexorable vegetable organism with its own laws of subsistence. The civil servants were grass. Nothing destroyed them, they were stronger than the pavement, they were stronger than time." Like some hideous dragon crouched in the underworld, "the organism breathed, it comprehended itself" (*P,* 29). Verdant nature is, of course, a traditional aspect of biblical Eden as it is of the pastoral idyll. In Puttermesser's fantasies, however, the repeated emphasis on green nature and its organic potency begins to sound a warning note. That Puttermesser's dream of heaven contains the seeds of its own monstrous hell is a prophecy subsequently fulfilled by the creation, and destruction, of the golem.

The appearance of the golem in the novella graphically demonstrates Puttermesser's enchantment with the uses of fantasy. By introducing this magical event into an otherwise familiar urban environment, Ozick dramatizes the dangerous power of the human mind, dabbling in creation, to unleash lethal forces in the concrete world. Yet the opening pages of the novella hardly prepare the reader for such extraordinary developments. Here we find Puttermesser, at the age of forty-six, entrenched in the vicissitudes of quotidian existence—further than ever, it would appear, from the realization of her dreams. Whether or not her love of fudge has persisted, Puttermesser is by no means in heaven. Unprotected by any celestial immunity to tooth decay, she has developed "peridontal disease" involving "sixty percent bone loss." Her "gums were puffy, her teeth in peril of uprooting. It was as if, in the dread underworld below the visible gums, a volcano lay watching for its moment of release" (PX, 79). Yet despite—or because of—the disappointments of actual life and the forces of deracination threatening even her teeth, she has not ceased to believe in the uses of fantasy. The pressure of these fantasies will, in fact, unleash the dread volcano lying in wait. Through the power of her "unironic, unimaginative, her plain but stringent mind," Puttermesser activates forces dangerous to herself, to others, and to the city she so fervently desires to save.

Puttermesser's predilection for fantasy, Ozick makes clear, might not be attributable to an excess of poetic imagination. Though idealist and dreamer, she is an intellectual and rationalist for whom Plato is favorite bedtime reading. (Her lover, who tires of waiting for her to finish the *Theaetetus*, finally abandons her.) Like other literal-minded idealists who are determined to realize their vision, Puttermesser is compelled not to invention but to implementation. Still employed at the Department of Receipts and Disbursements, she is more beguiled by the uses of fantasy than any poet to whom Plato might accusingly point, for she attempts to realize her ideals in action rather than in words. Out of the degenerate and disorderly universe of New York City she seeks to create a new world, an earthly paradise. Longing for social redemption, worshipping "this god of the ideal," Puttermesser sets a minor miracle in motion.[4] Out of her "desires as strong and strange as powers" there springs a golem.[5]

Apparently validating Puttermesser's faith in "the uses of fantasy," the golem vows to her maker: "You made me. I will be of use to you" (*PX*, 98). Puttermesser's ambition to construct an ideal city thus begins to materialize; the idealist becomes a social engineer.

Ozick's own use of fantasy, the literary invention of a golem, is a form of narrative reflexivity that serves both to distance the reader from depicted events and to suggest latent ironies and complexities of meaning. Just before the golem appears, Puttermesser, alone in her apartment, carries the Sunday *New York Times*, "as heavy as if she carried a dead child," to her bed. Already her active mind anticipates the impact of those scenes—of murder, larceny and rape—that inevitably blare from a metropolitan newspaper's pages. Instead of these images, however, Puttermesser confronts "a naked girl [who] lay in [her] bed. She looked dead—she was all white, bloodless" (*PX*, 92). Noting the grittiness of the creature's skin, Puttermesser shudders at the thought that some "filthy junkie or prostitute" has crawled into her bed. The narration of Puttermesser's discovery emphasizes rather than resolves the incongruity between the magical nature of the golem and the laws of ordinary reality. No sooner does Puttermesser assume a plausible social identity for the naked creature—an identity continuous with the urban reality trumpeted from the pages of the *Times*—than she perceives her to be an unfinished work of creation. Without hesitation, Puttermesser "reach[es] out a correcting hand" and begins to pinch and mold the creature's unfinished nose and mouth. Then, like a sculptor at work on a clay model, she focuses her attention on perfecting its features by lengthening a forefinger that strikes her as too short: "It slid as if boneless, like taffy, cold but not sticky, and thrillingly pliable. Still, without its nail a finger can shock." Here again the description emphasizes the incongruous nature of Puttermesser's response. Impressed by the golem's unfinished finger, Puttermesser immediately accepts the magical manifestation; she is even thrilled by the golem's pliability. To Puttermesser, moreover, "the body had a look of perpetuity about it, as if it had always been reclining there, in her bed." Her reaction hints at Puttermesser's emotional and psychological *readiness* for the appearance of this "child" in her bed. Meanwhile the narrator plays up the ironic contrast between this filthy creature of clay and the pristine bed in which she appears: "such a civilized bed, the home of Plato and other high-minded readings" (*PX*, 93-94). The suggested link between these superficially disparate phenomena—the lofty realm of "Intellect and Knowledge" and the chthonic origins of the golem—will gradually be made clear.

The narrator of "Puttermesser and Xanthippe" functions in much the same way as her counterpart in the earlier "biography." Although she now refrains from overtly addressing the author, her controlling presence and occasional, ironic asides arouse critical awareness and thus effect our continued disengagement from "Puttermesser's romance." In the earlier short story, the narrating persona predicted that Puttermesser would not marry (*P,* 31). In the subsequent novella Ozick confirms the reliability of the persona's detached perspective by demonstrating the truth of her prediction. Now forty-six, Puttermesser herself recognizes "that she would never marry," "would never give birth" (*PX,* 91, 97). She is not yet reconciled to childlessness," however, and "sometimes the thought that she would never give birth tore her heart." As she carries the *Times,* as heavy as a dead child, to the bed in which she will abruptly discover the golem, Puttermesser laments that unborn child. Recalling Goethe's poem *Der Erlkönig,* she romantically envisions a parent's tragic loss: "The child was dead. In its father's arms the child was dead" (*PX,* 92). Without repeating a previous warning—that we not "accommodate too obsequiously to Puttermesser's romance"—the narrator transmits a similar, if more obliquely stated, message: Puttermesser "imagined daughters. It was self-love; all these daughters were Puttermesser as a child." Egoistic self-love apparently fuels both Puttermesser's desire for a daughter and her predilection for fantasy: "She believed in the uses of fantasy. 'A person should see himself or herself everywhere,' [Puttermesser] said. 'All things manifest us' " (*PX,* 91). By juxtaposing Puttermesser's ardent longing for a daughter with the sudden appearance of a "child" in her bed, Ozick suggests the source of the golem's creation: the potent magic of human desire. By giving reign to her fantasies, moreover, Puttermesser unwittingly attempts to usurp the supreme role of God the Creator—envisioning a world that in "all things manifest[s]" her rather than Him. Between her faith in a monotheistic God and her belief in the uses of fantasy springs a contradiction that is gradually writ large in the text of Puttermesser's existence.[6]

This contradiction is complicated by the fact that Puttermesser employs traditional Jewish magic to summon the golem to life, just as she will later use magic to destroy her. Reading the "single primeval Hebrew word, shimmering with its lightning holiness" on the golem's forehead, Puttermesser utters "the Name of Names" aloud—whereupon "the inert creature, as if drilled through by electricity," leaps "straight from the bed" into life. This symbolic electrical force may emanate from the same source that galvanized, in a lightning flash, Dr. Frankenstein's monster: the heavens. Yet despite the evidence that a creative force beyond her own—in this case, the power summoned by invoking God's holy name—is needed to jolt matter into life, Puttermesser unconsciously begins to assume the role of ultimate creator. It later "disturbs her that she did not recall making [the golem]"—but as Puttermesser gazes upon her "handiwork," the narrator's language parodistically echoes the biblical account of creation: "She looked at the [golem's] mouth; she saw what she had made" (*PX*, 106, 95, 97).

An extension of Puttermesser's "desires as strong and strange as powers," the golem declares to her "maker": "I know everything you know. I am made of earth but also I am made out of your mind." She adds, "I express you. I copy and record you" (*PX*, 98, 123). Yet the golem proves to have a mind of her own—and, as a logical consequence of her origins, a mind that seeks to manifest itself everywhere. "Use me in the wide world," she instructs Puttermesser; yet subservience to her creator contradicts the willfulness of the mind the golem manifests. As soon as she springs to life, therefore, the creature challenges Puttermesser's will and intentions. To begin with, she rejects the Hebrew name that Puttermesser, who has "always imagined a daughter named Leah," bestows on her; the golem insists on being called by the pagan Greek name of Xanthippe. To no avail, Puttermesser voices her objection, saying, "Xanthippe was a shrew. Xanthippe was Socrates' wife" (*PX*, 97-98). Thus indirectly Ozick reinforces the connection, suggested earlier, between the golem's recalcitrant nature and the high-minded realm of Plato and rational ideas. Like Socrates' infamous wife, Puttermesser's surrogate daughter will prove a scourge rather than a helpmate.

The unlikely relation of rational ideas to Jewish magic is a theme Ozick develops by means of a major self-conscious narrative device: the interpolation of other texts within the writer's own, which inevitably draws attention to the literary artifice. The interpolation of sources of golem history throughout the ages also emphasizes Ozick's contemporary reworking of a traditional theme. Not only does Puttermesser's author update the ancient theme by providing an urban American setting for the golem; she reverses the tradition established since biblical times by making the golem female. Formed in the image of her female creator, Xanthippe envinces the new power of women in contemporary Western society. Only those who have experienced some degree of social and intellectual authority are likely, it would seem, to nurture the ambitions of a golem maker. A "classical feminist" deeply committed to the social, political and intellectual equality of women, Ozick does not present Puttermesser's golem making as a glorious matriarchal feat overturning male-centered religious tradition.[7] Rather, through the analogies established between Puttermesser and her male predecessors, Ozick suggests that her heroine falls prey to the same overweening ambition indulged, for millennia, by male dreamers and intellectuals.

The interpolated sources on the golem, it quickly becomes clear, establish Puttermesser's unambiguous affinity with her male counterparts. They also provide Ozick's less well informed readers with a brief but necessary introduction, spanning six pages of an eighty-page text, to the long history of the golem in Jewish lore. The immediate occasion for this helpful summary is Puttermesser's pressing curiosity to understand what she, the golem maker, has wrought. While she knows "the noble Dr. Gershom Scholem's bountiful essay 'The Idea of the Golem' virtually by heart," she traces "the history of the genus golem" in numerous other sources as well.[8] Originating, as Scholem points out, in a Hebrew word in the Bible, then evolving through medieval cabalistic texts and legends, the permutations of golem history culminate in the nineteenth century, although they may also be found in modern literary fables and tales.

By reading up on "the genus golem," Puttermesser seeks to discover why she—avowedly "no mystic, enthusiast, pneumaticist, ecstatic, kabbalist"—has been visited by this magical manifestation. Following the process of Puttermesser's inquiry, Ozick's readers benefit from the information she gains but through her narrative strategies are able to arrive at their own significantly different conclusions. What strikes Puttermesser as she reads is "the kind of intellect (immensely sober, pragmatic, unfanciful, rationalist like her own) to which a golem ordinarily occurred." The "Great Rabbi Judah Loew, circa 1520–1609," for example, was "a solid scholar, a pragmatic leader" who fashioned a golem out of clay in an attempt to save the Jews of Prague. Whether the foregoing parenthetical remark on the nature of Puttermesser's sober intellect is registered in her own consciousness or provided for the reader's benefit by the narrator, who has made several previous parenthetical appearances, remains ambiguous. In any event alerted to possible parallels, Ozick's readers begin to discern further analogies between Puttermesser and her precursors. We learn, for example, that Rabbi Loew was moved to create a golem when, as they had for Puttermesser, "the scurrilous politics of his city" had "gone too far." And when told that the great rabbi "entered a dream of Heaven" in order to discover the secret of golem making, readers are likely to recognize Puttermesser's own heavenly dream as having similarly paved the way (PX, 99-100).

Puttermesser's "sober, pragmatic, unfanciful, rationalist" intellect is in marked contrast to the traditional stereotype of the female mind as being weak, irrational, fickle. The traditional stereotype might help, in fact, to account for the consistently male identity of the golem maker and his golem in Jewish lore throughout the ages. Overturning this tradition as well as the stereotype, Ozick's account neither exalts nor deprecates Puttermesser's sober intellect. Committed to the principle of sexual equality, Ozick portrays Puttermesser as neither inferior nor superior to her male counterparts. Possessed of formidable rational powers long thought to belong solely to men, Puttermesser is shown to incur the same risks that attend the male golem maker's intellectual ambition.[9] Both the interpolated sources, as they are arranged in the narrative, and the narrator's parenthetical asides alert the reader to the morally problematic nature of Puttermesser's enterprise. Yet Puttermesser herself, because of her unqualified trust in the methods of the "reasoner" and the "refinements of . . . analysis," remains blind to the danger. Reading about the original golem makers' attempts to imitate creation by activating matter, she quickly perceives that they are "the plausible forerunners" of contemporary "physicists, biologists, or logical positivists."[10] Mistakenly vindicated by what she perceives as having "nothing irrational in it," Puttermesser concludes that "she would not be ashamed of what she herself had concocted" (PX, 104).

By fashioning her minihistory of the genus golem achronologically, Ozick ensures that her readers will not remain so complacently unaware. After providing the high-minded example of Rabbi Judah Loew in the sixteenth century, the narrator introduces various accounts going back to the time of the prophets Jeremiah and Daniel. "Even before that [time]," she continues, "thieves among the wicked generation that built the Tower of Babel swiped some of the contractor's materials to fashion idols, which were made to walk by having the Name shoved into their mouths; then they were taken for gods" (PX, 102). The achronological account of the history of the golem thus hints at the possible deterioration of the golem maker's idealistic intentions, like those of Rabbi Loew, into sheer will for power. The narrative handling of the interpolated texts ultimately serves to underscore the protagonist's own moral decline: the golem Xanthippe signals Puttermesser's descent from dreaming idealist to practical politician, culminating in her eventual declaration, "I have to be Caesar" (PX, 136).[11]

In the name of rational idealism, Puttermesser brings the golem to life and justifies her creation, unaware that she has released telluric forces that will not respond to the appeal of reason. In this way she indeed resembles her "scientific" precursors, whose initial enthusiasm for the pragmatic uses of the golem she also rehearses. The tasks she assigns Xanthippe quickly escalate from the traditional duties of servant and housekeeper to the implementation of a PLAN by which New York City can be rehabilitated and redeemed. With the golem's assistance she campaigns throughout the city for the office of mayor. Her party, "Independents for Socratic and Prophetic Idealism—ISPI for short," promises "to transform the City of New York into Paradise." Here again, the arrangement of narrative details comments ironically on Puttermesser's ambitions. In the acronym of the party's name as well as in its campaign poster, the snake of irony hisses audibly—the asp in ISPI—at Puttermesser's Edenic dream. The poster "shows an apple tree with a serpent in it. The S in ISPI is the serpent. Puttermesser . . . has promised to cast out the serpent" (PX, 128). Despite such a promise, the serpent lies dramatically coiled, as letter, sign, and symbol, within the text of the narrative. Symbolizing Adam and Eve's defiance of God's law in their temptation to acquire absolute knowledge and power, the serpent indicates the inherent flaw in Puttermesser's dream of Eden. She too will grow infatuated with power and dream of making "an entire legion of golems"— "herself the creator down to the last molecule of [their] ear-wax" (PX, 131).

Embedded in Ozick's narrative, as it is in the name and poster representing Puttermesser's political party, the serpent is a potent sign that draws the reader's attention to unseen forces ready to spring into action like the volcano, "in the dread underworld" of Puttermesser's infected gums, "waiting for its moment of release." Arresting the reader's attention, these patterns and images tend to slow the momentum of the plot. Calling attention to this effect, Ozick's narrator slyly remarks on the reader's probable inertia: "All this must be recorded as lightly and swiftly as possible; a dry patch to be gotten through, perhaps via a doze or a skip" (PX, 128). As Puttermesser is progressively more caught up in her luxuriant dream—earnestly believing she can apply her material magic to remaking reality into "a rational daylight place [that] has shut out the portals of night"— careless readers may tend to go along with the delusion. By dozing and skipping over the bright surface of visible reality, they will have submitted to some rather potent local magic: the illusions of art. The spell of the narrative, its stream of successive events, is itself a kind of luxuriant dream that catches the passive dreamer in its coils.

To break this spell, as we have seen, Ozick employs a variety of self-conscious devices, including the narrative persona who needles the reader into critical awareness and moral attention. As a further strategy Ozick divides "Puttermesser and Xanthippe" into twelve sections or chapters, each preceded by a Roman numeral and a descriptive title or heading. These headings frame the action while they distance the reader from its immediate effects—so that the often ironic relation between incident and meaning gradually emerges. One heading, for example, is entitled "Puttermesser's Fall, and the History of the Genus Golem." The fall recounted in the narrated events, however, is hardly a moral one. Ostensibly the title refers to Puttermesser's losing her job at the Department of Receipts and Disbursements. In this instance, she is merely the victim of a corrupt system of spoils. What the heading obliquely suggests, on the other hand, is a possible connection between the appearance of the golem and some moral blunder or fall on Puttermesser's part.

The title of a later chapter, "The Golem Destroys Her Maker," is also superficially misleading: Puttermesser is not literally destroyed, but later the golem is. The title is a comment, not on these literal events, but on Puttermesser's shaky status as idol maker: "The coming of the golem animated the salvation of the City, yes—but who, Puttermesser sometimes wonders, is the true golem? . . . Xanthippe did not exist before Puttermesser made her . . . [but] Xanthippe made Puttermesser Mayor, and Puttermesser sees that she is the golem's golem" (*PX*, 135-36). Having unleashed, with her material magic, the forces of nature, Puttermesser cannot control what she has wrought. Xanthippe daily grows larger, and her capacity to carry out Mayor Puttermesser's will is more than matched by her own monstrous will, size, and appetite. When the golem, whose "blood is hot," tries to slake her mounting lust on the city officials, they are quickly exhausted and finally ruined in the process. Of the "broad green City" she helps transform into a temporary Eden, Xanthippe has said earlier, "I can tear it all down." Now the golem begins to fulfill her prophecy (*PX*, 139-40).

Like the insatiably lustful pagan goddess in Ozick's story "The Dock-Witch," Xanthippe embodies the destructive potency of organic nature. That telluric forces can wreak havoc when human consciousness—pagan, romantic, or "scientific"—exalts them is a pervasive theme in Ozick's fiction. Fashioning a clay idol by means of her own Jewish magic, Puttermesser has entered into this dangerous worship.[12] So instead of slaying the dragon—the fearful "organism" that "breathes and comprehends itself"—Puttermesser has roused it in another form. Like all idolators, she is enslaved by the very powers she has sought to placate. Having unleashed those forces in order to perfect the material order, she becomes "the golem's golem." Now as the city grows "diseased with the golem's urge," Puttermesser's career as mayor is clearly over. In this sense destroyed, she must destroy the golem before riot and rage demolish what is left of the city.

Traditional tales of the fantastic, Tzvetan Todorov has pointed out, describe the conflict between reason and the "mirror" world of magic and distorted perception. Ozick significantly inverts these conventions to create a parable for our time, suggesting that reason may detonate its own fatal magic.[13] The golem is created, then justified by her maker's worship of "Intellect and Knowledge"; yet Puttermesser loves her creation as her "own shadow," an extension of her (godlike) self. In a similar act of self-love, the male protagonist of Ozick's book exalts the educator's power "to seize in the hand new mind, fresh clay, early intellect," and mold it like a "monarch" in his image.[14] The sinister irony is, of course, that one act of usurpation follows another. By exalting his own powers of creation over any other and declaring himself the highest law and authority, the usurper is in danger of creating his own alter ego. Summoned like Xanthippe by the usurper's magic, such a creature is likely, as a mirror of his creator's will, to defy the very power that made him.

Puttermesser's matriarchal urges are not depicted as morally superior to her male counterpart's patriarchal drives. Her overweening fantasies are, moreover, an extension of rational idealism rather than poetic imagination. Ozick is not suggesting, however, that rationalists are the only dreamers susceptible to forms of idolatry. As a writer who by her own statement "lust[s] after stories more and more," she also detects the whiff of idolatry permeating the rituals of art. Fashioning images that stun and captivate, inciting the beholder to wonder—and perhaps worship—at the altar of art, the artist is implicated in the idol making that preoccupies Ozick everywhere in her writing. This concern is voiced most directly in "Usurpation (Other People's Stories)," a novella that, by Ozick's testimony, suggests how "the story-making faculty itself can be a corridor to the corruptions and abominations of idol-worship, of the adoration of magical event." For Ozick, "belief in idols is belief in magic. And storytelling, as every writer knows, is a kind of magic act."[15] Because, like Puttermesser, "artists play with clay and then ask that the clay be honored," there is "in every act of creation the faint shadow of idolmaking."[16]

Readers of the Puttermesser stories might well assume that the self-conscious narrative devices that Ozick employs are themselves symptomatic of their creator's idolatrous self-love. They are, it might be said, the author's way of arranging her fictional universe so that "all things manifest her." Victor Strandberg has said, with some justification, that Ruth Puttermesser "is in some ways an alter ego of her maker."[17] Sharing much of her author's experience and many of her avowed interests—especially in the pursuit of "Knowledge and Intellect"—Puttermesser, it might then be suggested, is a kind of golem herself, forged by Ozick's own, highly original Jewish magic. When subjected to careful analysis, however, Ozick's self-conscious narrative techniques prove to work in quite the opposite way: even her most overt authorial ploys are ranged against the idol-making tendencies of art itself.

A conclusive example of this countering effect occurs in the final paragraph of the first Puttermesser story under discussion. Here, directly addressing the reader, the narrator says: "The scene with Uncle Zindel . . . could not occur because, though Puttermesser dares to posit an ancestry, we may not. Puttermesser is not to be examined as an artifact but as an essence. . . . Puttermesser is henceforth [in the subsequent novella, that is] to be presented as a given" (P, 38). Adopting the first person plural "we," the narrator appears to be speaking now on behalf of the author-biographer as well as herself. Obliquely she alludes to some operating principle—moral, aesthetic, perhaps both—that prohibits author and narrator from indulging the kind of fantasy in which Puttermesser "dares" to engage. Acknowledging their mortal limits, they apparently do not aim to usurp the role of ultimate Creator, the source of that human essence of which Puttermesser, though a fictional character, partakes. In other words, Puttermesser is not simply presented as the author's artifact but as a representative of the race descended from Adam and Eve. She is not the author's golem or clay idol, fashioned for the uses of fantasy by an arbitrary set of signs and symbols. As the image of a human being, her origins and her essence are ultimately a given of Creation—God-given, that is—even while she is conjured, shaped, and manipulated by the author. While the first half of this assertion underscores the moral and metaphysical basis of Ozick's art, the latter half recognizes the temporary and local powers of the artist. As Vladimir Nabokov once put it, in a now familiar phrase, an author "may impersonate an anthropomorphic deity" within the world of his fiction, but his godlike authority does not extend beyond the page.

Having alerted us to Puttermesser's ineffable essence, Ozick redirects attention to the playfully staged dialogue between the narrator and Puttermesser's silent biographer. The first Puttermesser story ends as the narrating persona calls out to the silent author: "Hey! Puttermesser's biographer! What will you do with her now?" (P, 38). To pose such a question in the concluding line of a story is, quite obviously, to flaunt the conditions of artifice. Yet Ozick remains true to her character's essence by offering an answer to this apparently rhetorical question—couched in the form of yet another fiction, published five years later. "Puttermesser and Xanthippe," the overt creation of self-conscious artifice, nonetheless testifies to Ozick's profoundly moral commitment as an artist. Like most of her other fiction, both the Puttermesser stories employ postmodernist narrative techniques to convey a deeply orthodox vision of reality. One of Ozick's abiding concerns, as I have demonstrated, is the multivalent forms of idolatry that have proliferated in our era—an era not merely secular in nature but one that exalts usurpation in every conceivable arena of life: practical and political, philosophical and artistic. In all spheres of social and cultural activity idols to which are attributed absolute power and authority are eagerly embraced: the glorified state, the arm of technology and progress, the "final solution," the mythical promise of artificial intelligence or simply those old and familiar gods, Moloch and Mammon. Among artists and literary scholars the ideal, or idol, of usurpation is no less evident. Among Ozick's contemporaries, the prominent Yale critic, Harold Bloom, for example, unambiguously exalts the usurper at the heart of all literary endeavor: "We read," Bloom says, "to usurp, just as the poet writes to usurp. Usurp what? A place, a stance, a fullness, an illusion of identification or possession; something we can call our own or even ourselves."[18] But to Cynthia Ozick this fullness, presence, essence, or identity is already ours—the given of Creation it is the artist's responsibility to fulfill rather than merely invent. To the testimony of this presence, as witness rather than usurper, she dedicates the narrative magic of her art.

NOTES

1. Cynthia Ozick, "Puttermesser: Her Work History, Her Ancestry, Her Afterlife," *New Yorker* 53 (9 May 1977): 38-44; "Puttermesser and Xanthippe," *Salmagundi* 55 (Winter 1982): 163-225; hereafter cited in the text as *P* and *PX*, respectively.

2. Cynthia Ozick, "Justice (Again) to Edith Wharton," *Commentary* 62 (October 1976): 48-57.

3. Cynthia Ozick, "Envy; or, Yiddish in America," *Commentary* 48 (November 1969): 33-53.

4. Cynthia Ozick, "Preface," *Bloodshed and Three Novellas* (New York: Alfred A. Knopf, 1976).

5. According to Gershom Scholem, the distinguished historian of Jewish religious tradition and texts, the idea of "the golem as a man created by magical art" originates in "certain Jewish conceptions concerning Adam, the first man." "Golem," he points out, "is a Hebrew word that occurs only once in the Bible, in Psalm 139:16. . . . Here probably, and certainly in the later sources, 'golem' means the unformed, amorphous." In the philosophical literature of the Middle Ages, "it is used as a Hebrew term for matter, formless *hylé*. . . . In this sense, Adam was said to be 'golem' before the breath of God had touched him"; see "The Idea of the Golem," in *On the Kabbalah and Its Symbolism,* trans. Ralph Manheim (London: Routledge & Kegan Paul, 1965), 159-61.

6. As Scholem points out, "obviously a man who creates a golem is in some sense competing with God's creation of Adam; in such an act the creative power of man enters into a relationship, whether of emulation or antagonism, with the creative power of God"; ibid., 159.

7. Identifying herself as a "classical feminist," Ozick has argued against those radical feminists who perceive "apartness," or separatism from men, as "the dominant aim, even chief quality of feminism." "Classical feminism—i.e., feminism at its origin, when it saw itself as justice and aspiration made universal, as mankind widened to humankind—rejected anatomy not only as destiny, but as any sort of governing force; it rejected the notion of 'female sensibility' as a slander designed to shut women off from access to the delights, confusions, achievements, darknesses, and complexities of the great world": "Literature and the Politics of Sex: A Dissent," *Ms.* 6 (December 1977): 79-80.

8. Scholem's essay is cited in notes 5 and 6, above.

9. The human mind, Ozick says, is "androgynous, epicene, asexual"; thus "the minds of men and women [are] indistinguishable": "Previsions of the Demise of the Dancing Dog," in *Art and Ardor* (New York: Knopf, 1983), 263.

10. In an essay originally delivered as a dedicatory address on the occasion of the "unveiling" of a new computer at the Weizmann Institute at Rehovot, Scholem makes a similar point: Despite "all the theological trappings," he says, "there is a straight line linking the two developments" of golem history and that of applied science and mathematics. Rabbi Loew of Prague "was not only the spiritual, but also the actual, ancestor of Theodor von Karman who . . . was extremely proud of this ancestor of his in whom he saw the first genius of applied mathematics in his family. But . . . Rabbi Loew was also the spiritual ancestor of two other departed Jews—I mean John von

Neumann and Norbert Wiener—who contributed more than anyone else to the magic of the modern Golem [the computer]"; see "The Golem of Prague and the Golem of Rehovot," in *The Messianic Idea in Judaism and Other Essays on Jewish Spirituality* (New York: Schocken Books, 1971), 336.

11. As Scholem points out, the translation of the idea of the golem from "Kabbalistic speculations on the spiritual plane" to "down-to-earth tales" in Jewish folk tradition also traces a descent. In cabalistic literature, the golem is associated with an "ecstatic experience" whereby "the figure of clay, infused with all those radiations of the human mind . . . became alive for the fleeting moment of ecstasy, but not beyond it." In the folk tales inspired by rumors of such cabalistic speculations, the golem, instead of representing "a spiritual experience of man, became a technical servant of man's needs, controlled by him in an uneasy and precarious equilibrium"; "The Golem of Prague and the Golem of Rehovot," 338.

12. As the narrator of Ozick's novella "Usurpation (Other People's Stories)" points out, Jewish magic is forbidden by Mosaic law. "And yet," he exclaims, "with what prowess we [Jews] have crept down the centuries after amulets, and hidden countings of letters, and the silver crown that heals: so it is after all nothing to marvel at that my own, my beloved, subject should be the preternatural—everything anti-Moses, all things blazing with their own wonder"; see *Bloodshed and Three Novellas,* 134-35. To this anti-Mosaic strain in Jewish tradition the magic of golem making obviously belongs.

13. Tzvetan Todorov, *The Fantastic: A Structural Approach to a Literary Genre,* trans. Richard Howard (Cleveland: Case Western Reserve Univ. Press, 1973), 122-23. In *An Essay on Man,* Ernst Cassirer discusses the connection between magic and scientific reason that Ozick endeavors to expose. Cassirer alludes to Sir James Frazer's "thesis that there is no sharp boundary separating magical art from our modes of scientific thought. Magic, too, however imaginary and fantastic in its means, is scientific in its aim." Although, as Cassirer says, Frazer's conception of myth and magic as "typically aetiological or explanatory" of the cosmos has been found inadequate by modern anthropologists, it does call attention to the hidden affinity between science and magic. The practitioners of both, as Ozick points out, seek mastery over the laws of nature. Sir James Frazer, *The Magic Art and the Evolution of Kings,* vol. 1 of *The Golden Bough,* 2d ed. (London: Macmillan & Co., 1900), 61ff., 220ff.; cited in Ernst Cassirer, *An Essay on Man: An Introduction to a Philosophy of Human Culture* (New Haven: Yale Univ. Press, 1944; reissued, 1972), 75-76.

14. Cynthia Ozick, *The Cannibal Galaxy* (New York: Knopf, 1983), 56; revised from "The Laughter of Akiva," *New Yorker* 56 (10 November 1980): 60.

15. Cynthia Ozick, "Preface," *Bloodshed and Three Novellas,* 10-12.

16. Catherine Rainwater and William J. Scheick, "An Interview with Cynthia Ozick (Summer 1982)," *Texas Studies in Literature and Language* 25, Special Issue: *Three Contemporary Women Novelists: Hazzard, Ozick, and Redmon* (Summer 1983): 260.

17. Victor Strandberg, "The Art of Cynthia Ozick," *Three Contemporary Women Novelists*, 309.

18. Harold Bloom, *Agon: Towards a Theory of Revisionism* (New York: Oxford Univ. Press, 1982), 17.

A Bibliography of Writings by

CYNTHIA OZICK

Susan Currier & Daniel J. Cahill

BOOKS

Trust. New York: New American Library, 1966.
The Pagan Rabbi and Other Stories. New York: Alfred A. Knopf, 1971.
Bloodshed and Three Novellas. New York: Knopf, 1976.
Levitation: Five Fictions. New York: Knopf, 1982.
Art and Ardor. New York: Knopf, 1983.
The Cannibal Galaxy. New York: Knopf, 1983.

SHORT STORIES

"The Sense of Europe." *Prairie Schooner* 30 (June 1956): 126-38.
"Stone." *Botteghe Oscure* 20 (Autumn 1957), 388-414.
"The Butterfly and the Traffic Light." *Literary Review* 5 (Autumn 1961): 46-54. [Reprinted in *The Pagan Rabbi and Other Stories*; in *Faith and Fiction: The Modern Short Story*, ed. Robert Detweiler and Glenn Meeter (1979).]
"The Pagan Rabbi." *Hudson Review* 19 (Autumn 1966): 425-54. [Reprinted in *Explorations: An Annual on Jewish Themes*, ed. Murray Mindlin and Chaim Bermont (1968); in *My Name Aloud: Jewish Stories by Jewish Writers*, ed. Harold U. Ribalow (1969); in *Best SF: 1971*, ed. Harry Harrison and Brian W. Aldiss (1972); in *The Pagan Rabbi and Other Stories*; in *Jewish American Stories*, ed. Irving Howe (1977); in *The Penguin Book of Jewish Stories*, ed. Emanuel Litvinoff (1979); in *More Wandering Stars: An Anthology of Jewish Fantasy and Science Fiction*, ed. Jack Dann (1981).]
"Envy; or, Yiddish in America." *Commentary* 48 (November 1969): 35-53. [Reprinted in *The Best American Short Stories, 1970*, ed. M. Foley and D. Burnett (1970); in *The Pagan Rabbi and Other Stories.*]
"The Dock-Witch." *Event* 1 (Spring 1971): 40-73. [Reprinted in *The Pagan Rabbi and Other Stories*; in *Best American Short Stories, 1972*, ed. M. Foley (1972).]

"The Doctor's Wife." *Midstream* 17 (February 1971): 53-71. [Reprinted in *The Pagan Rabbi and Other Stories.*]

"Virility." *Anon.*, February 1971 [?]. [Reprinted in *The Pagan Rabbi and Other Stories.*]

"An Education." *Esquire* 77 (April 1972): 98-102. [Reprinted in *Bitches and Sad Ladies: An Anthology of Fiction by and about Women*, ed. Pat Rotter (1975); in *Bloodshed and Three Novellas*; in *Familiar Faces: Best Contemporary American Short Stories* (1979).]

"Freud's Room." *American Journal*, 8 May 1973: 12-14. [Reprinted as the first of two fragments and retitled "From a Refugee's Notebook," in *Levitation: Five Fictions.*]

"Usurpation." *Esquire* 81 (May 1974): 124-28. [Reprinted in *Prize Stories 1975: The O. Henry Awards* (1975); in *Bloodshed and Three Novellas*; in *All Our Secrets Are the Same: New Fiction from Esquire*, ed. Gordon Lish (1976).]

"A Mercenary." *American Review* 23 (October 1975): 1-37. [Reprinted in *Best American Short Stories, 1976*, ed. M. Foley (1976); in *Bloodshed and Three Novellas.*]

"Bloodshed." *Esquire* 85 (January 1976): 100-101. [Reprinted in *Bloodshed and Three Novellas*; in *All Our Secrets Are the Same: New Fiction from Esquire*, ed. Gordon Lish (1976).]

"Puttermesser: Her Work History, Her Ancestry, Her Afterlife." *New Yorker* 53 (9 May 1977): 38-44. [Reprinted in *Levitation: Five Fictions.*]

"Shots." *Quest/77* 1 (July-August 1977): 68-72. [Reprinted in *Levitation: Five Fictions.*]

"The Sewing Harems." *Triquarterly* 40 (Fall 1977): 237-44. [Reprinted as the second of two fragments and retitled "From a Refugee's Notebook," in *Levitation: Five Fictions.*]

"Levitation." *Partisan Review* 46 (1979): 391-405. [Reprinted in *The Pushcart Prize 5*, ed. Bill Henderson (1980); in *Levitation: Five Fictions.*]

"The Laughter of Akiva." *New Yorker* 56 (10 November 1980): 50-173. [Revised version published in *The Cannibal Galaxy.*]

"The Shawl." *New Yorker* 56 (26 May 1980): 33-34. [Reprinted in *Best American Short Stories, 1981* (1981).]

"Puttermesser and Xanthippe." *Salmagundi* 55 (Winter 1982): 163-225. [Reprinted in *Levitation: Five Fictions.*]

"Rosa." *New Yorker* 59 (21 March 1983): 38-71.

"At Fumicaro." *New Yorker* 60 (6 August 1984): 32-58.

POEMS

"The Fish in the Net." *Epoch* 9 (Spring 1958): 36-37.

"Apocalypse." *Commentary* 28 (September 1959): 242.

"O Talk to Me of Angels." *San Francisco Review* 1 (September 1959): 81-82.

"The Street Criers." *Noble Savage* 2 (1960): 132-34.

"The Artist, Ha Ha." *Literary Review* 5 (Spring 1962): 407-8.

"The Engineers." *Literary Review* 5 (Spring 1962): 403-4.

"To My Uncle, A Craftsman." *Literary Review* 5 (Spring 1962): 405-6.

"The Arrest." *Literary Review* 5 (Summer 1962): 545.

"The Coming." *Literary Review* 5 (Summer 1962): 544.

"O." *Antioch Review* 22 (Summer 1962): 206.

"Short Historical Essay on Obtuseness." *Literary Review* 5 (Summer 1962): 543-44.

"Visitation." *Prairie Schooner* 36 (Fall 1962): 271.

"Footnote to Lord Acton." *Virginia Quarterly Review* 38 (Winter 1962): 100. [Reprinted in *Of Poetry and Power: Poems Occasioned by the Presidency and by the Death of John F. Kennedy,* ed. Edwin Glikes and Paul Schwaber (1964).]

"Revisiting." *Virginia Quarterly Review* 38 (Winter 1962): 99.

"The Seventeen Questions of Rabbi Zusyo." *Midstream* 8 (Winter 1962): 70.

"Stile." *Virginia Quarterly Review* 38 (Winter 1962): 99-100.

"Commuters' Train through Harlem." *Mutiny* 12 (1963): 15-16.

"Filling in the Lake." *Mutiny* 12 (1963): 15-16.

"Caryatid." *New Mexico Quarterly* 33 (Winter 1963-64): 426.

"Bridled." *Chelsea Review* 15 (June 1964): 64.

"Red-Shift." *Chelsea Review* 15 (June 1964): 65.

"A Riddle." *Judaism* 14 (Fall 1965): 436. [Reprinted in *Voices within the Ark: The Modern Jewish Poets,* ed. Howard Schwartz and Anthony Rudolf (1980).]

"Origins, Divergences." *Judaism* 14 (Fall 1965): 433.

"The Wonder Teacher." *Judaism* 14 (Fall 1965): 432-33. [Reprinted in *Voices within the Ark: The Modern Jewish Poets,* ed. Howard Schwartz and Anthony Rudolf (1980).]

"When That with Tragic Rapture Moses Stood." *Judaism* 14 (Fall 1965): 434-35.

"Yom Kippur, 5726." *Judaism* 14 (Fall 1965): 433.

"In the Synagogue." *Jewish Spectator* 35 (December 1970): 9.

"Chautauqua Poems." *Field* 8 (Spring 1973): 52.

"Fire-Foe." *Literary Review* 25 (Summer 1982): 611.

"In the Yard." *Literary Review* 25 (Summer 1982): 612.

"Urn-Burial." *Literary Review* 25 (Summer 1982): 613-16.

ARTICLES

"Geoffrey, James or Stephen." *Midstream* 3 (Winter 1957): 70-76.

"We Ignoble Savages." *Evergreen Review* 3 (November-December 1959): 48-52.

"The Jamesian Parable: The Sacred Fount." *Bucknell Review* 11 (May 1963): 55-70.

"The College Freshman: Portrait of a Hero as a Collection of Old Saws." *Confrontation* 1 (Spring 1968): 40-50. [Reprinted as "The College Freshman: A Teacher's Complaint" in *Reading, Writing, and Rewriting,* ed. W.

Moynihan, D. Lee, and H. Weil (1969); as "The College Freshman" in *The Conscious Reader*, ed. C. Shrodes, H. Finestone, and M. Shugrue (1974).]

"An Opinion on the Ovarian Mentality." *Mademoiselle* 66 (March 1968): 20, 25.

"Women and Creativity: The Demise of the Dancing Dog." *Motive* 29 (March-April 1969): 7-16. [Reprinted in *Woman in Sexist Society*, ed. Vivian Gornick and Barbara Moran (1971).]

"American: Toward Yavneh." *Judaism* 19 (Summer 1970): 264-82. [Reprinted in *Congress Bi-Weekly*, 26 February 1971; condensed and reprinted as "New Yiddish: Language for American Jews" in *Jewish Digest* 18 (February 1973); in *Art and Ardor*.]

"Alumnus as Dodo Bird." *Change: A Magazine of Higher Learning* 3 (Summer 1971): 35-39.

"24 Years in the Life of Lyuba Bershadskaya." *New York Times Magazine*, 14 March 1971, 27-29. [Written under the pseudonym Trudie Vocse.]

"Intermarriage and the Issue of Apostasy." *Sh'ma*, 19 March 1971, 74-75.

"We Are the Crazy Lady and Other Feisty Feminist Fables." *Ms.* 1 (Spring 1972): 40-44. [Reprinted in *The First Ms. Reader*, ed. Francine Klagsbrun (1973); in *The Conscious Reader: Readings Past and Present*, ed. C. Shrodes, H. Finestone, and M. Shugrue (1974); in *Woman as Writer*, ed. Jeannette Webber and Joan Grumman (1978).]

"Four Questions of the Rabbis." *Reconstructionist*, 18 February 1972, 20-23. See also "Rabbis Answer Cynthia Ozick," *Reconstructionist* 19 May 1971, 35-37.

"Literary Blacks and Jews." *Midstream* 18 (June-July 1972): 10-24. [Reprinted in *Bernard Malamud: Twentieth-Century Views*, ed. Joyce Field and Leslie Field (1975); in *Art and Ardor*.]

"A Bintel Brief for Jacob Glatstein." *Jewish Heritage* 14 (September 1972): 58-60.

"Germany Even without Munich." *Sh'ma*, 13 October 1973, 150-52.

"The Hole/Birth Catalogue." *Ms.* 1 (October 1972): 55-60. [Reprinted in *The First Ms. Reader*, ed. Francine Klagsbrun (1973); in *Motherhood: A Reader for Men and Women*, ed. Susan Cahill (1982); in *Art and Ardor*.]

"Some Antediluvian Reflections Intending to Shove Up the Generation Gap Certain Current Notions Not Held by the Writer." *American Journal*, 1 December 1972, 22-28.

"If You Can Read This, You Are Too Far Out." *Esquire* 79 (January 1973): 74, 78.

"Reconsideration: Truman Capote." *New Republic*, 27 January 1973, 31-34.

"Israel: Of Myth and Data." *Congress Bi-Weekly*, 15 June 1973, 4-8.

"All the World Wants the Jews Dead." *Esquire* 82 (November 1974): 103-7.

"Culture and the Present Moment: A Roundtable Discussion." *Commentary* 58 (December 1974): 35.

"Palestine Issue: A 'Spectacular Falsehood.' " *New York Times*, 22 November 1974, Sec. C, 38.

"A Response to Josephine Knopp's 'The Jewish Stories of Cynthia Ozick.' " *Studies in American Jewish Literature* 1 (1975): 49-50.

"A Liberal's Auschwitz." *Confrontation* 10 (Spring 1975): 125-29. [Condensed and reprinted in *Jewish Digest* 21 (November 1975); reprinted in *The Pushcart Prize 1* (1976).]

"The Riddle of the Ordinary." *Moment* 1 (July-August 1975): 55-59. [Reprinted in *Art and Ardor.*]

"Hadrian and Hebrew." *Moment* 1 (September 1975): 77-79.

"Notes towards a Meditation on Forgiveness." In *The Sunflower*, by Simon Wisenthan, with a Symposium. New York: Schocken Books, 1976, 183-90.

"Hanging the Ghetto Dog." *New York Times Book Review,* 21 March 1976, 48-57.

"Writers and Critics." *Commentary* 62 (September 1976): 8, 10.

"Justice (Again) to Edith Wharton." *Commentary* 62 (October 1976): 48-57. [Reprinted in *Art and Ardor.*]

[Response to "What Three Books Did You Most Enjoy This Year?"] in "Authors' Authors." *New York Times Book Review,* 5 December 1976, 103.

"How to Profit More from the Teachings of Clara Schact Than from All the Wisdom of Aristotle, Montaigne, Emerson, Seneca, Cicero, et al." *Esquire* 87 (May 1977): 92.

"Passage to the New World." *Ms.* 6 (August 1977): 70.

[Introduction to *Escape from Czarist Russia*, by Siphra Rigelson Ozick.] *Ms.* 6 (August 1977): 72.

"Does Genius Have a Gender?" *Ms.* 6 (December 1977): 56.

[Response to "Who Is the Living Writer You Most Admire?"] *New York Times Book Review,* 4 December 1977, 66.

"Query: Where Are the Serious Readers?" *Salmagundi* 42 (Summer-Fall 1978): 72-73.

"The Biological Premises of Our Sad Earth-Speck." *Confrontation* 15 (Fall-Winter 1978): 166-70. [Reprinted in *Art and Ardor.*]

"What Has Mysticism to Do with Judaism?" *Sh'ma,* 17 February 1978, 69-71.

"Letter to a Palestinian Military Spokesman." *New York Times,* 16 March 1978, Sec. A, 23.

"My Grandmother's Pennies." *McCall's* 106 (December 1978): 30-34.

[Reply to "Christmas Comes to a Jewish Home," by Anne Riophe.] *New York Times,* 28 December 1978, Sec. C, 1, 6.

"Notes toward Finding the Right Question (A Vindication of the Rights of Jewish Women)." *Forum* 35 (Spring-Summer 1979): 37-60. [Reprinted in *Lilith* 6 (1979).]

"Judaism and Harold Bloom." *Commentary* 67 (January 1979): 43-51.

[Response to "What Made You Decide to Become a Writer and Why?"] *New York Times Book Review,* 2 December 1979, 59.

"Pay Fair." *Savvy* 1 (January 1980): 80.

"Carter and the Jews: An American Political Dilemma." *New Leader*, 30 June 1980, 3-23.

"George Steiner's Either/Or: A Response." *Salmagundi* 50-51 (Fall 1980-Winter 1981): 90-95.

"Helping T.S. Eliot Write Better: Notes towards a Definitive Bibliography." *American Poetry Review* 10 (May-June 1981): 10-13. [Reprinted in *The Pushcart Prize 7* (1982).]

"I Call You 'Beloved.' " *The Hunter Magazine* 2 (September 1982): 3-5.

"What Literature Means." *Partisan Review* 49 (1982): 294-97.

"Spells, Wishes, Goldfish, Old School Hurts: The Making of a Writer." *New York Times Book Review*, 31 January 1982, 9.

"Works in Progress." *New York Times Book Review*, 6 June 1982, 11.

"The Lesson of the Master." *New York Review of Books*, 12 August 1982, 20-21. [Reprinted in *Art and Ardor*.]

"Bialik's Hint." *Commentary* 75 (February 1983): 22-28.

[Response to Meron Benvenisti's claim that removal to Israel of contents of PLO's Palestine Research Center in East Beirut was erasure of Palestinian culture and history.] *New York Times*, 3 March 1983, Sec. A, 26.

"Writers Domestic and Demonic." *New York Times Book Review*, 25 March 1983, 1.

[Response to Don Peretz and others rebutting identification of Palestine Research Center in Beirut as PLO intelligence matrix.] *New York Times*, 9 April 1983, Sec. A, 22.

[Response to query about what books novelists enjoy rereading.] *New York Times Book Review*, 12 June 1983, 15.

REVIEWS

[Review of *Works and Days and Other Poems*, by Irving Feldman.] *New Mexico Quarterly* 32 (Autumn-Winter 1962-63): 235-37.

"Literature or Segregated Writing" [*Soon, One Morning: New Writing by American Negroes, 1940–1962*, ed. Herbert Hill]. *Midstream* 9 (September 1963): 97-101.

"Cheever's Yankee Heritage" [*The Wapshot Scandal*, by John Cheever]. *Antioch Review* 24 (Summer 1964): 263-67.

"Novels for Adults" [*The Crossing Point* and *A Slanting Light*, by Gerda Charles]. *Midstream* 10 (March 1964): 101-4.

"America Aglow" [*The Wapshot Scandal*, by John Cheever]. *Commentary* 38 (July 1964): 66-67.

"A Contraband Life" [*Other People's Houses*, by Lore Segal]. *Commentary* 39 (March 1965): 89.

"Of Skill and Vision" [*Where Mist Clothes Dream* and *Song Runs Naked*, by Sara; *Stop Here My Friend*, by Merrill Joan Gerber]. *Midstream* 11 (June 1965): 106-8.

"The Evasive Jewish Story" [*Modern Jewish Stories*, ed. Gerda Charles]. *Midstream* 12 (February 1966): 78-80.

"Against the Grain" [*Testimony: The United States, 1885–1890*, by Charles Reznikoff]. *Congress Bi-Weekly,* 9 May 1966, 18.

[*The Children*, by Charity Blackstone; *We Came as Children*, by Karen Gershon.] *Book Week,* 30 October 1966, 16.

"Full Stomachs and Empty Rites" [*The Jewish Cookbook*, by Mildred G. Bellin]. *Congress Bi-Weekly,* 23 January 1967, 17-19. [Reprinted in *Jewish Digest* 12 (August 1967).]

"Assimilation and Downward Mobility" [*The Carpenter Years*, by Arthur A. Cohen]. *Congress Bi-Weekly,* 6 March 1967, 16-17.

"From Anger to Truth" [*Digging Out*, by Ann Richardson]. *Midstream* 13 (August-September 1967): 76-79.

"The Unresplendent Dynasties of 'Our Crowd' " [*Our Crowd*, by Stephen Birmingham]. *Congress Bi-Weekly,* 18 December 1967, 3-6.

"Reflections Pleasant and Unpleasant on Jewish Marriage and Divorce" [*The Jewish Wedding Book*, by Lilly S. Routtenberg; *Jews and Divorce*, by Jacob Fried]. *Congress Bi-Weekly,* 13 January 1969, 16-17. See also letter in reply to R.R. Seldin on *The Jewish Wedding Book, Congress Bi-Weekly,* 24 March 1969, 23.

"The Uses of Legend: Elie Wiesel as Tsaddik" [*Legends of Our Time*, by Elie Wiesel]. *Congress Bi-Weekly,* 9 June 1969, 16-20.

"Hortense Calisher's Anti-Novel" [*The New Yorkers*, by Hortense Calisher]. *Midstream* 15 (November 1969): 77-80.

"Ethnic Joke" [*Bech: A Book*, by John Updike]. *Commentary* 50 (November 1970): 106-14.

"Jews and Gentiles" [*The Goy*, by Mark Harris]. *Commentary* 51 (June 1971): 104-8.

"Forster as Homosexual" [*Maurice*, by E.M. Forster]. *Commentary* 52 (December 1971): 81-85. See also letter in reply to Albert Sherrard (about Forster), *Commentary* 53 (March 1972): 30-32; letter in reply to Anne Farber (about Forster), *Commentary* 53 (May 1972): 32-42; letter in reply to Leo Skir (about Forster), *Commentary* (May 1972): 42.

[Review of *In the Reign of Peace*, by Hugh Nissenson.] *New York Times Book Review,* 19 March 1972, 4.

[Review of *Open Heart*, by Frederick Buechner.] *New York Times Book Review,* 11 June 1972, 4.

[Review of *In the Days of Simon Stern*, by Arthur A. Cohen.] *New York Times Book Review,* 3 June 1973, 6.

"Mrs. Virginia Woolf" [*Virginia Woolf: A Biography*, by Quentin Bell]. *Commentary* 56 (August 1973): 33-44.

"Slouching toward Smyrna" [*Sabbatai Sevi: The Mystical Messiah*, by Gershom Scholem.] *New York Times Book Review,* 24 February 1974, 27-28.

"Book Month Forum." *Sh'ma,* 12 December 1975, 22-23.

[Review of *The Street of Crocodiles*, by Bruno Schulz.] *New York Times Book Review,* 13 February 1977, 4-5.

"The Loose Drifting Material of Life" [*The Diary of Virginia Woolf*, vol. 1, ed. Anne Olivier Bell]. *New York Times Book Review,* 2 October 1977, 7.

"The Mystic Explorer" [*From Berlin to Jerusalem: Memories of My Youth*, by Gershom Scholem]. *New York Times Book Review,* 21 September 1980, 1.

"Fistfuls of Masterpieces" [*The Collected Stories of Isaac Bashevis Singer*]. *New York Times Book Review,* 21 March 1982, 1.

[Review of *Pipers at the Gates of Dawn*, by Jonathan Cott.] *New York Times Book Review,* 1 May 1983, 7.

[Review of *Life and Times of Michael K.*, by J.M. Coetzee.] *New York Times Book Review,* 11 December 1983, 1.

MISCELLANEOUS

"Nine Anti-Rules for Writing a 'First Novel.' " *Writer* 80 (January 1967): 18.

"The Coat," "Elegy for the Soviet Yiddish Writers," by Chaim Grade. Translated by Cynthia Ozick. In *A Treasury of Yiddish Poetry.* Edited by Irving Howe and Eliezer Greenberg. New York: Holt, Rinehart and Winston, 1969, 338-45.

"The Last to Sing," "And All of These Are Gone," "A Prayer," by David Einhorn. Translated by Cynthia Ozick. In *A Treasury of Yiddish Poetry.* Edited by Irving Howe and Eliezer Greenberg. New York: Holt, Rinehart and Winston, 1969, 82-85.

"On the Road to Siberia," "God, a Boy," "A Voice," "Cain and Abel," by H. Leivick. Translated by Cynthia Ozick. In *A Treasury of Yiddish Poetry.* Edited by Irving Howe and Eliezer Greenberg. New York: Holt, Rinehart and Winston, 1969, 118, 123-26.

"A Song about Elijah the Prophet," by Itzik Manger. Translated by Cynthia Ozick. *Congress Monthly,* 28 April 1969, 13.

"Father-Legend," by H. Leivick. Translated by Cynthia Ozick. *Midstream* 17 (April 1971): 4.

"Tradition and Revolt in Yiddish Poetry," by Tabachnik. Translated by Cynthia Ozick. In *Voices from the Yiddish: Essays, Memoirs, Diaries.* Edited by Irving Howe and Eliezer Greenberg. Ann Arbor: University of Michigan Press, 1972, 269-89.

"Responses (Part I) Symposium," *Response* 6 (Fall 1972): 87-93.

"Two Propositions." *Confrontation* 9 (Fall 1974): 128.

"Palestine Issue: A 'Spectacular Falsehood' " [Letter]. *New York Times,* 22 November 1974, Sec. A, 38.

"Foreword," *Dark Soliloquy: The Selected Poems of Gertrude Kolmar* [Gertrud Chodziesner]. New York: Seabury Press, 1975, vii-ix.

"Ozick and Schulweis," *Moment* 1 (May-June 1976): 77-80. [Debate.]

"Foreword," *The Worlds of Maurice Samuel: Selected Writings.* Edited by Milton Hindus. Philadelphia: Jewish Publication Society of America, 1977, xv-xx.

"3 Women: The Real Thing Is Somewhere Off Camera" [Film Review]. *Ms.* 5 (19 June 1977): 22-26.

ANNE TYLER

Medusa Points & Contact Points

Mary F. Robertson

John Updike, a fan of Anne Tyler's work, remarked in a review that "Tyler, whose humane and populous novels have attracted (if my antennae are tuned right) less approval in the literary ether than the sparer offerings of Ann Beattie and Joan Didion, is sometimes charged with the basic literary sin of implausibility."[1] Indeed, Tyler's novels do not seem a promising hunting ground for critics, who seek advances in the experimental surface of fiction. Her most palpable narrative virtues are by and large traditional ones: memorable charcters, seductive plots, imaginative and hawk-eyed descriptions. Tyler is adept with the simile, acute as a psychologist, and quite good at the meditative pause in dramatization, although the reflections usually come as ruminations of a character rather than as autonomous philosophical sorties like George Eliot's.

On first opening Tyler's novels—and perhaps until having read several—a reader is apprehensive that he or she has only encountered still more domestic dramas, seemingly oblivious of the public dimension of the life of men and women in society. A social critic might feel that Tyler's very limitation of subject matter confirms an ideology of the private family to the detriment of political awareness, and a feminist reader might think that only female actions having more public importance than Tyler's seem to have can help the cause of women. In this essay, however, I shall argue that Tyler's unusual use of narrative patterns accomplishes much that should interest the femi-

Photo by Diana Walker, Liaison Agency, Inc.

nist and the social critic alike. To see how, perhaps Updike's word *implausibility* should be examined. This trait in Tyler's work might be a sticking point for some serious readers because of prejudices about what is realistic in the plots of novels about families. Words such as *zany* and *magical* that appear regularly on her book jackets amount to labels that are likely to encourage such prejudices, to invite readers to resist the uncomfortable psychological and political seriousness of Tyler's vision, and to settle for a "good read" instead. Such prejudices, however, are ultimately thwarted by Tyler's fiction; in fact, thwarted prejudices are exactly the point. Tyler's implausible narrative form is a door through which the reader passes to a deeper sense of realism.

Families are, of course, a traditional subject of fiction. Novels about families can be divided into two groups: those that explore the interior psychology of a family—*Mansfield Park, Sons and Lovers,* and *To the Lighthouse* are diverse examples—and those that use family sagas to represent larger historical changes—works ranging from *Absalom, Absalom* to *Giant* and *The Thorn Birds.* In either case, the genre depends traditionally on features that produce certain narrative expectations in the reader. Foremost, perhaps, is a clear conception of the boundary between the insiders of a family and its outsiders. The typical family novel reserves its emotional center for the insiders. No matter how many forays or entanglements the members of the family have with outsiders, such a novel gains its power from a clear definition of the traits of both the individual members and the family as a whole. One narrative consequence of this conventional boundary that a reader, accustomed to it, might not notice is that dialogues or interchanges among members of a family are usually more portentous for the themes and outcomes of the book than those between members of the family and outsiders. Even if family problems are not solved thematically in such moments, these moments are the points in the narrative at which the significance of the story accrues. There is a centripetal impetus in such interchanges in the traditional family novel that the narrative design does nothing to question.

This conventional attachment of weight to family interchanges produces a preference for formal purity in the narrative shape of the novel as a whole. The strategy of maintaining the boundary between insiders and outsiders is reflected in the reader's awareness of what is plot—action concerning the family history—and what is subplot—contingent action concerning outsiders who function thematically and narratively to push a character to some momentous choice as he or she develops the family's destiny but who then either recede or are absorbed into the family, for example, through marriage. Such peripheral matters as affairs or business dealings function, if anything, to make clear by contrast the central skein of reciprocal effects of members of the family on one another. Often, too, the chapters of such novels are organized according to the points of view of insiders to reflect the central significance of the family.

Independent of the particular thematic content of individual family novels, such generically conventional narrative patterns constitute a second-order system of signs. They imply a certain ideological relationship among family, identity, and history. The family is shown or implied to be the principal determinant of adult identity and the primary social unit. In conventional family novels a kind of binary thinking rules the narrative. The characters can either submit to or reject the family's ways and values; the family as a whole can either triumph or be destroyed. In either instance the concept of the private, inward-turning family remains coherent and ideologically definitive. Something about families, happy or not, makes them one of the very names of narrative order. If they "break down" in divorce, miscommunication, betrayal, or catastrophe, the reader is as uneasy as if people spoke to him or her in disrupted, nonsensical syntax. If families survive in even some good measure, the reader feels that something has been set right with the universe. In addition, even when the family is historically representative of general cultural movements, such an emphasis on the power of the family projects a certain idea of history. History is implicitly reduced to a narrative about families of unquestioned centrality. Families are perhaps the human race's oldest mode of plotting history, and long after more primitive family chronicles have been outgrown as the dominant mode of recording history, the family survives metaphorically in political histories of monarchies and nation-states.

Anne Tyler's narrative strategies disrupt the conventional expectations of the family novels, and thus the disruptions themselves also constitute a second-order system of signs that helps to dislodge the ideology of the enclosed family and the notion that the family is the main forum for making history.[2] These disruptions are undoubtedly responsible for the feeling of implausibility in Tyler's fiction; Tyler does not respect the usual patterns of the genre. The first "itch" caused by her narratives comes at what I shall call Medusa points. These are points at which a certain pattern obtains in the dialogues and interchanges among members of the family. The second itch arises from Tyler's unwillingness to manage the narrative so as to form a clear line of demarcation between insiders and outsiders. The outsiders assume roles that are more than contingent yet not quite surrogates for family roles. The points at which this ambiguity occurs I shall call contact points.[3] The third itch, the result of the first two, is that the pure narrative shape of the family novel is upset. Because the boundary between insiders and outsiders is continually transgressed, the progress of Tyler's novels is felt more as an expansion of narrative disorder than as a movement toward resolution and clarification. This larger narrative movement of disorder usually includes both negative and positive moments. A member of the family typically both sheds—somehow becomes unencumbered from his other family relations—and incorporates—forms significant new relationships with outsiders. If the reader is alert to the meaning of the disruptions of usual expectations of the genre, it becomes clear that Tyler's most pervasive structural preoccupation is with the family as a sign of order or disorder in personality and society.

This structural obsession with the family as a contender for the signs of identity manifests itself especially in Tyler's three most recent novels. In *Earthly Possessions* a middle-aged housewife named Charlotte, who has been thinking of leaving her preacher-husband, Saul, and her two children, goes to the bank to withdraw money for that purpose and is taken hostage by a bank robber, Jake Simms.[4] Until the end of the book she is held captive in this stranger's peripatetic stolen car, which he has chained shut on the passenger's side, and is allowed out only under close surveillance. This sudden traumatic intimacy, symbolized by the closed space of the car, is a parody of the very familial claustrophobia Charlotte had planned to throw off. Yet it proves to be an important opportunity for revelations about otherness and helps her to arrive at some mature distinctions she had not been in the habit of making. Since Tyler interweaves flashbacks to Charlotte's childhood and married life throughout the book, the implications of her eventual choice to risk at gunpoint leaving the robber and returning to her family can be appreciated fully.

In *Morgan's Passing* the overall tone is more lighthearted, but the structural pattern is similar.[5] The two chief characters are Gower Morgan, an eccentric—who cannot resist impersonating others—with seven children and an unflappable wife, and Emily Meredith, a young married woman. The story opens with Morgan's delivering Leon and Emily Meredith's baby in a car after telling them untruthfully that he is a doctor. At first Morgan haunts the Merediths in a creepy way by trailing them; finally he is let into their lives as a valued friend. After a few years he reciprocates by allowing them into the life of his family. Later yet, he and Emily fall in love, have an affair, leave their marriages for each other, and produce a new child. This account does not begin to do justice to the disorder to be found in either of Morgan's households, nor to the ambiguous way his presence confounds the distinction between insider and outsider, no matter where he resides; but for the moment it is enough to show that, once again, a stranger disrupts a family's ordered life and alters its self-definition irrevocably.

In *Dinner at the Homesick Restaurant* the action takes us from the time when Pearl Tull, the self-sufficient mother, is dying, back through the history of her marriage and her children's adulthood, full circle to her funeral, when her long-lost husband, Beck, shows up for the day.[6] This book might be read only as a dramatization of what one therapist calls the family crucible; Tyler is very good at showing how neurotic traits ricochet off one another in a family and are passed on to the next generation. If that were all, however, the novel would be nothing special. Its particular virtue lies in the way it places the family's children, Jenny, Ezra, and Cody, in various exogenous relationships that prove as formative and valuable to them as do their family ties.

On numerous occasions in these novels there is a pattern of misconnection—what I call a Medusa point in the narrative—such as this one between Ezra Tull and his mother:

"I'm worried if I come too close, they'll say I'm overstepping. They'll say I'm pushy, or . . . emotional, you know. But if I back off, they might think I don't care. I really, honestly believe I missed some rule that everyone else takes for granted; I must have been absent from school that day. There's this narrow little dividing line I somehow never located." "Nonsense: I don't know what you're talking about," said his mother, and then she held up an egg. "Will you look at this? Out of one dozen eggs, four are cracked." [*HR*, 127]

Here is a similar interaction between Morgan and his wife, Bonny, who tries to assume the role of bride's mother for her engaged daughter:

"Morgan, in this day and age, do you believe the bride's mother would still give the bride a little talk?" "Hmm?" "What I want to know is, am I expected to give Amy a talk about sex or am I not?" "Bonny, do you have to call it *sex*?" "What else would I call it?" "Well . . ." "I mean, sex is what it is, isn't it?" "Yes, but, I don't know . . ." "I mean, what would *you* say? Is it sex, or isn't it?" "Bonny, will you just stop *hammering* at me?" [*MP*, 110]

In *Earthly Possessions* the pattern is not dramatized but revealed through Charlotte's memories. A stubborn separateness at the center of the relationship of Charlotte with each member of her family— mother, father, husband— is emphasized. Though Charlotte's father adores her in one way, he makes her feel she can never please him. She cares all her life for her grotesquely obese mother, but never breaks through to her candidly about her fears and feelings. She is separated most from her husband, whom she plans to leave almost from the beginning and did not even really make an active decision to marry. Here is the way they become engaged:

In May he bought me an engagement ring. He took it out of his pocket one night when the three of us were eating supper—a little diamond. I hadn't known anything about it. I just stared at him when he slipped it on my finger. "I thought it was time," he told me. "I'm sorry, Mrs. Ames," he said. "I can't wait any longer, I want to marry her." Mama said, "But I—" "It won't be right away," he said. "I'm not taking her off tomorrow. I don't even know what my work will be yet. We'll stay here as long as you need us, believe me. I promise you." "But—" Mama said. That was all, though. I should have refused. I wasn't helpless, after all. I should have said, "I'm sorry, I can't fit you in . . . But I didn't." [EP, 76-77]

None of these characters tries maliciously to damage his or her family interlocutors; in general, they try to help each other in the mundane ways of life. But in their minds and hearts they feel cut off, paradoxically because each feels suffocated by the other. After exposure to several Tyler novels a reader learns to bypass themes of the individual novels and understands that such nonsequiturs as occur in the conversation between Morgan and Bonny and such failures of communication as Charlotte's are best not read as individuals' character problems but as a narrative pattern drawn by Tyler to make a point about family relations in general. These points in the narrative assume a significance that stands apart from their particular content. Through them Tyler shows that situations calling for responses considered proper in certain spousal and filial roles petrify people in both senses of the word: the constant intimate gaze threatens to turn people to stone and also scares them into stratagems to evade the threat, just as Perseus could not look at the Medusa directly but mediated the slaying with the mirror. Thus the phrase "Medusa points" seems useful for such moments in Tyler's narratives when a character refuses or is unable to respond to a family member in the way that member desperately needs or desires. These Medusa points are registered, if not in the reader's petrification, at least in exasperation, because what is "supposed to happen" in a family novel—that is, connection between intimates or at least a definitive antagonism—does not happen. Thus the narrative pattern is mirrored in the reading process as resistance.

The Perseus-Medusa image is appropriate for *Dinner at the Homesick Restaurant* in an even more special way. Tyler seems deliberately to invoke Eudora Welty's *The Golden Apples*, in which this myth is quite important.[7] The connection becomes explicit when Beck Tull, who leaves his wife and children early in the book, just as King McLain does in *The Golden Apples*, returns to Pearl's funeral—King returns to Katie Rainey's funeral; Tyler writes: "King-like, he sat alone" (*HR*, 297). *The Golden Apples* is itself a mysterious and complex book, far more dreamlike and mythical than *Homesick*, but the two books dwell on the same two problems: people's existence in time and the profound ambivalence of human beings about identification with others. People suffer from their separateness and are especially drawn to merging with strangers who are exotic to them; yet, no sooner have they done so than they feel the petrification begin to set in and they fantasize evasion, abandonment, wandering. At the end of *The Golden Apples*, Virgie Rainey remembers the picture that hung on her piano teacher's wall of Perseus holding the Medusa's head. She thinks:

Cutting off the Medusa's head was the heroic act, perhaps that made visible a horror in life, that was at once the horror in love—the separateness. . . . Virgie saw things in their time, like hearing them—and perhaps because she must believe in the Medusa equally with Perseus—she saw the stroke of the sword in three moments, not one. In the three was the damnation . . . beyond the beauty and the sword's stroke and the terror lay their existence in time—far out and endless, a constellation which the heart could read over many a night. . . . In Virgie's reach of memory a melody softly lifted, lifted of itself. Every time Perseus struck off the Medusa's head there was the beat of time, and the melody. Endless the Medusa, and Perseus endless. [*GA*, 275-76]

Tyler shares with Welty the modified view of the heroic Perseus and Medusa reflected in this passage. The principal difference from the classical view lies in Virgie's recognition that the struggle is never finished. Likewise the Medusa is never really killed in Tyler's novels. Indeed, in Tyler's fiction the Medusa points signify primarily by their irony because they are the points in the narrative at which the occurrence of climactic movements, connections, and definitive severances is expected but never witnessed. Thus in and of themselves these Medusa points signify Tyler's refusal to regard the family as the most significant agent of character development and social representation. A crucial stylistic difference between Tyler and Welty aids this narrative message. Welty's poeticizing style, uplifted and abstract, creates a transcendent aura somewhat at odds with the content of Virgie's insight about time. The style itself has a way of lifting and resolving what is unresolved in the subject. In contrast, Tyler's more ordinary prose stylistically places the Medusa syndrome in real his-

torical time. Her prose enacts stylistically the full force of the "fall
into time" of those potential Perseuses—characters or readers—who
would finish off forever the Medusa of a too complete family communication or would be totally vanquished by it.

In each of the Tyler novels mentioned certain characters are
identified most strongly with the Medusa influence. In *Homesick*,
Pearl Tull, after being left with three young children and forced to
become the breadwinner, defensively develops a rigid, claustrophobic
family style. She has no friends, does not visit with the customers at
the store where she works, does not encourage her children to bring
friends home. For years, in her stubborn pride, she refuses to admit to
her children that their father has left them—the abandonment was
simply never mentioned as such during all the time they were growing up. Besides this steely silence, Pearl encourages an unhealthy self-
sufficiency and iron discipline. When the young Ezra, who is the most
sensitive of the three children and the one who takes on the role of
family nurturer, asks Pearl whether she would let him stay home
from school one day if on that day alone money grew on trees, she
answers with a severe "No," and in response to further pleading
erupts, "Ezra, will you let it be? Must you keep at me this way? Why
are you so obstinate?" (*HR*, 18). A thousand such exchanges in the life
of the family produce personalities inclined to give up on real candor
and expression of feelings in the family arena. We see this when Cody,
the oldest son, is about to leave for college. Pearl has finally brought
herself to mention the most pervasive fact in each of their lives—
their father's absence:

"Children, there's something I want to discuss with you." Cody was talking about a job. He
had to find one in order to help with the tuition fees. "I could work in the cafeteria," he was
saying, "or maybe off-campus. I don't know which." Then he heard his mother and looked
over at her. "It's about your father," Pearl said. Jenny said, "I'd choose the cafeteria." "You
know, my darlings," Pearl told them, "how I always say your father's away on business." "But
off-campus they might pay more," said Cody, "and every penny counts." "At the cafeteria
you'd be with your classmates, though," Ezra said. "Yes, I thought of that." "All those coeds,"
Jenny said. "Cheerleaders. Girls in their little white bobby sox." "Sweater girls," Cody said.
"There's something I want to explain about your father," Pearl told them. "Choose the
cafeteria," Ezra said. "Children?" "The cafeteria," they said. And all three gazed at her coolly,
out of gray, unblinking, level eyes exactly like her own. [*HR*, 30]

In time Tyler's reader learns that the trick at such moments in the
narrative is not to read them conventionally as the portrayal of
psychological cripples and tragic family failures. The Medusa points
are semantically complex because, while they depict the characters

as stony to others in the family, they show at the same time (in the children's oblique comments just quoted, for example) the healthy partial escape from total petrification. Such points show characters who have learned to turn their eyes away from the monster of family self-absorption and to seek their maturity and identity by means of other resources.

The second generic disruption in narrative form that develops an independent significance in Tyler's novels is the altered treatment of outsiders. Pushed, like the characters, to swerve from the in-conclusiveness of the Medusa moments and denied the satisfaction of the partial closures usually provided in the family interchanges, the reader must look closer at the supposedly marginal characters of the novel to find a new pattern of significance. The reader then realizes that Tyler shapes an unusual nexus of characters that forces him or her to take seriously Morgan's remark that "our lives depend on total strangers. So much lacks logic, or a proper sequence" (*MP*, 225). If said in a certain tone, of course, this statement *could* suggest an alienation like that of Joan Didion's characters and might reflect anomic acceptance of provisional but meaningless encounters with strangers—even intimates who feel like strangers. But alienation is not the contract offered by Tyler through such a thought. The concept of alienation depends on a firm conceptual boundary between the strange and the familiar, inside and outside; Tyler's narrative disposi-tion of characters trangresses this boundary without eradicating it. The outsiders take over some of the usual functions of family, but their ultimate difference from family is their most significant trait. Such characters are signs of permanent human strangeness, but Tyler's work presents this strangeness as the very resource by which to prevent alienation.

Throughout her life an alienated woman, Pearl Tull, on her death-bed, reflects on the foolishness of holding herself inviolate from disruption: "It was such a relief to drift, finally. Why had she spent so long learning how? . . . She kept mislaying her place in time, but it made no difference" (*HR*, 33). This drift is not a feckless passivity such as that which leads Jenny, Emily, and Charlotte into their first marriages, but an ability to open oneself to the disorder and uncer-tainty that strangers bring into one's life; it is the ability to be enriched by these strangers, even to be derailed by them, without trying to erase their radical difference from oneself. Narratively, this theme of disorder is registered in a tension produced by Tyler's blur-ring of the boundary between insiders and outsiders. In their surface organization, whether linear or flashback in manner, her novels give the impression that she is interested in tracing chronological developments of certain families; but the real movements—spiritual, emotional, even material—occur in the marginal relations of members of the family with outsiders. Eventually, the image of the family in each novel becomes an empty presence. The reader feels like a person in a canoe who, while being carried forward by the straight-running current, is also swept sideways by a strong crosswind. In the phenomenological movement of reading, the reader, like the characters, is forced to drift into supposedly contingent, incomplete relations that nevertheless prove to be the most important sources of meaning—the "real story," as a Sherwood Anderson character would say. The reader must be willing to "mislay his or her place" in the ostensible generic order of the novel. The family shape remains in some form to the end of each of these three Tyler novels, but the significant spiritual, emotional, and material movements are produced by the crosswinds of strangeness.

Thus Tyler differs from many radical contemporary writers who give us fragmentary texts in order to challenge us to find the unity beneath them. Hers is an opposite vector. She gives us the semblance of order in the overall family design of the novels, but hollows out such order from within by means of the relations of the family with strangers, thereby sugggesting the inability of the family to transcend time and disorder, and the provisionality of everyone's life. Rather than the mounting feeling of inevitability to which we are accustomed in family narratives, Tyler's plots impart the feeling almost of random branching. She seems to need a minimum of three generations in her books, not to represent larger historical movements or stronger family definition, but to allow for the free play of interruption of a family's order by the unexpected people who embody the Perseus movement against the Medusa. Her plots reveal along the horizontal axis a continual questioning of the proper vertical boundary between family and not-family. The margin thus always threatens the center, even as it paradoxically also provides an escape valve that enables the family to persist, in a manner of speaking. Intriguingly, then, while Tyler would seem to be the last candidate for the ranks of the postmodernists, who are usually perceived as stylistically radical, her assault on the notion of what is a proper family makes her close in spirit to other postmodernists who regularly engage in what might be called category assassination, questioning just about every conventional distinction between one concept and another that we use to order our lives and thought.

Dinner at the Homesick Restaurant exhibits the features and principles just discussed. Family chronology seems to be respected in the linear movement of the characters' lives contained within the circle of Pearl's expiring life. Most of each chapter is told from the viewpoint of one member of the family—the first and the penultimate from Pearl's point of view and the others from the points of view of her children and her grandchild. In the final chapter the three generations are assembled at a meal to which the abandoning father has returned. Superficially, therefore, the form might seem to imply that families triumph, that we need the order they provide, that all the suffering and disappointment merely contributes to the family's growth. But the real story in *Homesick* does not confirm the family's heroism or even its lasting identity; it shows, rather, how the children have changed the signification of the family identity almost beyond recognition. The maturity of the members of the family is allied with successful disorder, a genuinely scattering movement in time. When Beck Tull left her, Pearl patterned her life on a model she had noted in her youthful diary: "Bristlecone pines, in times of stress, hoard all their life in a single streak and allow the rest to die" (*HR*, 279). Pearl's child, Cody, also tries to adopt this posture, but his son, Luke, belies his success. Jenny and Ezra, in contrast, develop the capacity to drift—that is, to discard both Pearl's notions of daily order in their lives and the conceptual order of family definition. The significance of their lives develops through their turning away from agony over the Medusa points in family life toward the energizing and formative contact points with sundry persons outside the family. They allow the disorder—from the point of view of what is proper—to open new routes without necessarily abandoning the old routes entirely. They exhibit the truth of Morgan's rhetorical assertion: "Aren't we all sitting on stacks of past events? And not every level is neatly finished off, right? Sometimes a lower level bleeds into an upper level. Isn't that so?" (*MP*, 143).

In *Homesick*, Ezra is the character who most fully embodies the narrative paradox of maintaining the outline of family relations while forming a mature identity through contact points outside the family. He lives his whole life at home, caring for Pearl, yet the center of his life is outside that home in the restaurant, in which at first he works for Mrs. Scarlatti and which he then inherits from her. The long intimacy between Ezra and Mrs. Scarlatti does not fit any of the usual categories. He never addresses her except as Mrs. Scarlatti, yet he is her "significant other" in her final illness in the hospital. The nature of their interaction in the hospital shows that Tyler considers it important that peripheral but significant figures remain confirmed in their recalcitrant otherness. Ezra brings her some soup he has made, knowing that

after he left someone would discard his soup. But this was his special gizzard soup that she had always loved. . . . He only brought the soup out of helplessness; he would have preferred to kneel by her bed and rest his head on her sheets, to take her hands in his and tell her, "Mrs. Scarlatti, come back." But she was such a no-nonsense woman; she would have looked shocked. All he could do was offer this soup. . . . He only sat, looking down at his pale, oversized hands, which lay loosely on his knees. [*HR*, 115]

Mrs. Scarlatti, then, has her own rigidities, but they do not paralyze Ezra with guilt as his mother's did. In fact, even before she dies, he begins to alter her restaurant radically, changing the menu from fancy French to down-home cooking, tearing out walls, leaving the kitchen exposed to the dining room and so on. When she unexpectedly makes a sufficient temporary recovery to return home and finds what he has done, she cries: " 'Oh, my God,' . . . She looked up into his eyes. Her face seemed stripped. 'You might at least have waited till I died,' she said. 'Oh!' said Ezra. 'No, you don't understand; you don't know. It wasn't what you think. It was just . . . I can't explain, I went wild somehow!' " (*HR*, 130). Tyler shows here that a person's contact points with outsiders are still subject to betrayals and difficulties; differences are not erased in some blissful harmony with outsiders that cannot be attained with insiders. But the fact that relationships with outsiders ocur makes the crucial difference in the characters' ability to grow and be themselves. Even though Mrs. Scarlatti is appalled at Ezra's changes, she does not revoke her decision to leave him the restaurant, and though he is grief-stricken, her death clearly releases new energies in him. He soon changes the name from "Scarlatti's" to "The Homesick Restaurant," and he thrives by arranging matters more in his own way.

Jenny, another character who, like Ezra, escapes the rigid patterns of her early life, makes her own disorderly way through three marriages. She becomes a pediatrician, exerting in her work the same strong will as her mother, but each of her marriages represents a move away from rigidity to disorder. Her final marriage is to Joe, a man whose wife has left him with six children. He says he married Jenny because he "could see she wasn't a skimpy woman. . . . Not rigid. Not constricted. Not that super-serious kind" (*HR*, 193). But of course she had been more so in her younger days when she was closer to Pearl's influence. It may be implausible to us that she could run a household of nine and still not stint on a demanding career, but that seems beside the point that Tyler wishes to make. Jenny is shown to have moved through the nervous-breakdown stage into an impressive equanimity gained from learning to drift through demands upon her. She is perhaps at risk for turning everything into a joke; nevertheless, she is a compelling example of a character's ability to outgrow a destructive background. And not only does she show greater tolerance for the literal physical disorder of her new household, but in her way she accomplishes in her final marriage what Ezra accomplishes in his relationship with Mrs. Scarlatti; with her third marriage she breaks the purity of the family line decisively by blurring the boundary between who is real family and who is not. By the end, most of her immediate family is not even her own, but consists of stepchildren she has accepted the responsibility of nurturing.

Ezra and Jenny's brother, Cody, in *Homesick*, does not manage to form a flexible and freely determined personality as his siblings do. He is the classic example of the child who unwittingly replicates the very childhood condition he tries to flee. He considers Ezra his oldest enemy because Ezra was always liked more than he, and he keeps a distance from his mother and siblings most of his adult life. Yet Cody's hate is just the outer skin that hides his eternal longing to be like Ezra. For much of the book the reader feels that Cody is a villain. The reader would like to roast him over hot coals when, a Cain to Ezra's Abel, in a calculated way he woos Ezra's fiancée, Ruth, away from his lovable brother. Ruth and Ezra had seemed destined only for each other, since they are both eccentric in the same way. The defection of Ruth to Cody is an interesting example of those implausible turns in Tyler's narrative design for which a higher logic must be sought than character psychology alone would provide. It is difficult to credit that Cody, the rich city slicker, would fall in love with this barefoot country girl and even more difficult to believe that she would go with him. True, the episode does teach us something profound about the dialectics of longing, but Tyler wishes above all to use the implausibility to make a narrative argument that people will often choose strangeness over similarity for their own self-preservation. Her narrative ethos, borne out in the other novels too, seems to say that such a choice is somehow right, as if Ezra and Ruth are too much alike for their own good. Tyler does not seem to allow relationships between like and like to flourish. While Cody and Ruth's marriage is not especially happy, it is loyal, and we do not, as we expect, hear Ruth complaining later that she should have married Ezra. She seems to have known she needed something different in life from living with her soul twin. And, through Ruth, Cody is able in part to incorporate that lost part of himself—the brother whom he so wished to be like. Thus, Cody too is a character affected beneficially by disorder and strangeness.

Cody's son, Luke, is the only third-generation member of the family to have a viewpoint chapter of his own. What emerges is the likeness, much to Cody's overt disgust, between Luke and Ezra. Cody rails at it and probably damages the boy somewhat by absurdly and jealously accusing Ruth of having had Ezra's son rather than his own. Cody feels that the resemblance is the vengeance of fate, but we see it as a kind of fortunate prevention of a too-pure family identity, for Cody has tried to seal off his own family just as Pearl had. Cody's rigidity is reflected in his profession, that of efficiency expert, doing time-and-motion studies for industry. He tells us: "Time is my favorite thing of all. . . . Time is my obsession: not to waste it, not to lose it. It's like . . . I don't know, an object to me; something you can almost take hold of. If I could just collect enough of it in one clump, I always think. If I could pass it back and forth and sideways, you know? If only Einstein were right and time were a place or river you could choose to step into at any place along the shore" (*HR*, 228). This insight is the opposite of Virgie's perception about time in *The Golden Apples* or Pearl's drift. Cody dreams of killing the Medusa in one final stroke, but he is forced through Luke and Ezra to submit to time, like everyone else, as the repetition of ceaseless conflict. Cody might fight disorder, but it is always there to exert a pressure on him to be more flexible than he might otherwise be.

Running through *Homesick* like a bolt through a door hinge is a series of six family dinners he has tried to make "just like home" that Ezra plans at the restaurant. The inability of the family ever to complete a meal eventually becomes comical in spite of our sympathy for Ezra's disappointments. Yet this unfinished-dinner pattern is the book's strongest narrative emblem for Tyler's complex vision of order, disorder, and the family. Ezra is the "feeder," unlike his mother, who, Cody reflects, was a "non-feeder if there ever was one . . . neediness: she disapproved of neediness in people. Whenever there was a family argument, she most often chose to start it over dinner" (*HR*, 162-63). Tyler never uses gender stereotypes; men can be nurturing as well as women, and women can exhibit patriarchal attitudes. Indeed, Pearl is at first the reason Ezra's dinners are never finished before someone walks out. In being stalled by someone's bitterness the dinners are emblems of the Medusa syndrome, but in going on anyhow, eventually by including more outsiders, they are also emblems of Perseus' slaying of the Medusa through the fruitful disorder of contact points. The first four breakdowns during meals occur because Pearl thinks that one character or another is insufficiently concerned about the family's integrity: Ezra's business partnership will dissolve the family; Jenny is too familiar with Ezra's eccentric friend, Josiah; Jenny does not heed her mother's opinion; Cody has "set up shop too far from home." The fifth breakdown occurs because Cody reacts jealously when his wife talks to Ezra; his jealousy often cuts his family off entirely from innocent interchanges with others. Through the failure of meals, which are usually the classic expression of family order, Tyler shows symbolically the family's inability to thrive when its ideals are hermetic.

Ezra occupies an ambiguous position in this narrative pattern, and eventually his actions prevent the total petrification of the family. No one wishes more than he that the family care about one another, and, he cries, "I wish just once we could eat a meal from start to finish" (HR, 111). Yet he is not annihilated when things fall apart; he does not give up but placidly and resiliently keeps the institution going, even in apparent defeat. Significantly, however, in keeping the tradition going, Ezra does not follow an orthodox plan for family meals. They occur in a public place, the restaurant, where the members of the family are always in marginal relation to others, such as Mrs. Scarlatti, the kitchen crew, the friend, Josiah (whom Pearl had made unwelcome in her house), and the other customers. That is, Ezra upholds the tradition of the family meal in one way, yet he revises it, loosens its joints, forces it to articulate with outsiders who remain outsiders. Though it is true that the family never stops arguing and never finishes the meals, even its minimal survival as a unit thus "depends on total strangers" in order to keep it from being turned into stone altogether.

With the last dinner, not only has Ezra's more public sphere replaced Pearl's tightly guarded kitchen as the family meeting place, but the composition of the family has become less pure. The direct descendents among the grandchildren, Cody's Luke and Jenny's Becky, are vastly outnumbered by Joe's gaggle of children, who are technically outsiders. Beck starts to swell with grandfatherly pride when he looks around the table, but Cody says, "It's not really that way at all. . . . Don't let them mislead you. It's not the way it appears. Why, not more than two or three of these kids are even related to you. The rest are Joe's by a previous wife" (HR, 300). Furthermore, Beck's unexpected presence conveys no sense of the missing piece that triumphantly closes the circle in an image of final reconciliation and unity. On the contrary, it is clear that he returns as a stranger and will always be a stranger, like a bird alighted on a branch, about to depart at any moment. When Joe's baby chokes on a mushroom, distracting everyone, Beck slips out before the meal is over. Ezra, beside himself at another unfinished dinner, organizes the whole party to run out in different directions to find Beck. Cody is the one to do so and brings him back after finally hearing his father's side of the story of the abandonment. There is a hint that Cody will be somewhat liberated from his constricting beliefs after receiving this information, but, if so, only because Beck makes real for Cody his father's separate existence, forces Cody to see him not as Cody's projection but as a person with his own needs and rights. Beck agrees to go back to the meal for "one last course," but says, "I warn you, I plan to leave before the dessert wine's poured." The reason he must leave is that he feels obliged to return to a woman he is dating and will marry now that Pearl is dead. The progenitor does not finally offer an image of re-union, wholeness; he too, in fact, moves in the direction of another connection peripheral to the original family. The meal is more nearly finished than any of the previous ones, but it is not finished with everyone who would symbolically confirm the intactness of the Tull family present. Thus "Homesick" in the name of the restaurant is a pun: people go there who yearn for the nurturing of home, but the restaurant stands equally as an alternative to the home which, if too much ingrown, or if conceived of as the place of a golden age, is sick. The Tull family is finally like this restaurant itself: the shell of the original still stands, but the interior has been demolished and re-fashioned through the beneficial agency of significant outsiders. The tones and meanings are now quite as different as Ezra's food is from French cuisine. Thus the overall narrative shape that might have signified that the family is a real sign of order and growth is so heavily qualified by the actual patterns of meaning and growth as to be voided as a narrative and thematic signifying system.

Space does not permit detailed documentation of the way *Morgan's Passing* and *Earthly Possessions* exhibit a similar narrative semiosis questioning the traditional family as a sign of order, but it is important to recognize that such narrative semiosis exists in each novel, in which plot and character patterns show meanings independent of their special content. The charming Morgan himself, a Hermes-like figure lurking at boundaries, provides a vehicle to show that energy comes from the disorderly transactions both within and between families. Just as Morgan is the character who shakes up the Merediths' lives for the better, so, in *Earthly Possessions*, Jake, the bank robber, pulls Charlotte roughly out of her trancelike life and forces her to recognize that the Medusa is not so much in her husband's domestic style as it is in her own inner, unspoken dream of perfect order for herself. She finally perceives that there is no need to unload those she had thought responsible for her unhappiness.

Tyler also has a suitably wry sense that the most disorderly characters themselves have a fascination with or craving for order. Morgan says comically as he shakes out Emily's purse,

"Look at that! You're so orderly." Emily retrieved her belongings and put them back in her purse. Morgan watched, with his head cocked. "I too am orderly," he told her. "You are?" "Well, at least I have an interest in order. I mean order has always intrigued me. When I was a child, I thought order might come when my voice changed. Then I thought, no, maybe when I'm educated. At one point I thought I would be orderly if I could just once sleep with a woman." . . . Emily said, "Well?" "Well what?" "Did sleeping with a woman make you orderly?" "How can you ask?" he said. He sighed. [MP, 140]

Similarly, Jake the robber detests the irregularity of his life on the lam, and his conscience causes him to head the stolen car for the home of a girl he had made pregnant. This dangerous adventure thus soon bogs down in domestic problems such as the girl's nausea and the care of the cat she has brought with her.

In *Homesick*, the narrative pattern of family dinners is symbolic of disorderly movement within an apparently fixed figure; in *Morgan*, Tyler makes the same point, that nothing in our lives can or should stay rigid, through the symbolism of both Emily's puppets and the leotards she always wears. Leon Meredith explains in a condescending manner that, whereas he can improvise in his management of the puppet shows which are their livelihood, "Emily makes them according to a fixed pattern. *They're* not improvised." Emily thinks to herself, however, "This was true, in a way, and yet it wasn't. Emily did have a homemade brown-paper pattern for the puppets' outlines, but the outlines were the least of it. What was important was the faces, the dips and hills of their own expressions, which tended to develop unexpected twists of their own no matter how closely she guided the fabric through the sewing machine" (*MP*, 131-32).

Later, when Morgan has become her new husband and is characteristically chafing at the very disorder he brings with him, he complains,

We don't have any chance to be alone. . . . Mother, Brindle, the baby . . . it's like a transplant. I transplanted all the mess from home. It's like some crazy practical joke." . . . "I don't mind it," Emily said. "I kind of enjoy it." "That's easy for you to say," he told her. "It's not your problem, really. You stay unencumbered no matter what, like those people who can eat and eat and not gain weight. You're still in your same wrap skirt. Same leotard." Little did he know how many replacement leotards she had had to buy over the years. Evidently, he imagined they lasted forever. [*MP*, 307]

In *Earthly Possessions*, Charlotte's found trinket saying "Keep on truckin'" is the symbol equivalent to the dinners of *Homesick* and Emily's puppets and leotards in *Morgan*. When she finds it, Charlotte takes it as a sign that now is the time to leave Saul. After her abduction, however, she returns to Saul with a different sense of the phrase; now the phrase suggests endurance, and the novel finishes this way: "Maybe we ought to take a trip, he says. Didn't I use to want to? But I tell him no. I don't see the need, I say. We have been traveling for years, traveled all our lives, we are traveling still. We couldn't stay in one place if we tried. Go to sleep, I say. And he does" (*EP*, 222). Yet Tyler is no Hegelian of domesticity, portraying disorder merely as an antithetical way station to greater order, recapturing drift for the greater benefit of the concept of the private family. Charlotte does go back to Saul, but Jenny and Emily both rightly obtain divorces. Tyler designs narratives in which there is constant oscillation between shedding and incorporation without any suggestion of some final resting place, either totally within the family or totally outside it.

While freedom from suffocation of family life is a favorite theme of feminist writers, Tyler's prescription about means differs notably from those writers, such as Tillie Olsen, to whom *drift* is a red-flag word signaling loss of coherent identity and personal purpose. Olsen's Eva in "Tell Me a Riddle" is a famous example of a character who evinces this sense of loss. While raising her family, Eva had to abide by the idea that "empty things float," but the story represents such drift as a tragic forfeiture of her own identity, which she can only recover bitterly as she is dying. Ruth, in Marilynne Robinson's *Housekeeping* might seem closer to Tyler, since she asserts the value of drift and sheds domestic encumbrances by choosing the equivalent of Huck Finn's "lighting out for the territory" and leaving with her eccentric Aunt Sylvie for a vagrant life on the railroad boxcars. Yet that pattern obviously perpetuates the old either-or dilemma for those stifled by family closeness. Sylvie and Ruth become pariahs. For Tyler, the negative freedom of merely shedding is undesirable. In her novels, drift signifies not only such emptiness of infinite potential, but also a movement toward a positive condition of greater fullness accomplished through commitments in exogeneous exchanges. For Tyler, drift must include the second phase of incorporation, taking into one's life, however temporarily, others who do not

merge with oneself but remain different; otherwise one merely re-
produces within oneself the Medusa influence of family life.

In Tyler's narratives that represent this oscillation between shedding and incorporation, metonymies of household effects are abun-
dant. They might remind the reader of Kafka's *Metamorphosis*, but
the difference from Kafka is instructive. In Kafka's story both the
emptying and refilling of Gregor's room are symptoms of alienation.
In *Homesick* Ezra's demolition of Scarlatti's restaurant is a sign of his
rejection of Mrs. Scarlatti's dominance, a temporary alienation perhaps, but the demolition also allows for the constructive substitution
of his own adult identity, which is being formed through his life
outside his family. He does go nearly bankrupt at first, but when the
restaurant fills up again, it does not parallel Gregor's trash-filled
room, which is a sign that Gregor no longer matters. On the contrary,
the crowded restaurant testifies to Ezra's significance. The same is
true of the overstuffed households of Emily and Morgan and
Charlotte and Saul. Both women realize there is no exit from the
disorder of claims upon them by people who are technically outsiders
to their own families, but it does not feel like hell to them because
they have learned to respect true difference as nourishing. Tyler's
stories might be seen as affirmative complements to Kafka's fable
about the damaging effects on personality of a rigid family identity.

The bountiful environments portrayed in Tyler's conclusions
suggest that Updike is right to contrast Tyler with Beattie and Didion,
whose "spareness" is a result of their vision of alienation. A critic
who believes that alienation is still the only authentic response to the
world will not like Tyler. Her work makes room for the alienated
moment, but it finally makes one wonder whether the alienated
attitude does not rest on a secret, stingy resentment that the world
and its many people are different from oneself.

Even Tyler's physical settings underscore her rejection of alienation and her theme that disorder is a remedy for excessive family
order. In each novel a building structure symbolizes the paradox that
one can best be oneself if one is connected in some significant way
with those in the public who are different from oneself. Charlotte's
house has a room with an outside door which serves as a photography
studio that is open to the public. Ezra's "homesick" restaurant similarly connotes both the public and the private life. The Merediths'
apartment, into which Morgan eventually moves with Emily, is located above a public crafts shop with a common hallway. Further
suggesting connectedness of the private to the public scene, Tyler's
novels are emphatically urban rather than suburban. Charlotte's

neighborhood changes from strictly residential to partly commercial when Amoco buys the property next door for a filling station. Ezra's is a city restaurant in Baltimore, and Morgan's people reside in Baltimore too. Morgan says, "We're city people. . . . We have our city patterns, things to keep us busy" (*MP*, 164). The city is of course the place where one is maximally involved with the difference of other people in one's daily affairs.

Tyler's insistence on the public and urbane quality even of family life calls to mind the argument of an urban theorist, Richard Sennett, whose ideas seem remarkably apposite to Tyler's vision. In *The Uses of Disorder*, Sennett argues that our contemporary society, with its preference for sequestered surburban life or for the highly rationalized city of city planners, instantiates an adolescent mode of personality development in our public life.[8] According to Sennett, adolescence is marked by a rigid drive for a "purified identity," which enables the powerless youth to mediate his self-image and his image of the outside world (*UD*, 17-18). Beneficial as it is at that stage, this drive is "extremely dangerous if it remains fixed in a person's life, if it meets no challenge and becomes a permanent modality. . . . It can lead to a language that similarly does away with the 'factness' of new people or new experiences . . . and assumes that one has had the meanings of experience without the threat of actively experiencing" (*UD*, 22-25). Suburbs and rationalized cities, by restricting the number of contact points for citizens, lock our public life into such a defensive, closed-off mode that we never learn the essential lesson of adulthood, which the real city teaches us—how to live with the "unachieved situations" that the radical differences of others impose on us. Sennett says that this "*intense family life is the agent, the middleman for the infusion of adolescent fear into the social life of modern cities. . . . It is exactly the character of intense families to* diminish the diversity of contact points that have marked out a community life in the teeming cities at the turn of the century" (*UD*, 67).

Whatever we might feel about certain corollary arguments in Sennett's book, which, if followed, could produce municipal anarchy, his diagnosis seems cogent, and Tyler's novels echo it. They enact thematically the growth from adolescent notions of identity to the adult willingness to live with unachieved situations of involvement with people's otherness. In her quiet way, Tyler stakes out a position against the whole existentialist nausea over "otherness" and makes it seem puerile. Emily reflects toward the end of *Morgan's Passing*, "You could draw vitality from mere objects, evidently—from these seething souvenirs of dozens of lives raced through at full throttle. Morgan's mother and sister (both in their ways annoying, demanding, querulous women) troubled her not a bit, because they weren't hers. They were too foreign to be hers. Foreign: that was the word. . . . She drew in a deep breath, as if trying to taste the difference in the air. She was fascinated by her son, who did not seem really, truly her own, though she loved him immeasurably" (*MP*, 289). Tyler's typical narrative patterns mirror this theme by refusing the kind of unswerving focus on members of a family as the repository of meaning that we expect in a family novel and by spinning the plots off at tangents that are not just detours from which we return. Likewise, her endings are not merely inconclusive and ambiguous as so many modernist fictional endings are, but instead convey more aggressive images of continuing flux, of the unachieved situation, understood and welcomed as such, like that we saw in *Homesick*'s final dinner, or in Morgan and Emily's improvisational spirit at the end of *Morgan*, or in Charlotte's thoughts as she returns to Saul in *Earthly Possessions*.

Tyler's emphasis on continuing flux, moreover, bears upon a serious problem with which feminist writers struggle: the difficulty of depicting feminist men and women using their knowledge in plausible ways in actual society. A careful reader can see that Tyler has to a great extent come to terms with that problem. A main ingredient, if not the essence, of the patriarchal attitude is a hypostatization of category differences—family/outsiders, for example—that makes it possible to transcend the disorderly flux of real relations among members of different classes. It might plausibly be argued that the whole notion of "proper" family is patriarchal; it was surely not the mothers who cared whether their children were bastards or whether blood relatives were treated better than outsiders. The nature of patriarchal thought, as of all ideologies, is Medusa-like in its reifications. The feminine personality has traditionally been allowed a dispensation from this way of thinking, but only at the price of being segregated from the world of significant action, which seems to require firm categories, and of being marked as amorphous—thus the fear of drift as regressive by many feminists. It seems difficult to dramatize people who are both taken seriously by society and consistently question prevailing conceptual boundaries, precisely for the reason that actual society does not take them seriously; indeed, they are marginalized as implausible, unrealistic, or irresponsible. Delightful or not, for example, Gower Morgan is probably perceived by many readers as little more than a humorous, self-indulgent stunt man and Ezra, Jenny, and Emily as memorable for their weirdness. If taken seriously as possible types of real people, they threaten the system that depends on ideological purities of various sorts. A reader who indulges in Tyler's novels for their "zaniness," however, does himself or herself a disservice. Tyler is rare in her ability to portray practical and constructive ways in which impatience with the "drive for purification" can translate into concrete, constructive action. Here these boundary-doubters are actually seen acting in a recognizable world.[9] None of what might seem at first implausible in Tyler is really so unrealistic. It is not even so farfetched these days that one might be taken hostage, and a person who was might have gained from *Earthly Possessions* some realistic instruction, not only in the psychology of the outlaw, but in the real horizons of his or her ordinary life, which had conveniently gone unnoticed. Likewise, the implausible semifriendship that develops between Morgan's first wife and Emily, once Bonny's anger at Morgan's leaving has cooled, is not really so uncommon these days among divorced families. *Time* magazine and the U.S. Census tell us that the typical nuclear family is much in the minority now, but ideologically the model still has a grip on us. Thus Tyler's idea that a respect for the difference of "significant others" in such disorderly family structures can liberate us is valuable in a practical way.

Indeed, Tyler's narrative vision of family disorder seems to have been derived directly from her sense of her own life's problems and patterns. The fact that she is married to an Iranian is bound to have had some influence on Tyler's theme of difference. Her essay "Still Just Writing" shows that as a writer and mother her personal anxiety is with the problem of interruption of her work and, by extension, the threat of "disorderly" deviations from her path as a writer. She seems to have learned the coping mechanism of drift from her father rather than from her mother. She explains that whenever his schedule was interrupted, even to the extent of having to cancel a long-awaited foreign sojourn at the last minute, he just whistled Mozart and occupied himself with whatever was available to him at the time. She claims to have found that the threatening detours actually enrich her work. This equanimity, however, is not without recognition of the dangers. Clear-eyed she says, "What this takes, of course, is a sense of limitless time, but I'm getting that. My life is beginning to seem unusually long. And there's a danger to it: I could wind up as passive as a piece of wood on a wave. But I try to walk a middle line."[10] This sense of limitless time should not be read, I think, as the classic feminine suspension above a real-world sense of deadlines and irrevocable actions. It is more like Virgie Rainey's "beat of time." A musical beat is a concrete commitment, a movement from the virtual to the actual, just as the productive interruption in Tyler's novels is. Virgie's phrase is also a way of recognizing that our short-sighted desire for finalities is often blind to time's amplitude and to the way unexpected turns taken by the beat can make life more interesting and fulfilling.

Although she lacks his stylistic genius, Faulkner is in a way the American author to whom Tyler seems closest. He too depicted the way a "drive toward purification" could ruin personalities and the whole culture of the South. Just as he saw at the center of the ideal of white supremacy the taboo against miscegenation as the chief means of sapping the vital energy of the South, so Tyler shows that the desire for family purity leads to entropy. The social critic might respect Tyler's family novels about private existence as significant for public life. If, as Sennett says, the family is the "middleman" institution between our psychological fears and our public life, then a novelist who alters the narrative line of the family novel to open it up to the radical disorder of outside influences that are not merely contingent does her part to suggest a new possibility for our actual history. She also does her part in altering the very idea of history, which, in the guise of recording events in time, more often artificially kills time, the beat of time, through concepts, such as the family, that deny history's real randomness and disorder.

NOTES

1. John Updike, review of *Dinner at the Homesick Restaurant, New Yorker* 58 (5 April 1982): 193-95.

2. Jane Marcus has called attention to the dissatisfaction with the Victorian patriarchal family among certain influential women of the modernist period. In *"The Years* as Greek Drama, Domestic Novel, and Götterdämmerung," *Bulletin of the New York Public Library*, Winter 1977, 277, she quotes the anthropologist Jane Harrison as saying, "Family life never attracted me. At its best it seems to me rather narrow and selfish; at its worst a private hell. . . . On the other hand, I have a natural gift for community life. . . . I think, as civilization advances, family life will become, if not extinct, at least much modified and curtailed." Marcus suggests, in this article and in "Pargeting 'The Pargeters,' " *Bulletin of the New York Public Library*, Spring 1977, 416-35, that in *The Years* Virginia Woolf experiments narratively with altering the traditional family novel by organizing it around relationships between sisters and aunts and nieces rather than around fathers and sons or fathers and daughters. Marcus reads *The Years* tragically, however, as an *Antigone* for the women and a *Götterdämmerung* for the patriarchs. As I shall argue, Tyler starts from a position well beyond the tragic view of the

demise of the traditional family. Furthermore, it is doubtful that Woolf really meant to let go of the ideal of family unity; she wished rather to broaden or change the definition of such unity to include the important transmissions and transactions among the female members of a family.

3. The phrase is Richard Sennett's in *The Uses of Disorder* (New York: Vintage Books, 1970), which I shall discuss later.

4. Anne Tyler, *Earthly Possessions* (New York: Berkley Books, 1977); hereafter cited in the text as *EP*.

5. Anne Tyler, *Morgan's Passing* (New York: Berkley Books, 1980); hereafter cited in the text as *MP*.

6. Anne Tyler, *Dinner at the Homesick Restaurant* (New York: Berkley Books, 1982); hereafter cited in the text as *HR*.

7. Eudora Welty, *The Golden Apples* (New York: Harcourt, Brace and World, 1947); hereafter cited in the text as *GA*.

8. Sennett, *Uses of Disorder*, passim; hereafter cited in the text as *UD*.

9. An interesting contrast, for example, is with *The White Hotel* by D.M. Thomas, in which Lisa Erdman also has little time for ordinary family boundaries, but is depicted as even moderately victorious only in an imagined purgatorial place after her death.

10. Still Just Writing," in *The Writer on Her Work*, ed. Janet Sternburg (New York: W.W. Norton, 1980), 11.

A Bibliography of Writings by

ANNE TYLER

Elaine Gardiner & Catherine Rainwater

BOOKS

If Morning Ever Comes. New York: Alfred A. Knopf, 1964.
The Tin Can Tree. New York: Knopf, 1965.
A Slipping-Down Life. New York: Knopf, 1970.
The Clock Winder. New York: Knopf, 1972.
Celestial Navigation. New York: Knopf, 1974.
Searching for Caleb. New York: Knopf, 1976.
Earthly Possessions. New York: Knopf, 1977.
Morgan's Passing. New York: Knopf, 1980.
Dinner at the Homesick Restaurant. New York: Knopf, 1982.

SHORT STORIES

"The Bridge." *Archive* 72 (March 1960): 10-15.
"I Never Saw Morning." *Archive* 73 (April 1961): 11-14. [Reprinted in *Under*

Twenty-Five: Duke Narrative and Verse, 1945-1962, ed. William Blackburn (1963), 157-66.]

"The Saints in Caesar's Household." *Archive* 73 (April 1961): 7-10. [Reprinted in *The Young Writer at Work*, ed. Jessie Rehder (1962), 75-83; in *Under Twenty-Five*, ed. William Blackburn (1963), 146-56.]

"The Baltimore Birth Certificate." *Critic* 21 (February-March 1963): 41-45.

"I Play Kings." *Seventeen* 22 (August 1963): 338-41.

"The Street of Bugles." *Saturday Evening Post* 236 (30 November 1963): 64-66.

"Nobody Answers the Door." *Antioch Review* 24 (Fall 1964): 379-86.

"Dry Water." *Southern Review*, N.S., 1 (Spring 1965): 259-91.

"I'm Not Going to Ask You Again." *Harper's* 231 (September 1965): 88-89.

"As the Earth Gets Old." *New Yorker* 42 (29 October 1966): 60-64.

"Two People and a Clock on the Wall." *New Yorker* 42 (19 November 1966): 202-17.

"The Genuine Fur Eyelashes." *Mademoiselle* 64 (January 1967): 102-3, 136-38.

"The Tea-Machine." *Southern Review*, N.S., 3 (Winter 1967): 171-79.

"The Feather behind the Rock." *New Yorker* 43 (12 August 1967): 26-30. [Reprinted in *A Duke Miscellany: Narrative and Verse of the Sixties*, ed. William Blackburn (1970), 154-62.]

"A Flaw in the Crust of the Earth." *Reporter* 37 (2 November 1967): 43-46.

"Who Would Want a Little Boy?" *Ladies Home Journal* 85 (May 1968): 132 + .

"The Common Courtesies." *McCall's* 95 (June 1968): 62 + . [Reprinted in *Prize Stories 1969: The O. Henry Awards*, ed. William Abrahams (1969), 121-30.]

"With All Flags Flying." *Redbook* 137 (June 1971): 88 + . [Reprinted in *Prize Stories 1972: The O. Henry Awards*, ed. William Abrahams (1972), 84-87.]

"Outside." *Southern Review*, N.S., 7 (Autumn 1971): 1130-44.

"The Bride in the Boatyard." *McCall's* 99 (June 1972): 92 + .

"Respect." *Mademoiselle* 75 (June 1972): 146.

"A Misstep of the Mind." *Seventeen* 31 (October 1972): 118 + .

"Spending." *Shenandoah* 24 (Winter 1973): 58-68.

"The Base-Metal Egg." *Southern Review*, N.S., 9 (Summer 1973): 682-86.

"Neutral Ground." *Family Circle* 85 (November 1974): 36 + .

"Half-Truths and Semi-Miracles." *Cosmopolitan* 177 (December 1974): 264 + .

"A Knack for Languages." *New Yorker* 50 (13 January 1975): 32-37.

"The Artificial Family." *Southern Review*, N.S., 11 (Summer 1975): 615-21. [Reprinted in *The Pushcart Prize: Best of the Small Presses*, ed. Bill Henderson (1976), 11-18.]

"The Geologist's Maid." *New Yorker* 51 (28 July 1975): 29-33. [Reprinted in *Stories of the Modern South*, ed. Benjamin Forkner and Patrick Samway, S.J. (1978), 343-54.]

"Some Sign That I Ever Made You Happy." *McCall's* 103 (October 1975): 90+.

"Your Place Is Empty." *New Yorker* 52 (22 November 1976): 45-54. [Reprinted in *Best American Short Stories* and *Yearbook of the American Short Story*, ed. Martha Foley (1977), 317-37.]

"Holding Things Together." *New Yorker* 52 (24 January 1977): 30-35.

"Average Waves in Unprotected Waters." *New Yorker* 53 (28 February 1977): 32-36.

"Under the Bosom Tree." *Archive* 89 (Spring 1977): 72-77.

"Foot-Footing On." *Mademoiselle* 83 (November 1977): 82+.

"Uncle Ahmad." *Quest/77* 1 (November-December 1977): 76-82.

"Linguistics." *Washington Post Magazine*, 12 November 1978, 38+.

"Laps." *Parents' Magazine* 56 (August 1981): 66-70.

"The Country Cook." *Harper's* 264 (March 1982): 54-62.

"Teenage Wasteland." *Seventeen* 42 (November 1983): 144-48.

ARTICLES

"Youth Talks about Youth: 'Will This Seem Ridiculous?' " *Vogue* 145 (1 February 1965): 85+.

"Olives Out of a Bottle" [Interview with Tyler]. *Archive* 87 (Spring 1975): 70-90.

"Because I Want More Than One Life." *Washington Post*, 15 August 1976, Sec. G, 1+.

"Trouble in the Boys' Club: The Trials of Marvin Mandel." *New Republic* 177 (30 July 1977): 16-19.

"Chocolates in the Afternoon and Other Temptations of a Novelist." *Washington Post Book World*, 4 December 1977, 3.

"Writers' Writers: Gabriel Garcia Marquez." *New York Times Book Review*, 4 December 1977, 70.

"My Summer." *New York Times Book Review*, 4 June 1978, 35-36.

[Tyler's favorite books for 1978.] *Washington Post Book World*, 3 December 1978, 1+.

"Please Don't Call It Persia." *New York Times Book Review*, 18 February 1979, 3+.

"Still Just Writing." In *The Writer on Her Work: Contemporary Women Writers Reflect on Their Art and Situation*. Ed. Janet Sternburg. New York: W.W. Norton, 1980, 3-16.

"A Visit with Eudora Welty." *New York Times Book Review*, 2 November 1980, 33-34.

REVIEWS

"For Barthelme, 'Words Are What Matters' " [*Sadness*, by Donald Barthelme]. *National Observer*, 4 November 1972, 21.

"Stories of Escape and Love in 'Beasts of the Southern Wild' " [*Beasts of the Southern Wild*. by Doris Betts]. *National Observer*, 5 January 1974, 15.

"In Unerring Detail, the Story of a Good Woman" [*The Mystic Adventures of*

Roxie Stoner, by Berry Morgan]. National Observer, 9 November 1974, 25.

"Of Bitches, Sad Ladies, and Female Politics" [Bitches and Sad Ladies, ed. Pat Rotter]. National Observer, 22 February 1975, 31.

"The Nabokov Act Returns, Dazzling Us with Mirrors" [Tyrants and Other Stories, by Vladimir Nabokov]. National Observer, 22 March 1975, 25.

"Thought? Action? Or a Bit of Both?" [Emily Stone, by Anne Redmon; Hers, by A. Alvarez; Are We There Yet? by Diane Vreuls]. National Observer, 19 April 1975, 25.

"Stead Pulls a Surprise: A Hotelful of Madmen" [The Little Hotel, by Christina Stead]. National Observer, 17 May 1975, 23.

"When the Novel Turns Participant, the Reader Switches Off" [Looking for Mr. Goodbar, by Judith Rossner]. National Observer, 14 June 1975, 19.

"The Topic Is Language—with Love and Skill" [The Message in the Bottle, by Walker Percy]. National Observer, 19 July 1975, 21.

" 'The Lonely Hunter': The Ballad of a Sad Lady' [The Lonely Hunter, by Virginia Spencer Carr]. National Observer, 16 August 1975, 17.

"Georges: Two Women Who Chose to Write as Men" [George Sand: A Biography, by Curtis Cate; George Eliot: The Emergent Self, by Ruby V. Redinger]. National Observer, 20 September 1975, 23.

"A Photo Album of Snips and Surprises" [Beyond the Bedroom Wall, by Larry Woiwode]. National Observer, 18 October 1975, 21.

"Tales of an Apocalypse Served Up in a Tureen" [The Collected Stories of Hortense Calisher]. National Observer, 22 November 1975, 21.

"Barthelme's Joyless Victory" [The Dead Father, by Donald Barthelme]. National Observer, 27 December 1975, 17.

" 'The Voice Hangs On, Gay, Tremulous' " [Letters Home, by Sylvia Plath]. National Observer, 10 January 1976, 19.

"When the Camera Looks, It Looks for All of Us" [Jacob A. Riis, by Alexander Alland; The Light of Other Days, by Robert French and Kieren Hickey; Through Camera Eyes, by Nelson Wadsworth; The Photographic Eye of Ben Shahn, ed. Davis Pratt; Native Americans, by Joseph Farber and Michael Dorris; Gypsies, by Joseph Koudelks]. National Observer, 14 February 1976, 19.

"Stretching the Short Story" [Mr. Wong, by Elizabeth Jane Howard; Dream Children, by Gail Godwin]. National Observer, 13 March 1976, 21.

"Women Writers: Equal but Separate" [Literary Women, by Ellen Moers]. National Observer, 10 April 1976, 21.

"Fairy Tales: More than Meets the Ear" [The Uses of Enchantment, by Bruno Bettelheim]. National Observer, 8 May 1976, 21.

"Gregory Hemingway Remembers Papa" [Papa, by Gregory Hemingway]. National Observer, 5 June 1976, 21.

"On the Uses of Genius, Daydeams, and Idle Hours" [Creativity, by Silvano Arieti]. National Observer, 10 July 1976, 17.

[Review of The Master and Other Stories, by Sue Kaufman; and Angels at the

Ritz and Other Stories, by William Trevor]. *New York Times Book Review*, 11 July 1976, 7.

[Review of *Crossing the Border, Fifteen Tales*, by Joyce Carol Oates.] *New York Times Book Review*, 18 July 1976, 8 +.

"The New Improved Short Story" [*Mademoiselle Prize Stories; Prize Stories, 1976: The O. Henry Awards; The Talisman and Other Stories*, by Carlos Baker; *Children and Lovers*, by Helga Sandburg; *The Lists of the Past*, by Julie Hayden]. *National Observer*, 7 August 1976, 17.

"A Breathless Dash through a Whirlwind Life" [*Miss Herbert*, by Christina Stead]. *National Observer*, 14 August 1976, 17.

"Writers Talk about Writing" [*Writers at Work*, ed. George Plimpton]. *National Observer*, 11 September 1976, 19.

[Review of *A Sea-Change*, by Lois Gould.] *New York Times Book Review*, 19 September 1976, 4-5.

"The Woman Who Fled from Her Self" [*Lady Oracle*, by Margaret Atwood]. *National Observer*, 9 October 1976, 25.

"*The Autumn of the Patriarch:* Marquez's Latest Examines a Dictator's Empty Power" [*The Autumn of the Patriarch*, by Gabriel Garcia Marquez]. *National Observer*, 13 November 1976, 23.

[Review of *Polonaise*, by Piers Paul Read.] *New York Times Book Review*, 28 November 1976, 8 +.

"Boundaries and Bonds: Concerning Strangers in Strange Lands" [*Sleep It Off, Lady*, by Jean Rhys; *How I Became a Holy Mother*, by Ruth Prawer Jhabvala]. *National Observer*, 11 December 1976, 18.

"Books for Those Awkward Years" [*What About Me?* by Colby F. Rodowsky; *Girl Missing*, by Christopher Nostlinger; *The Amazing Miss Laura*, by Hila Colman; *Father's Arcane Daughter*, by E.L. Koningsbury; *Very Far Away from Anything Else*, by Ursula Le Guin; *Allegro Maud Goldman*, by Edith Konecky]. *National Observer*, 25 December 1976, 15.

"The What-Ifs Enliven an X-Shaped Novel" [*Henry and Cato*, by Iris Murdock]. *National Observer*, 5 February 1977, 19.

"Life in Prison with a Sunny Innocent" [*Falconer*, by John Cheever]. *National Observer*, 12 March 1977, 19.

"Even in a Crisis, That Inner Voice Goes On" [*A Quiet Life*, by Beryl Bainbridge]. *National Observer*, 9 April 1977, 21.

"Farewell to the Story as Imperiled Species" [*Prize Stories 1977: The O. Henry Awards*, ed. William Abrahams; *Winter's Tales*, ed. James Wright; *The Sea Birds Are Still Alive*, by Toni Cade Bambara; *Yellow Roses*, by Elizabeth Cullinan; *Slow Days, Fast Company*, by Eve Babitz; *In Miro District*, by Peter Taylor]. *National Observer*, 9 May 1977, 23.

"Herbert Gold, Two Bags, $20, and California. What?" [*Waiting for Cordelia*, by Herbert Gold]. *National Observer*, 6 June 1977, 19.

"Repeat Performance" [*The Pushcart Prize, 2*, ed. Bill Henderson]. *New York Times Book Review*, 19 June 1977, 15.

"The 'Ad! Da! of Mr. Nabokov" [*Nabokov: His Life in Part*, by Andrew Field].
   National Observer, 4 July 1977, 17.
"Meg and Hannah and Elaine" [*Flight of the Seabird*, by William Lavender;
   The Goat, the Wolf, and the Crab, by Gillian Martin; *Landfill*, by Julius
   Horowitz]. *New York Times Book Review*, 31 July 1977, 7.
"Three Novels" [*Gillian Unbuttoned*, by Alfred Gillespie; *Not Quite a Hero*,
   by Milton Ross; *Water Under the Bridge*, by Sumner Locke Elliot]. *New
   York Times Book Review*, 28 August 1977, 7.
"Apocalypse in a Teacup" [*The Collected Stories of Hortense Calisher*].
   Washington Post Book World, 18 September 1977, 3.
"Starting Out Submissive" [*The Women's Room*, by Marilyn French]. *New
   York Times Book Review*, 16 October 1977, 7 + .
"Rank Smell of Success" [*The Ice Age*, by Margaret Drabble]. *Washington
   Post Book World*, 23 October 1977, 1-2.
"Mother and Daughter and the Pain of Growing Up" [*Listening to Billie*, by
   Alice Adams; *The Grab*, by Maria Katzenbach]. *Detroit News*, 5 February
   1978, Sec. G, 2.
"Her World of Everyday Chaos" [*Inquiry Time*, by Beryl Bainbridge]. *Detroit
   News*, 19 March 1978, Sec. G, 3.
"After the Prom" [*Burning Questions*, by Alix Kates Shulman]. *Washington
   Post Book World*, 26 March 1978, Sec. G, 3.
"Looking Backward" [*Victim of the Aurora*, by Thomas Keneally; *The Cas-
   pian Circle*, by Donné Raffat]. *New York Times Book Review*, 26 March
   1978, 12-13.
"Two Women" [*Listening to Billie*, by Alice Adams; *I Hardly Knew You*, by
   Edna O'Brien.] *Quest/78* 2 (March-April 1978): 84-85.
"Lady of the Lone Star State" [*Prince of a Fellow*, by Shelby Hearon]. *Wash-
   ington Post Book World*, 2 April 1978, 4.
"Letters from Bess about Bess" [*A Woman of Independent Means*, by Eliz-
   abeth Forsythe Hailey]. *New York Times Book Review*, 28 May 1978, 4 + .
"The Artist as an Old Photographer" [*Picture Palace*, by Paul Theroux]. *New
   York Times Book Review*, 18 June 1978, 10 + .
"The Poe Perplex" [*The Tell-Tale Heart: The Life and Works of Edgar Allan
   Poe*, by Julian Symons]. *Washington Post Book World*, 9 July 1978, 3.
"Pretty Boy" [*Splendora*, by Edward Swift]. *New York Times Book Review*, 6
   August 1978, 14 + .
"Till Death Do Us Part" [*A Death of One's Own*, by Gerda Lerner]. *Wash-
   ington Post Book World*, 13 August 1978, 14 + .
"An Affair to Remember" [*Adjacent Lives*, by Ellen Schwann.] *Washington
   Post Book World*, 3 September 1978, 1 + .
"The Resilient Institution" [*Families*, by Jane Howard]. *Quest/78* 2 (Sep-
   tember-October 1978): 61-62.
"Betty the Likeable Lady" [*The Times of My Life*, by Betty Ford]. *Washington
   Post Book World*, 29 October 1978, 1 + .

[Review of *The Stories of John Cheever*.] *New Republic* 179 (4 November 1978): 45-47.

[Review of *I, etcetera*, by Susan Sontag.] *New Republic* 179 (25 November 1978): 29-30.

"Mirage of Love Past" [*The Sea, the Sea*, by Iris Murdock]. *Washington Post Book World*, 26 November 1978, 5.

"Damaged People" [*The Cement People*, by Ian McEwan]. *New York Times Book Review*, 26 November 1978, 11.

"Generations on a Farm" [*A Woman's Place*, by Anne Eliot Crompton]. *New York Times Book Review*, 10 December 1978, 69.

"Brother A and Brother B" [*The Cutting Edge*, by Penelope Gilliatt]. *New York Times Book Review*, 21 January 1979, 14.

"Of Different Feathers" [*Happy Endings*, by Margaret Logan]. *Washington Post*, 16 February 1979, Sec. D, 8.

"Chile: The Novel as History" [*Sweet Country*, by Caroline Richards]. *Washington Post Book World*, 18 February 1979, 1 + .

[Review of *Stealing Home*, by Phillip O'Connor.] *Washington Post Book World*, 18 March 1979, 1 + .

"Unlikely Heroines" [*Sanjo*, by Evelyn Wilde Mayerson; *Favours*, by Bernice Rubens]. *New York Times Book Review*, 6 May 1979, 13 + .

[Review of *Territorial Rights*, by Muriel Spark.] *New Republic* 180 (26 May 1979): 35-36.

"A Family Fugue" [*The Blood of Paradise*, by Stephen Goodwin]. *Washington Post Book World*, 27 May 1979, 3.

"California Nightmares" [*The White Album*, by Joan Didion.] *Washington Post Book World*, 17 June 1979, 1 + .

"Two Novels: Growing Up" [*Wild Oats*, by Jacob Epstein; *The Ballad of T. Rantula*, by Kit Reed]. *New York Times Book Review*, 17 June 1979, 14 + .

[Review of *The Basement*, by Kate Millet.] *New Republic* 181 (7 and 14 July 1979): 35-36.

"Two Sets of Bleak Lives" [*Where the Cherries End Up*, by Gail Henley; *Days*, by Mary Robison]. *New York Times Book Review*, 29 July 1979, 13.

"Her Younger Self" [*About Time*, by Penelope Mortimer]. *New York Times Book Review*, 19 August 1979, 14.

[Review of *Endless Love*, by Scott Spencer.] *New Republic* 181 (15 September 1979): 35-36.

"European Plots and People" [*From the Fifteenth District*, by Mavis Gallant]. *New York Times Book Review*, 16 September 1979, 13.

"Dreams of Inertia" [*Burger's Daughter*, by Nadine Gordimer]. *Saturday Review* 6 (29 September 1979): 44 + .

"Mary McCarthy" [*Cannibals and Missionaries*, by Mary McCarthy]. *Washington Post Book World*, 14 October 1979, 4-5.

"Novel with Notes" [*Love, Etc.*, by Bel Kaufman]. *New York Times Book Review*, 21 October 1979, 14.

"Moments Sealed in Glass" [*Vanishing Animals*, by Mary Morris]. *Washington Post Book World*, 23 December 1979, 11.

"Artistic Ambivalence" [*I Passed This Way*, by Sylvia Ashton-Warner]. *Quest/80* 4 (January 1980): 77.

[Review of *The Transit of Venus*, by Shirley Hazzard.] *New Republic* 182 (26 January 1980): 29-30.

"Woman Coping" [*A Woman's Age*, by Rachel Billington]. *New York Times Book Review*, 10 February 1980, 15 +.

"Pale People, but Rich Cosmic Dreams" [*Life before Man*, by Margaret Atwood]. *Detroit News*, 17 February 1980, Sec. C, 2.

"Everyday Events" [*A Matter of Feeling*, by Janine Boissard]. *New York Times Book Review*, 9 March 1980, 10 +.

"Gardner Wrestles Anew with the Devil" [*Freddy's Book*, by John Gardner]. *Chicago Sun-Times Book Week*, 9 March 1980, 11.

"At the Still Center of a Dream" [*The Salt Eaters*, by Toni Cade Bambara]. *Washington Post Book World*, 30 March 1980, 1-2.

"A Master's Voice: When Robert Penn Warren Speaks, the Words are Golden" [*Robert Penn Warren Talking*, ed. Floyd C. Watkins and John T. Hiers]. *Chicago Sun-Times Book Week*, 13 April 1980, 12.

[*Review of Three by Irving*, by John Irving.] *New Republic* 182 (26 April 1980): 32-33.

"Adventures in a Charmed Universe" [*Stone Fox*, by John Reynolds Gardiner]. *New York Times Book Review*, 27 April 1980, 45 +.

"In the 'Wood,' Mere Flashes of a Wicked Mind" [*Another Part of the Wood*, by Beryl Bainbridge]. *Detroit News*, 27 April 1980, sec. F, 4.

[Review of *Girl in the Swing*, by Richard Adams.] *New York* 13 (19 May 1980): 72-73.

"Bridging Gaps of Dazzling Width" [*Maybe*, by Lillian Hellman]. *Detroit News*, 1 June 1980, sec. E, 2.

[Review of *Off Center*, by Barbara Grizzuti Harrison.] *New Republic* 182 (7 June 1980): 31-32.

"Feminism and Power: A New Social Contract?" [*Powers of the Weak*, by Elizabeth Janeway]. *Chicago Sun-Times Book Week*, 8 June 1980, 12.

"Clothes Make the Man" [*Sunday Best*, by Bernice Rubens]. *Washington Post Book World*, 15 June 1980, 5.

[Review of *China Men*, by Maxine Hong Kingston.] *New Republic* 182 (21 June 1980): 32-34.

"Finding the Right Voices" [*Women in Crisis II; Flannery O'Connor's South*, by Robert Coles]. *Detroit News*, 22 June 1980, sec. E, 2.

"Capote Cleans Out His Attic" [*Music for Chameleons*, by Truman Capote]. *Chicago Sun-Times Book Week*, 3 August 1980, 13.

"The Return of Sarah Stern" [*The School Book*, by Anne Bernays]. *New York Times Book Review*, 3 August 1980, 14.

"An Honorable Heroine" [*Rich Rewards*, by Alice Adams]. *New York Times Book Review*, 14 September 1980, 13 +.

"A Chance to Spill Out the Soul" [*American Dreams: Lost and Found*, by Studs Terkel]. *Detroit News*, 21 September 1980, sec. E, 2.

"Mary Lee Settle: Mining a Rich Vein" [*The Scapegoat*, by Mary Lee Settle]. *Washington Post Book World*, 28 September 1980, 1 + .

"A Good Family" [*Hard Laughter*, by Anne Lamott]. *New York Times Book Review*, 12 October 1980, 11 + .

"The Fine, Full World of Welty" [*The Collected Stories of Eudora Welty*]. *Washington Star*, 26 October 1980, sec. D, 1 + .

"A Czech in Mourning for His Country" [*The Book of Laughter and Forgetting*, by Milan Kundera]. *Chicago Sun-Times Book Week*, 2 November 1980, 12.

"The Tenants of Tothill House" [*Setting the World on Fire*, by Angus Wilson]. *New Republic* 183 (8 November 1980): 33-34.

"Coming of Age on Rass Island" [*Jacob Have I Loved*, by Katherine Peterson]. *Washington Post Book World*, 9 November 1980, 11 + .

"Staking Out Her Territory" [*A Place Apart*, by Paula Fox]. *New York Times Book Review*, 9 November 1980, 55.

"Novels of Other Times and Places" [*Clear Light of Day*, by Anita Desai]. *New York Times Book Review*, 23 November 1980, 1 + .

"Portrait of a Bag Lady" [*If Birds Are Free*, by Evelyn Wade Mayerson]. *Washington Post Book World*, 23 November 1980, 10.

"A Clamor of Voices" [*First-Person America*, ed. Ann Banks]. *Detroit News*, 28 December 1980, sec. F, 2.

"When No One Was Looking" [*When No One Was Looking*, by Rosemary Wells]. *New York Times Book Review*, 1 February 1981, 28.

"An Art of Distance" [*The Collected Stories of Elizabeth Bowen*]. *New Republic* 184 (7 February 1981): 36-38.

"The Stoics and Trudgers" [*American Rose*, by Julia Markus]. *New York Times Book Review*, 8 March 1981, 9 + .

"An Elegannt First Novel" [*Dale Loves Sophie to Death*, by Robb Foreman]. *New Republic* 184 (4 April 1981): 35-36.

"The Soul without the Scent of Lavender" [*The Collected Stories of Caroline Gordon*]. *New York Times Book Review*, 19 April 1981, 6 + .

"Looking for Mom" [*Rainbow Jordan*, by Alice Childress; *Anna and the Infinite Power*, by Mildred Ames; *I'm Still Me*, by Betty Jean Lefta]. *New York Times Book Review*, 26 April 1981, 52 + .

"Men Will Be Boys" [*The Men's Club*, by Leonard Michaels]. *New Republic* 184 (2 May 1981): 31-32.

"South Africa after Revolution" [*July's People*, by Nadine Gordimer]. *New York Times Book Review*, 7 June 1981, 1 + .

"The View from the Village" [*Dandil*, by Gholam-Hossien Sa'edi]. *New Republic* 185 (25 July 1981): 36-37.

"Girl Mothers" [*Baby Love*, by Joyce Maynard]. *New York Times Book Review*, 16 August 1981, 8-9.

"A Community Portrait" [*Neighborhood*, by Linda Girich, et al.]. *New Republic* 185 (25 November 1981): 26 + .

"The Fall of a Star" [*Poppa John*, by Larry Woiwode]. *New Republic* 185 (9 December 1981): 36-38.

"The Glass of Fashion" [*The Language of Clothes*, by Alison Lurie]. *New Republic* 185 (23 December 1981): 32 + .

"Life in the Ingrown Household" [*Against the Grain*, by James Hanley]. *New York Times Book Review*, 17 January 1982, 7 + .

"All in the Family" [*A Mother and Two Daughters*, by Gail Godwin]. *New Republic* 186 (17 February 1982): 39-40.

[Review of *A Bigamist's Daughter*, by Alice McDermott.] *New York Times Book Review*, 21 February 1982, 1 + .

"Ordinary Family, with a Difference" [*White Horses*, by Alice Hoffman]. *New York Times Book Review*, 28 March 1982, 11.

"The Imagination of Disgust" [*Flaws in the Glass*, by Patrick White]. *New Republic* 186 (31 March 1982): 40-42.

"1900" [*1900*, by Rebecca West, ed. Jane Marcus]. *Saturday Review* 9 (April 1982): 55-58.

"South Bronx Story" [*Forsaking All Others*, by Jim Breslin]. *New Republic* 187 (19 July 1982): 42-43.

"The Complexities of Ordinary Life" [*Dancing Girl*, by Margaret Atwood]. *New York Times Book Review*, 19 September 1982, 2 + .

"The Mosaic of Life" [*Grace Abounding*, by Maureen Howard]. *New Republic* 187 (4 October 1982): 35-36.

"The Growing up of Lily Shields" [*My Old Sweetheart*, by Susanna Moore]. *New York Times Book Review,* 17 October 1982, 14.

"Kentucky Cameos" [*Shiloh and Other Stories*, by Bobbie Mason]. *New Republic* 187 (1 November 1982): 36 + .

"Avignon at War" [*Constance; or Solitary Practices*, by Lawrence Durrell]. *New Republic* 187 (6 December 1982): 36 + .

"Death to the Dictator" [*A Coin in Nine Hands*, by Marguerite Yourcenar]. *New Republic* 188 (10 January 1983): 42-43.

[Review of *No Fond Return of Love*, by Barbara Pym.] *New York Times Book Review,* 13 February 1983, 1 + .

"A Widow's Tale" [*Praisesong for the Widow*, by Paule Marshall]. *New York Times Book Review*, 20 February 1983, 1.

"The Ladies and the Tiger" [*Right-Wing Women*, by Andrea Dworkin]. *New Republic* 188 (20 February 1983): 34-35.

"Stories within Stories" [*Ararat*, by D. M. Thomas]. *New Republic* 188 (4 April 1983): 30-32.

"A Civilized Sensibility" [*Bartleby in Manhattan and Other Essays*, by Elizabeth Hardwick]. *New Republic* 188 (20 June 1983): 32-33.

[Review of *Modern Baptists*, by James Wilcox.] *New York Times Book Review*, 31 July 1983, 1 + .

"Varieties of Inspiration" [*In Praise of What Persists*, ed. Stephen Berg]. *New Republic* 189 (12 September 1983): 32-33.

"The Ledfords and All of Us" [*Generations: An American Family*, by John Egerton]. *New York Times Book Review*, 6 November 1983, 3 + .

[Review of *I Will Call It Georgie's Blues*, by Suzanne Newton]. *New York Times Book Review*, 13 November 1983, 40.

"End of a Love Affair" [*Pitch Dark*, by Renata Adler]. *New Republic* 189 (5 December 1983): 27-28.

"Mothers and Mysteries" [*At the Bottom of the River*, by Jamaica Kincaid]. *New Republic* 189 (31 December 1983): 32-33.

"1944 and All That" [*I Wish This War Were Over*, by Diana O'Hehir]. *New Republic* 190 (19 March 1984): 36-37.

Compilers' note: We wish to make special acknowledgment to Stella Nesanovich for "An Anne Tyler Checklist, 1959-1980," *Bulletin of Bibliography* 38 (April-June 1981): 53-64. We have included some items from her checklist that were not available in standard indices.

ALICE WALKER

The Dialect & Letters of *The Color Purple*

Elizabeth Fifer

Varying in content, length, function and time of composition, the letters in Alice Walker's *The Color Purple*,[1] provide a personalized format and a flexible vehicle for narration that—despite the prohibition *"You better not never tell nobody but God. It'd kill your mammy"* (*CP*, 3)—produce a triumph of storytelling. God is Celie's first audience, Nettie her second; as observers of these two intimate relationships, we must relate the letters of Celie and Nettie to one another. Celie is the main narrator, Nettie a secondary witness among the myriad relatives whose stories fill many of the letters. By learning Celie's dialect as employed in these letters, we enter into her astonished and astonishing consciousness as her self-awareness grows; and by considering the effects Walker achieves through the development of two distinctly different narrative voices—Celie's dialect and Nettie's conventional, educated diction—we come to understand Celie's plight within a larger cultural context.

In the act of writing, a frightened pregnant girl, struggling to understand her situation by forming it into language, enters the public world denied her by her position ("Don't nobody come see us" [*CP*, 4]). Forbidden by Alphonse the "father" and tampered with by Albert the husband, Celie's self-expression is itself audacious and liberating. With it, she can analyze and judge, raising her consciousness through an examination of other women's lives. All her acts of thought, of psychology and philosophy, all her triumphs are

It is her ability to write that frees Celie. W/o writing, she has no outlet for her creative (or distructive) energy.

made available and possible by the writing itself. Celie participates in the creation of meaning for herself through language. Without language, silence would have ensured madness or, as in her mother's case, an early death. It is not only an exterior adventure that frees Celie, or the people she meets through her extended family, but the language that she makes of them. Her letters shape her experience and thus transform it.

In *The Color Purple,* Celie's—and Nettie's—development of a feminist consciousness is gradual, but the plots of both lives form a mosaic, the design of which parallels the rise of feminism in the 1970s: Walker's heroines gain a "consciousness" just as if they were feminist heroines of the last decade. This sort of archetypal character development risks becoming anachronistic, even when it is accomplished through strong characters, such as the eccentric and unrestricted Shug, or when accomplished within unusual cultural contexts, such as the polygamous, patriarchal East African Olinka society, whose rigid and dangerous practices radicalize Nettie. Fortunately, the letter format adds vitality to what might otherwise become a melodramatic plot. The letters skillfully reinvent and reenvision the events by shuffling their chronological order and juxtaposing different conversations that seem as if they might have happened simultaneously. In between the letters problems are solved; their solutions appear as faits accompli, charged with their narrator's delayed excitement and delight. When Sofia is released from prison or after she and Harpo are reunited, the reader must participate in the text by imagining the missing dramas, the pieces of past action that led to the characters' present solutions. The letters themselves, like a vast soliloquy or endless after-dinner story, encompass and interconnect all the characters in two alternating voices; Celie and Nettie shape themselves before our eyes, helping us understand a grief that stretches over thirty years. The poignancy of Celie's grief lies in her need for her sister and her inability to reach her or the children born in terror by her stepfather. Celie's recounting of her life, her controlling and shaping it, replaces sister love and mother love; paradoxically, their flight saves Nettie, Adam, and Olivia, just as Celie's struggle to communicate her feelings in their absence saves her and gives her autonomy.

In her previous novel, *Meridian,*[2] Walker also explored, in the plight of suffering mothers and unwanted children and of other equally mismatched and desperate relationships, the sorrow of those struggling for expression. Meridian's mother's hopeless cry, "It's not fair" (*M*, 40), is echoed by Celie's reproach to God, "You must be sleep"

(*CP*, 151). And both major characters are nonconformist rebels, "artists," trying to forge a new language adequate to the complexity and ambiguity of their worlds. Meridian creates, in social action if not in poetry; Celie creates, in writing and in sewing if not in painting. The quality of self-expression—and the quality of its personalized format—makes a vital difference for characters precariously suspended in both novels between humor and horror; both Meridian and Celie are storytellers.

Though the plots of both novels follow a predictable cycle of birth, marriage, separation, and reunion, Walker's narrative strategies are more effective in supporting the narrative in *The Color Purple* than the intellectual digressions and experimental juxtapositions that suport the narrative of *Meridian*. Read together, the letters in *The Color Purple* seem less like parts of a puzzle than parts of a mystery, incomplete and transient by their very nature, without the immediate possibility of closure: "I will write more when things start looking up" (*CP*, 145); "Oh, Celie! Will I ever be able to tell you all?" (*CP*, 121); "I don't know nothing, I think. And glad of it" (*CP*, 105).

If the secrets of the letters are hidden forever without apologies in their interstices, their therapeutic effects on the writers themselves are clear enough. Celie, the main author, is an actor in all the dramas she recounts; through her writing she can accept and reconcile herself even to the unpleasant truths, as in the following passage where she tries to cure Harpo, her stepson, of wife-beating:

> Harpo, I say, giving him a shake, Sofia *love* you. You *love* Sofia.
> He look up at me best he can out his fat little eyes. Yes Ma'am? he say.
> Mr. _____ marry me to take care of his children. I marry him cause my daddy made me. I don't love Mr. _____ and he don't love me. [*CP*, 57]

Her letters are an elaborate literary mask, subjective, emotional, affording Celie all the advantageous intimacy of first-person narration and Walker all the distance and control of omniscient narration.

Ironically, these oddly eloquent letters are not exchanged immediately. One group is writen and not sent, while the other is sent but not read by its intended reader. This paradoxically hermetic quality is reinforced by the variety of effects the letters contain—they are many small overlapping worlds replete with high drama and melodrama, eccentric characters, internal dialogue, monologue, straight narration, direct address, poignant unanswered questions, dreams, stories, jokes, vignettes, overheard conversations, scenarios with repeated themes, cycles of confession and forgiveness, mysteries and their solutions, philosophic digressions, and more. The extraordinary compression of these diverse elements is a masterful achievement.

Although the broad sweep of the letters is governed by great cyclic events in lives or seasons, each letter reports the state of the writer in a scenario or vignette that may unfold unpredictably in several parts through a succession of letters. As such the letters provide energy for the plot through their own local effects, their twists, surprises, and ironies, which the reader may appreciate most when Celie does not. In fact, Walker enjoys counterpointing Celie's innocence with the reader's suspicions. Some of the most moving instances of the reader being allowed to move ahead of Celie are contained in the scenes in which she and Shug unwittingly fall in love.

Not only do the chronological positions of the letters and the interrelations between them control the reader's response; the dialect Celie uses is another sort of mask through which author and audience must peer at each other. By influencing our understanding of the characters, it allows Walker to assume the position of a medium, one whose spirits have their own intentions.[3] Celie's letters are her only possible rebellion against Alphonse's prohibition, "You better not never tell nobody" (CP, 3). By using dialect, the only language she knows, when all public communication is forbidden, she discovers and exploits a powerful tool in her development of awareness through self-expression. When Darlene tells her she could better herself if she would improve her speech, she refuses: "What I care? I ast. I'm happy" (CP, 183). Her dialect creates the reality—it is uneducated but personal, difficult but precise.

The languages of Celie and of Nettie, her sister, each honed fine within its oddly formal conventions, are both stylized and fluid. Their letters possess personal interior voices, but Celie's dialect adds an insider's language that immediately establishes a sense of community, an efficient capacity to express forbidden subjects, and a disarming exterior effect. Since Nettie has been educated and has changed her diction, leaving behind the world of private language Celie inhabits, when Nettie's letters are finally opened and read, many years after their separation, it is the educated language of the outside world that must be translated, not the other way around. Celie vividly recounts not only the joy of meeting Nettie again but also her bewilderment at the new self Nettie has created with her new language: "What with being shock, crying and blowing my nose, and trying to puzzle out words us don't know, it took a long time to read just the first two or three letters" (CP, 122). Celie's ability to express herself in dialect and her pride in her language are possible because she functions in a closed society, in which only one language is spoken. When Nettie finally returns to her, Celie bridges the gap by allowing Nettie's language to permeate her world: "Speak a little funny but us gitting use to it" (*CP*, 244).

Although Celie can speak to God about family matters, her letters become more emotively personal when she gains a human auditor. Shug's discovery of Nettie's hidden letters have at least three important effects on Celie and her narrative. First, Celie can begin to respond to, and be changed by, Nettie's history and experience. Second, she is released from the guilt of incest when she learns "Pa is not pa!" (*CP*, 150). Third, Celie is better able to implement her own variety of Walker's narrative strategy when she moves from passively addressing a benign but distant God to addressing a human being directly.

As Celie realizes, the shock of language is the shock of reality and selfhood. The letters help her to recognize what Nettie has faced in Africa during the years of their separation, but she also learns about herself and understands how she appears to others, even what she can become. Through the language of the letters, she goes beyond the arbitrarily set limits of her culture, strengthening a self barraged by the claims and traditions of patriarchy. Without the letters Celie's physical, psychological, social, and economic status would have made her both invisible and silent: "You skinny, you shape funny . . . you black, you pore, you ugly, you a woman . . . you nothing at all" (*CP*, 175-76). After all her mistreatment by him, through both indifference and aggression, the ability to call her husband Albert "a lowdown dog" (*CP*, 170) comes finally from her power in union with Nettie—her letters have conveyed her trials so well, and Nettie's have answered with such warmth and support, that Celie can say defiantly to a startled Albert, "Nettie and my children coming home soon . . . and all us together gonna whup your ass" (*CP*, 170). Language gives Celie the power to affirm her own existence, to announce herself to the world: "I'm pore, I'm black, I may be ugly . . . a voice say to everything listening. But I'm here" (*CP*, 176).

And Celie has other valuable attributes to compensate for her poverty of opportunity—curiosity, faith, and, most important, the power to enter and change the lives around her. She herself becomes as flexible, open, and continually evolving as the language she uses, allowing her creation to influence and define its creator: "all I'm telling you ain't coming just from me. Look like when I open my mouth the air rush in and shape words" (*CP*, 176). This comment

reinforces the remarkable illusion sustained by the Celie letters—
that they are shaped by outside events, that they are transparent
windows on her life, that they are created without authorial manipulation of reality by a powerless person buffeted by forces she can
hardly control.

By making Celie a repository for the stories of all her "peoples,"
Walker stresses the social context of her novel. A "wise innocent,"
Celie moves from relaying knowledge about the world as it is, as
through her stoic reaction to her sister-in-law Sofia's terrible beating
at the hands of the police—"scare me so bad I near drop my grip. But I
don't. . . I start to work on her" (*CP*, 77)—to visions of how it could
be, as she smokes out "all the evil" from the house she inherits from
Alphonse, the stepfather who raped her, "making a place for good"
(*CP*, 208). Her culture, intractable to some, bears little initial resemblance to the world outside in its wisdom, morality and opportunity. But the forces that shape Celie's world, reflected in the com-
plaints we hear—"you made my life a hell on earth" (*CP*, 171)—and
the pathos and hopelessness of her situation, are slowly transcended
by the understanding and the distance that self-expression requires.

Celie, like the narratives she tells, becomes stronger and better
defined as she moves from mere reporting to the dramas or scenarios
with extensive dialogue, to the insights of psychological analysis, and
finally, to humor. When her sister-in-law Sofia, captive of a white
mayor and his family, asks why one of her charges was born, Celie
replies straightforwardly, "Us don't have to wonder that bout
darkies" (*CP*, 88). For Walker, dialect provides its own world view, its
own answers, its own determination: it does not reduce, it com-
presses; it does not simplify, it focuses; it achieves distinction without cliché: "If us want to do better . . . our own self is what we have to
hand" (*CP*, 230).

Walker's use of dialect also helps her emphasize the context of her
narrators—they are outsiders, strangers, speakers of a foreign language. Celie and Nettie cannot even count on understanding each
other after their separation and the change in Nettie's diction. They
cannot react immediately to each other's experiences either, but only
imagine them. When Nettie and Celie finally do meet, after thirty
years, the result, inevitably, is further shock and disorientation: "Us
totter toward one nother like us use to do when us was babies. Then
us feel so weak when us touch, us knock each other down . . . . sit and
lay there on the porch inside each other's arms" (*CP*, 243).

Not the least of the ambiguous attractions of dialect is its ability
to convey primitive and childlike effects. Celie's language traps us at

the outskirts of the developing sensibility of a child approximating what passes for adult discourse ("teefs" for teeth, "boohoo" for crying); but her language manages the crises of her world effectively. Her language makes the dangerous less threatening. Like Celie's sewing, careful and precise, creating and connecting, "a needle not a razor in my hand" (*CP*, 125), language keeps Celie from the destructiveness that would be the natural result of her justified rage at her mistreatment. Celie's lesbian sexuality itself is somehow, through dialect, presented in childlike innocence, or at least it becomes less erotic and more coy—"us run off to my room like two prankish girls" (*CP*, 69); "titties gonna perk up, button gonna rise again" (*CP*, 124-25).

That Walker's use of dialect retains its positive virtues without relinquishing its sinister possibilities or its painful history is made especially apparent in Celie's unblinking, and therefore humorous, repetition of the typically chauvinistic language used to denigrate her ideal of womanhood, the free-spirited singer Shug: "Her pappy say, Tramp . . . she dying . . . of nasty woman disease . . . strumpet in short skirts . . . slut, hussy, heifer and streetcleaner" (*CP*, 40). Celie realizes sorrowfully that the minute the liberated Shug is sick and unable to fight back, the preacher "take her condition for his text" and even her husband, Albert, Shug's lover, lets the church "say amen gainst Shug" (*CP*, 41). But even the insults in dialect that men use take on a different meaning when Celie repeats them for Nettie in the letters, in the context of her anger and fierce protectiveness toward Shug: "Streetcleaner . . . somebody got to stand up for Shug" (*CP*, 40). Celie's own rebellion is prompted by the community's single-minded rejection of another nonconformist; in rallying to Shug's side Celie is saying that she, too, rejects the community's norms, its limitation of women through verbal sanctions. By inviting Shug into her home, she opposes the community, and in particular, her own father-in-law, who comments ascerbically that "not many women let they husband whore lay up in they house" (*CP*, 50). Celie acknowledges and overcomes the power of the language she must use to her own advantage; since both she and Albert love Shug, his father calling the singer a "whore" makes the husband and wife one at last, "the closest us ever felt" (*CP*, 50). Here Albert joins the world of women in rejection of his father's norms. His alliance with Celie to heal Shug prefigures his later maturation when he "gets religion" and tries to win Celie back.

As Celie saves Shug's life, nursing her back to health, Shug saves Celie as well. Although Shug's uncompromising language is mediated by an admiring Celie reporting in the letters, the presence of this appropriated language gives Celie a new perspective on her own life and marriage. When Albert tries to be tender, the half-dead Shug, still "too evil" to accept his advances, laughs in his face, telling him to "turn loose my goddam hand . . . I don't need no weak little boy" (*CP*, 43). Celie admires Shug's mouth "just pack with claws" (*CP*, 45) and the voice that says "I don't miss nothing" (*CP*, 45). At her first appearance since her illness Shug sings the song Celie inspires her to write: "Something I made up. Something you help scratch out my head" (*CP*, 48); helping Shug to make that song marks the beginning of Celie's movement from feminist language to useful work. Each piece of Shug's advice changes Celie's language and becomes part of Celie's progress.

When Shug replaces Albert's unsatisfactory love with her own, she introduces Celie to a new language to describe the body and its joys: "You never enjoy it at all? . . . why Miss Celie . . . you still a virgin . . . a little button git hotter and hotter and then it melt" (*CP*, 69). She develops Celie's creative powers by suggesting a new material, a new idiom. Shug is not only another mask for Celie to wear, a role for her to embody as she realizes in letters to Nettie the drama of her life; love for Shug and dialogue with this woman change Celie's focus, enabling her to use her talents in new ways. This is most humorously apparent when Celie stops being subservient to Albert and begins to make, wear, and finally sell pants. She moves in dialogues with Shug from surprise to enthusiastic embracing of the "male prerogative": "What I need pants for? I say. I ain't no man." Shug replies, "You do all the work around here" (*CP*, 124). Her first material is from the "male domain"—the stiff, unyielding cloth of an old army uniform. But she moves from this material to the soft, flexible stuffs that finally put her in demand: "I sit in the dining room making pants after pants . . . one day I make the perfect pair of pants . . . then orders start to come . . . pretty soon I'm swamp" (*CP*, 181). Shug's inventiveness sketches in the next developments—raised prices, a factory with employees. Shug's audacity and Celie's skills unite as Shug "sings out" her optimism, faith, and energy. She has enough vision for two lives, and her energy buoys Celie. Through their conversations, Shug rehearses the scenes Celie will make part of her life. When Celie realizes Shug's insight and accepts it, she sheepishly remembers her former self: "Now that my eyes opening, I feels like a fool" (*CP*, 168). Each woman relives her past and recreates her future for the other. In the process they relieve each other of guilt and supply each other with enabling language; Shug expiates her cruel teatment of Annie Julia, and Celie forgives herself for submitting to her stepfather.

Shug shows Celie how to have a feminist consciousness—"Why any woman give a shit what people think is a mystery to me" (*CP*, 171)—and their lesbian relationship forms the centerpiece of the novel. Her love for Celie is part of Shug's humanity, an outgrowth of her nurturing influence. Before she and Celie become lovers, she discusses sexual response and even advises Celie in her relationship with Albert. Celie moves from feeling as if she were a man when she desires Shug to feeling the innocent love of a "little lost baby" (*CP*, 97) when the relationship is consummated. This sexual expression is important to the meaning of the novel and reinforces Shug's message—you have to live with a belief that God loves the things you love (*CP*, 167). It is precisely this attitude toward the language of her own world that allows Celie self-expression and self-knowledge.

The color purple, the book's title, encapsulates both its theme and its narrative assumptions by presenting a striking example of God's love for what is most idiosyncratic and mundane; it dares us to ignore His works and to be pessimistic in the face of such a varied and pleasing creation: "I think it pisses God off if you walk by the color purple in a field somewhere and don't notice it" (*CP*, 167). As Shug judges but still accepts the evil she sees clearly around her, she inspires Celie to rid herself of the burden of the past, to live again in her old house, the grounds miraculously lush, the rooms transformed with ducks and elephants. Without Shug's animating influence, Celie would have been merely an observer of the loves and hurts of others, curiously anesthetized to her own passions, without a script, without an audience, without a language.

Nettie, Celie's sister and other mentor before she leaves to be a missionary in Africa (and after Celie finds the letters Albert kept and hid), is controlled, religious, and idealistic where Shug is erratic, vibrant, and ribald. When Nettie's letters enter, Celie's and Nettie's worlds mingle and combine, each influencing the other. Celie gains the confidence to tell an astonished Albert and his table of relatives that her children are being brought up in Africa, with "good schools, lots of fresh air and exercise" (*CP*, 170), and that they are coming home soon. Nettie's relief that Celie has not died bearing all Mr. _____'s children helps her bear her own trials more stoically.

Sharply different from Celie's letters in their content and style, Nettie's letters move the novel out beyond Celie's microscopic world. Both historic and "pedagogical," they introduce and maintain a different language, and consequently a different consciousness, far distant from the raw emotion of Celie's letters. Their larger African context—epic and unfamiliar—puts Celie's letters into perspective;

their emotional coolness helps us bear Celie's trials, intersecting, juxtaposing, providing counterpoint and parallel lines of development. If Celie, rapt and silent, recording her pain to God, illustrates her bondage and moves us with her simplicity, then Nettie, rational teacher and witness to the destruction of another culture, develops a larger context for pain and suffering, both her own and the African people's. If Celie's concerns are practical and parochial, seriocomic at times, full of folk wisdom, having, in other words, the virtues and vices of her dialect language, Nettie's concerns are utopian, religious, anthropological, and only secondarily personal. While the drama of Nettie's love for Joseph hovers in the foreground, the death throes of the Olinka culture constantly extend the background. Nevertheless, the substance of Nettie's letters emphasizes how Celie's total environment of emotional relationships is bounded and circumscribed by a ruthless, brutal, and destructive exterior world.

Nettie introduces the abstract questions that reinforce the reader's understanding of the layers of black oppression: black responsibility for slavery, black complicity in the white takeover of the Olinka lands, the complexity of being a black missionary working to further white ends in Africa. Nettie's letters, carefully plotted narratives in themselves, also provide further explanations of Celie's letters; they manipulate the way we experience Celie's letters by intervening to reveal what Celie herself could not know about her situation.

Nettie's more formal language supports her more formal attitudes, which stand in vivid contrast to Celie's more open, less self-conscious style. Walker also uses Nettie's letters to build the super-structure of the plot, as when she parallels the small-world suffering of Celie with the larger sufferings of the Olinka people. Celie's new-found love for Albert and her retelling of the Creation story are an ironic comment on the expulsion of the Olinkas from their African paradise, and the Southern marriages echo the polygamy of the African marriages, as other women take over when the first wife and mother is removed.

Intertwining complexly, the letters explore issues freely, not debating but demonstrating through language. Even Albert's mean-spiritedness culminates, many years later, in his spiritual renewal, as he realizes that "meanness kills" (CP, 191). When Celie cannot find her mother's and father's graves, Shug shows her that women can be each other's whole family: "Us each other's peoples now" (CP, 156). Squeak becomes Mary Agnes the singer by saving Sofia from jail, and her long odyssey to the stage culminates, twelve years later, in her giving of the children and Harpo back to the now free Sofia. Even Harpo's wish to be strong ends gently, "Harpo holding his daddy in his arms" (*CP*, 191). From all the suffering comes, finally, the joy of recognition and combination, the meeting of enduring characters who escape the inexpressible grief of their own silences to bring language head first like a new baby crying out, as Celie says, "into the Creation" (*CP*, 170). Self-expression, like human sexuality and God's creation of the world, is an act that generates its own imperatives. In *The Color Purple*, Walker's narrative techniques realize and embody this primary truth; how we tell the stories of our lives determines the significance and outcome of the narratives that are our lives.

NOTES

1. (New York: Harcourt Brace Jovanovich, 1982), hereafter cited in the text as *CP*.

2. (New York: Harcourt Brace Jovanovich, 1976), hereafter cited in the text as *M*.

3. Walker refers to herself as "A.W., author and medium" (*CP*, 245).

A Bibliography of Writings by

ALICE WALKER

Elizabeth Fifer

BOOKS

In Love and Trouble: Stories of Black Women. New York: Harcourt, Brace and World, 1967.

Once: Poems. New York: Harcourt, Brace and World, 1968.

The Third Life of Grange Copeland. New York: Harcourt Brace Jovanovich, 1970.

Revolutionary Petunias and Other Poems. New York: Harcourt Brace Jovanovich, 1971.

Langston Hughes. New York: Crowell, 1973.

Goodnight Willie Lee, I'll See You in the Morning. New York: Dial, 1975.

Meridian. New York: Harcourt Brace Jovanovich, 1976.

I Love Myself When I am Laughing . . . :A Zora Neale Hurston Reader. Old Westbury, New York: Feminist Press, 1979.

You Can't Keep a Good Woman Down. New York: Harcourt Brace Jovanovich, 1981.

The Color Purple. New York: Harcourt Brace Jovanovich, 1982.

SHORT STORIES

"The Diary of an African Nun." *In Love and Trouble,* 113-18. [Reprinted in *Freedomways* 8 (Summer 1968).]

"To Hell with Dying." *In Love and Trouble,* 129-38. [Reprinted in *Tales and Stories of Black Folks,* ed. Toni Cade Bambara (1971).]

"Roselilly." *In Love and Trouble,* 3-9. [Reprinted in *Ms.* 1 (August 1972).]

"Her Sweet Jerome." *In Love and Trouble,* 24-34. [Reprinted in *We Be Word Sorcerers,* ed. Sonia Sanchez (1973).]

"The Revenge of Hannah Kemhuff." *In Love and Trouble,* 60-80. [Reprinted in *Ms.* 2 (July 1973).]

"Everyday Use." *In Love and Trouble,* 47-59. [Reprinted in *Harper's* 244 (April 1973); in *Women and Fiction,* ed. Susan Cahill (1975).]

"The Third Life of Grange Copeland." *Redbook* 137 (May 1971): 173-95.

"A Sudden Trip Home." *Essence* 2 (September 1971), 58-59. [Reprinted in *You Can't Keep a Good Woman Down.*]

"Strong Horse Tea." *Black Short Story Anthology,* ed. Woodie King. New York: New American Library, 1972, 133-40.

"First Day (a Fable after Brown)." *Freedomways* 14, no. 4 (1974): 314-16.

"Advancing Luna and Ida B. Wells." *Ms.* 6 (July 1977): 75-79 + . [Reprinted in *You Can't Keep a Good Woman Down.*]

"Laurel." *Ms.* 7 (November 1978): 64-66 + . [Reprinted in *You Can't Keep a Good Woman Down.*]

"How Did I Get Away with Killing One of the Biggest Lawyers in the State? It Was Easy." *Ms.* 9 (November 1980): 72-75. [Reprinted in *You Can't Keep a Good Woman Down.*]

"Nineteen Fifty-five." *Ms.* 9 (March 1981): 54-57 + . [Reprinted in *You Can't Keep a Good Woman Down.*]

"Lover." *Essence* 11 (April 1981): 86-87 + . [Reprinted in *You Can't Keep a Good Woman Down.*]

"A Letter of the Times; or, Should This Sado-Masochism Be Saved?" *Ms.* 10 (October 1981): 63-64. [Reprinted in *You Can't Keep a Good Woman Down.*]

POEMS

"Once." *Once,* 23-26. [Reprinted in *Poetry* (February 1971); in *Poetry of Black America,* ed. Arnold Adoff (1973); in *New Voices in American Poetry,* ed. David Allen Evans (1973); in *No More Masks,* ed. Florence Howe and Ellen Bass (1973).]

"South." *Freedomways* 11, no. 4 (1971): 368.

"Hymn." *Once,* 41-42. [Reprinted in *Afro-American Literature: An Intro-*

duction, ed. Robert Hayden, David J. Burrows, Frederick R. Lapides (1971).]

"Burial." *Revolutionary Petunias,* 12-15. [Reprinted in *Harper's* 244 (March 1972); in *We Become New,* ed. Lucille Iverson and Kathryn Ruby (1975); in *The American Poetry Anthology,* ed. Daniel Halpern (1975).]

"Eagle Rock." *Revolutionary Petunias,* 20-22. [Reprinted in *Freedomways* 11, no. 4 (1971).]

"For My Sister Molly Who in the Fifties." *Revolutionary Petunias,* 16-17. [Reprinted in *Harper's* 244 (March 1972); in *We Become New,* ed. Lucille Iverson and Kathryn Ruby (1975).]

"The Girl Who Died #1." *Revolutionary Petunias,* 42. [Reprinted in *Broadside Series* 60 (June 1972).]

"He Said Come." *Revolutionary Petunias,* 50. [Reprinted in *Broadside Series* 60 (June 1972).]

"J, My Good Friend." *Revolutionary Petunias,* 24. [Reprinted in *Broadside Series* 60 (June 1972).]

"'Lost My Voice? Of Course' (For Beanie)." *Revolutionary Petunias,* 44. [Reprinted in *Broadside Series* 60 (June 1972).]

"Revolutionary Petunias." *Revolutionary Petunias,* 29. [Reprinted in *Broadside Series* 60 (June 1972).]

"In These Dissenting Times." *Revolutionary Petunias,* 2. [Reprinted in *Poetry of Black America,* ed. Arnold Adoff (1973).]

"The Old Warrior Terror." *Revolutionary Petunias,* 47. [Reprinted in *New Voices in American Poetry,* ed. David Allen Evans (1973).]

"Beyond What." *Revolutionary Petunias,* 69. [Reprinted in *Images of Women in Literature,* ed. Mary Anne Ferguson (1973); in *We Become New,* ed. Lucille Iverson and Kathryn Ruby (1975).]

"Chic Freedom's Reflection." *Once,* 37-38. [Reprinted in *No More Masks,* ed. Florence Howe and Ellen Bass (1973).]

"Love." *Once,* 23-36. [Reprinted in *No More Masks,* ed. Florence Howe and Ellen Bass (1973).]

"Mornings of an Impossible Love." *Once,* 53-59. [Reprinted in *New Voices in American Poetry,* ed. David Allen Evans (1973).]

"So We've Come at Last to Freud." *Once,* 61-62. [Reprinted in *A Rock against the Wind,* ed. Lindsay Patterson (1973); in *I Hear My Sisters Saying,* ed. Carol Konek and Dorothy Walters (1976).]

"Janie Crawford." *Aphra,* Fall 1974, 52. [Reprinted in *Goodnight Willie Lee, I'll See You in the Morning;* in *Black Collegian* 9 (May-June 1979).]

"Early Losses: A Requiem." *New Letters* 41 (December 1974): 7-12. [Reprinted in *Goodnight Willie Lee, I'll See You in the Morning.*]

"Black Mail." *Revolutionary Petunias,* 38-39. [Reprinted in *American Poetry Anthology,* ed. Daniel Halpern (1975).

"Expect Nothing." *Revolutionary Petunias,* 30. [Reprinted in *American Poetry Anthology,* ed. Daniel Halpern (1975).]

"Abduction of Saints." *Freedomways* 15, no. 4 (1975): 266-67. [Reprinted in *Goodnight Willie Lee, I'll See You in the Morning.*]

"Facing the Way." *Freedomways* 15, no. 4 (1975): 265-66. [Reprinted in *Goodnight Willie Lee, I'll See You in the Morning.*]

"Forgive Me If My Praises." *Goodnight Willie Lee, I'll See You in the Morning.* [Reprinted in *Black Scholar* 10 (November- December 1978).]

"Goodnight Willie Lee, I'll See You in the Morning." *Iowa Review* 6 (Spring 1975): 40-41. [Reprinted in *Goodnight Willie Lee, I'll See You in the Morning.*]

"Talking to my grandmother who died poor some years ago (while listening to Richard Nixon declare 'I am not a crook')." *Black Scholar* 6 (June 1975): 62. [Reprinted in *Goodnight Willie Lee, I'll See You in the Morning.*]

"Your Soul Shines." *Goodnight Willie Lee, I'll See You in the Morning*, 50. [Reprinted in *Nimrod* 21, nos. 2-22 (1977).]

"When We Held Our Marriage." *Nimrod* 21, nos. 2-22 (1977): 296.

"Malcolm." *Goodnight Willie Lee, I'll See You in the Morning*, 38. [Reprinted in *Black Collegian* 9 (May-June 1979).]

"My Daughter is Coming." *Callaloo* 5, no. 2 (1979): 33.

"Overnight." *Callaloo* 5, no. 2 (1979): 109.

"If Those People Like You." *Ms.* 7 (April 1979): 21.

"I'm Really Very Fond." *Ms.* 7 (April 1979): 21.

"When Golda Meir was in Africa." *Ms.* 7 (April 1979): 21. [Reprinted in *Black Scholar* 10 (March-April 1979).]

"Women." *Women Working.* Old Westbury, New York: Feminist Press, 1979, 201-3.

"Each One, Pull One." *Freedomways* 11 (1980): 87-99.

ARTICLES

"The Civil Rights Movement: What Good Was It?" *American Scholar* 36 (Autumn 1967): 550-54.

"But Yet and Still the Cotton Gin Kept on Working. . . ." *Black Scholar* 1 (January-February 1970): 17-21.

"The Black Writer and the Southern Experience." *New South* 25 (Fall 1970): 23-26.

"The Unglamorous but Worthwhile Duties of the Black Revolutionary Artist, or . . . of the Black Writer Who Simply Works and Writes." *Black Collegian* 2, no. 1 (1971): 5 + .

"The Growing Strength of Coretta King." *Redbook* 137 (September 1971): 96 + .

"A Talk by Alice Walker '65: Convocation 1972." *Sara Lawrence Alumni Magazine* (Summer 1972): 6-8.

"View from Rosehill Cemetery: A Tribute to Dr. Martin Luther King, Jr." *South Today* 4 (1973): 11.

"Staying Home in Mississippi: Ten Years after the March on Washington." *New York Times Magazine*, 26 August 1973, 9 + .

"In Search of Our Mothers' Gardens." *Ms.* 2 (May 1974): 64 + .
"In Search of Zora Neale Hurston." *Ms.* 3 (March 1975): 74 + .
""Can I Be My Brother's Sister?" *Ms.* 4 (October 1975): 64-65. [Published under the pseudonym Straight Pine.]
"Beyond the Peacock: The Reconstruction of Flannery O'Connor." *Ms.* 4 (December 1975): 77 + .
"Saving the Life That Is Your Own: The Importance of Models in the Artist's Life." *Women's Center Reid Lectureship: Papers by Alice Walker and June Jordan.* New York: Barnard College Women's Center (1976), unpaged.
"Lulls." *Black Scholar* 7 (May 1976): 2-12. [Reprinted in *Ms.* 6 (January 1977).]
"My Father's Country Is the Poor." *New York Times,* 21 March 1977, 27. [Reprinted in *Black Scholar* 8 (Summer 1977).]
"Secrets of the New Cuba." *Ms.* 6 (September 1977), 71 + .
"Zora Neale Hurston—A Cautionary Tale and a Partisan View." Foreword to *Zora Neale Hurston: A Literary Biography,* by Robert Hemenway (Urbana: University of Illinois Press, 1977), pp. xi-xviii.
"Other Voices, Other Moods." *Ms.* 7 (February 1979): 50 + .
"One Child of One's Own." *Ms.* 8 (August 1979): 47 + .
"Embracing the Dark and the Light." *Essence* 13 (July 1982): 67 + .
"Nuclear Exorcism: Beyond Cursing the Day We were Born." *Mother Jones* (September-October 1982): 20-21.

REVIEWS

[Review of *The Almost Year,* by Florence Engel Randall.] *New York Times Book Review,* 11 April 1971, 22.
"Jane Didn't Stay in a Corner" [*The Autobiography of Miss Jane Pittman,* by Ernest J. Gaines]. *New York Times Book Review,* 23 May 1971, 6.
"Can't Hate Anybody and See God's Face" [*Fannie Lou Hamer,* by June Jordan]. *New York Times Book Review,* 29 April 1973, 8.
"Judith Jamison Dances 'Cry.'" *Ms.* 1 (May 1973): 66-67.
[Review of *The Friends,* by Rosa Guy.] *New York Times Book Review,* 4 November 1973, 26.
[Review of *Another Life,* by Derek Walcott.] *Village Voice,* 11 April 1974, 26.
[Review of *Black Animal,* by N.J. Loftis.] *Parnassus* 2 (Spring 1974): 5-14.
"Like the Eye of a Horse" [*Cruelty,* by Ai]. *Ms.* 3 (July 1974): 41-42.
"A Daring Subject Boldly Shared" [*Loving Her,* by Ann Allen Shockley]. *Ms.* 3 (April 1975): 120 + .
"A Writer Because of, Not in Spite of, Her Children" [*Second Class Citizen,* by Buchi Emecheta]. *Ms.* 4 (January 1976): 40.
"Black Sorority Bankrolls Action Film" [*Countdown at Kusini,* produced by Delta Sigma Theta, directed by Ossie Davis]. *Ms.* 5 (July 1976): 45.
[Review of *Good Morning Revolution: Uncollected Writings of Social Protest,* by Langston Hughes, ed. Faith Berry.] *Black Scholar* 7 (July-August 1976): 53-55.

[Review of *Ruby*, by Rosa Guy.] *Black Scholar* 8 (December 1976): 51-52.
"A Walk through 20th-Century Black America" [*A Short Walk*, by Alice Childress]. *Ms.* 8 (December 1979): 46.
"Porn at Home" [excerpts from *Take Back the Night: Feminist Papers on Pornography*, ed. Laura Lederer and Lynn Campbell]. *Ms.* 8 (February 1980): 67 + .
"Breaking Chains and Encouraging Life" [*Conditions: Five, the Black Women's Issue*, ed. Lorraine Bethel and Barbara Smith.] *Ms.* 8 (April 1980): 35.
"The Divided Life of Jean Toomer" [*The Wayward and the Seeking: A Collection of Writings by Jean Toomer*, ed. with an introduction by Darwin T. Turner]. *New York Times Book Review*, 13 July 1980, 11 + .
[Review of *Gifts of Power: The Writings of Rebecca Jackson (1795-1871), Black Visionary, Shaker Eldress*, ed. Jean McMahon Humez.] *Black Scholar* 12 (September-October 1981): 64-67.
[Review of *Nuclear Madness: What You Can Do*, by Helen Caldicott, with the assistance of Nancy Herrington and Nahum Stiskin.] *Black Scholar* 13 (Spring 1982): 81.
"The Strangest Dinner Party I Ever Went To" [*Fireless Cookery: A Traditional Energy-Efficient Method of Slow Cooking*, by Heidi Kirschner]. *Ms.* 11 (July-August 1982): 58 + .

MISCELLANEOUS

"The Experience." In "The Negro College Dead-End." *Moderator*, March 1966, 13-14.
"Black Writers' Views on Literary Lions and Value." *Negro Digest*, January 1968, 10 + . [Alice Walker's statement appears on p. 13.]
"On 'The Diary of an African Nun' " [reply to a letter by Rev. Donald J. O'Leary]. *Freedomways*, First quarter 1969, 70-73.
"Women on Women" [transcript of panel discussion sponsored by *American Scholar*, moderated by Lillian Hellman]. *American Scholar* 41 (Autumn 1972), 599-626. [Alice Walker contributes on 601-2, 604, 606, 609-12, 617-18, 620.]
"Alice Walker." In *Interviews with Black Writers*, ed. John O'Brien. New York: Liveright, 1973, 185-211.
"Eudora Welty: An Interview." *Harvard Advocate*, Special Issue, 1973, 68-72. [Cited elsewhere under title "Something to Do with Real Life."]
[Letter on the founding of the national Black Feminist Organization]. *Ms.* 3 (August 1974): 4-6.
"An Interview with Alice Walker," by Jessica Harris. *Essence* 7 (July 1976): 33.
"Anais Nin: 1903-1977." *Ms.* 5 (April 1977): 46.
"On Anais Nin: 1903-1977" [reply to letter by Lani M. Nolan]. *Ms.* 6 (August 1977): 8.
"On Refusing to Be Humbled by Second Place in a Contest You Did Not

Design: A Tradition by Now." Dedication to *I Love Myself When I am Laughing . . .And Then Again When I Am Looking Mean and Impressive: A Zora Neale Hurston Reader*, ed. Alice Walker. Old Westbury, New York: Feminist Press, 1979, 1-5.

"Silver Writes." *Perspectives: The Civil Rights Quarterly* 14 (Summer 1982): 22-23.

"*The Color Purple* Didn't Come Easy." *San Francisco Chronicle Review*, 10 October 1982, 1.

"Letters Forum: On Anti-Semitism." *Ms.* 11 (February 1983): 13-16.

Compiler's note: The assistance of Susan Kirschner, of Lewis and Clark College, and Christy Roysden of Lehigh University, in the compilation of this bibliography is gratefully acknowledged.

MAXINE HONG KINGSTON

Narrative Technique & Female Identity

Suzanne Juhasz

Maxine Hong Kingston's two-volume autobiography, *The Woman Warrior* and *China Men*, embodies the search for identity in the narrative act. The first text places the daughter in relation to her mother, the second places her in relation to her father; they demonstrate how finding each parent is a part of finding oneself. For Kingston, finding her mother and father is to name them, to tell their stories. Language is the means with which she arrives at identity, first at home, and then in the world. But because a daughter's relation to her mother is psychologically and linguistically different from her relation to her father, so is the telling of these stories different.[1]

Although the two texts are superficially similar, they are generated from different narrative patterns. In *The Woman Warrior* alternating movements toward and away from the mother take place within a textual field in which a linear progression, defining first the mother, then the daughter, takes place. In *China Men* narrative movement goes in one direction only, toward the father. But because this impulse in the latter book is continually diffused into generalization and idealization, it begins over, again and again. Such narrative structures suggest the evolution of female identity, which is formed in relation to the mother through the achievement of individuation in the context of connection, in relation to the father through the understanding of separation, the creation of substitutes for connection. Taken together, *The Woman Warrior* and *China Men* compose a woman's autobiography, describing a self formed at the source by gender experience.

To say this is neither to ignore nor to minimize the question of national identity everywhere present in Kingston's writing. Born in the United States to Chinese immigrant parents, her search for self necessarily involves a definition of home. Is it America, China, or some place in between? For Kingston the question of national identity complicates the search for self. Yet it is possible to understand how gender identity and national identity can be versions of one another, how home is embodied in the mother and father who together stand for the primary source of the self. For Kingston, in fact, who has never been there, China is not so much a physical place as it is a construct used by her parents to define their own identities. America too, especially for her parents, is a psychological state as much as it is a place. My own focus here on sexual identity is therefore not meant to negate the other dimension of the problem, but rather to reveal sexual and national identities as parts of one another. For it is as a Chinese-American woman that Kingston seeks to define herself.

The narrator's search for home in both books is for a place and a self. That search involves rejections of source as well as connections to it, even as the achievement of identity is a combination of individuation and attachment: "Whenever my parents said 'home,' they suspended America. They suspended enjoyment, but I did not want to go to China. In China my parents would sell my sisters and me. My father would marry two or three more wives, who would spatter cooking oil on our bare toes and lie that we were crying for naughtiness. They would give food to their own children and rocks to us. I did not want to go where the ghosts took shapes nothing like our own."[2]

The movement of both texts is toward her own definition of home as a place to which she *can* return. "The simple explanation makes it less scary to go home after yelling at your father and mother. It drives the fear away and makes it possible someday to visit China, where I now know they don't sell girls or kill each other for no reason" (*WW*, 238). The explanation is the writing of the book, telling stories of home—of China and America in general, but of mothers and fathers in particular. "I want to hear the stories about the rest of your life," the narrator of *China Men* says to her father: "the Chinese stories." Her purpose is thereby to know *him*: "I want to know what makes you scream and curse, and what you're thinking when you say nothing; and why when you do talk, you talk differently from mother."[3] In the first chapter of *The Woman Warrior*, telling the forbidden story—told to her, nevertheless, by her mother—of an aunt who committed suicide, the narrator explains, "Unless I see her life branching into mine, she gives me no ancestral help" (WW, 10). Telling her aunt's story is a way to bring their two lives together, to discover commonality. At the same time, however, it reveals their differences as well. Telling their stories, in fact, both frees her from them and binds her to them, which is the process of finding home. "Thank you, Mother, thank you, Father," says the narrator in her fantasy of herself as a woman warrior: "They had carved their names and addresses on me, and I would come back" (WW, 44).

The Chinese phrase for story telling is "talking-story," and it defines the narration of both books. It is as well the subject of both books, because finding words, telling stories, is in Kingston's writing the other major metaphor, along with home, for the process of achieving identity. Chinese into English, silence into speech: when they appear in her books, these themes are subject and technique. The narrator of *The Woman Warrior*, who literally could not speak in public as a child, later cries to another silent Chinese-American girl, "If you don't talk, you can't have a personality. You'll have no personality and no hair" (WW, 210). The narrator's fantasy of the powerful woman, the woman warrior of the title, involves a female avenger with words actually carved on her back: "The ideographs for *revenge* are 'report a crime' and 'report to five families.' The reporting is the vengeance—not the beheading, not the gutting, but the words. And I have so many words—'chink' words and 'gook' words too—that they do not fit on my skin" (WW, 63). That power, equated with the ability to talk-story, is specifically associated with her mother: "I saw that I too had been in the presence of great power, my mother talking-story" (WW, 24).

Talking-story, discourse itself, is central to the difference between the two books, representative in turn of the difference in the relationships between daughters and mothers, daughters and fathers. The narrator's mother talks to her; her father does not. "Whenever she had to warn us about life, my mother told stories . . . a story to grow up on" (WW, 5). *The Woman Warrior* begins and ends with the narrator's mother talking-story. By the end of the book, the daughter's independent identity can be understood through her connection to her mother; talking-story is indicative of both parts of the mother-daughter relationship: "Here is a story my mother told me, not when I was young but recently, when I told her I also talk-story. The beginning is hers, the ending mine" (WW, 240). Her father, in contrast, does not talk. Screams and curses define his speech, but more important yet is his silence: "You kept up a silence for weeks and months" (*CM*, 8).

At the core of the relationship between daughter and mother is identification. The mother-child bond has always been the primary one, and girls never have to break it in the way boys do, by understanding that they are of different sexes. Through her stories, the narrator's mother passes on her version of reality to her daughter: "She tested our strength to establish realities," explains the narrator as *The Woman Warrior* begins. The matter is complicated, however, by the fact that the mother often tells lies. In *China Men* the narrator specifically contrasts men's stories with "the fairy tales and ghost stories told by women" (*CM*, 37). "No, no," says the narrator's mother to her in *The Woman Warrior*, "there aren't any flags like that. They're just talking-story. You're always believing talk-story" (*WW*, 213). To find her own identity the daughter needs to ascertain the difference between herself and her mother. Discovering a separate identity for her mother is one way to help her find her own self. Discerning the relation between her mother's "truths" and "lies" is representative of this process.

With her father the narrator needs not to loosen a connection but to make one. His discourse, and especially the lack of it, is indicative of the fundamental separateness between daughter and father, a separateness that arises because the father is neither a daughter's primary love nor is he of the same sex. The narrator's father screams or curses at her, "Wordless male screams that jolted the house upright and staring in the middle of the night" (*CM*, 8). His curses defile women: "Your mother's cunt. Your mother's smelly cunt" (*CM*, 8). Worse are his long silences, whereby he "punished us by not talking . . . rendered us invisible, gone" (*CM*, 8). To believe that her father does not mean *her* with his curses, to find out who he really is, the daughter has to invent him: "I'll tell you what I suppose from your silences and few words, and you can tell me that I'm mistaken. You'll just have to speak up with the real stories if I've got you wrong" (*CM*, 10). In the face of silence, invention is her only possible recourse. Yet it cannot be trusted in the same way that the narrator of *The Woman Warrior* trusts her imaginings about the lives of women relatives. Furthermore, it would be better, in the end, if he would tell her himself.

Therefore, although the two texts are conceived of by their author as "one big book [, she] was writing them more or less simultaneously," and although their surface stylistic features are similar, there is a profound difference between them. Whereas she "thought there would be a big difference between the men and the women,"

Kingston does not in fact "find them that different."[4] On the surface, the texts do look and sound alike. Both tell stories of relatives, stories interspersed with memories of the narrator's own childhood, in a matter-of-fact tone and declarative sentences that permit the speaker a fluid interchange between fact and fantasy, reportage and poetry. Yet the results are different, indicating more profound differences in narrative structure. Kingston herself points to their different sources. "In a way," she says, "*The Woman Warrior* was a selfish book. I was always imposing my viewpoint on the stories. In *China Men* the person who 'talks-story' is not so intrusive. I bring myself in and out of the stories, but in effect, I'm more distant. The more I was able to understand my characters, the more I was able to write from their point of view and the less interested I was in relating how I felt about them."[5] "More distant": This distance is, I think, a necessary result of the difference in finding a father rather than a mother, and it produces a text that creates not a universal or an androgynous but a female understanding of masculine experience. The essential separation between daughter and father is bridged by fantasy that, while it may do its work with intelligence and love, is never empathetic and is always idealized. For all its attention to detail, the text it produces is curiously—or not so curiously—abstract. *The Woman Warrior* is a messier book, but for me it is more satisfying than *China Men*. Yet, taken together as they are meant to be, they offer valuable insights into the nature of female identity, as it is created in relation not simply to women, not simply to men, but to both sexes, both parents.

The Woman Warrior is "messy" insofar as its narrative patterns are several and intertwined. *Complex* is really a better word for the various kinds of narrative movements that taken together reflect the dynamics of the mother-daughter relationship. The move to individuate and the move to connect both arise from the essential attachment between daughter and mother; the need for separation thus exists in the context of connection. In consequence, the identity that the text establishes for its narrator is achieved through a process involving both individuation and attachment.

The largest narrative pattern has a linear direction. The first three stories move toward defining the mother, thereby distinguishing her from the daughter; the two final stories go on to define the daughter, distinguishing her from the mother. But within each of the stories other movements occur in alternating patterns, maintaining the necessary tension between separation and connection. The text as a whole, for example, can be seen as an alternation between the stories the mother tells and the stories the daughter tells. Each teller's stories, in turn, alternate between true stories and stories that are not true.

The mother creates her relationship with her daughter through the kinds of story she tells her, stories whose purpose is sometimes to keep the two women alike and sometimes to make them different, as when, for example, the mother tries to offer her daughter a life other than her own. Seeking to know her mother, the daughter begins by thinking that what she has to understand is the difference between her mother's "truths" and "lies." Ultimately, however, she comes to discover not so much which ones are lies but why they are lies, and it is this kind of awareness that helps her to see her mother as another person.

At the same time, the daughter's own narrative style also alternates between "truths" and "lies." Her truths are her actual memories of her own past; but to write her history beyond herself, she invents or imagines stories—of her dead aunt in China, of her mother's young womanhood, of the woman warrior. This process of imaginative empathy should be understood not as prevarication but as fiction. It is, however, not the literal truth, and it establishes both connection with her subject, by means of empathy, and separation as well—the story is, after all, her own creation.

In each of the stories, these alternating rhythms create the double movement of individuation in the context of connection that enables the narrator to establish identity. In the first story, "No Name Woman," for example, the mother's telling of the aunt's story gives rise to her daughter's version of it, yet the daughter's version is revisionary. The daughter's story, in turn, both deepens her connection to her female heritage and creates some separation from it and thereby control over it.

The daughter begins her search for identity in *The Woman Warrior* by looking, not at her mother, but at another female relative, an aunt who took her own life in China, a woman whose own identity has been denied because the family never speaks of her. It is perhaps less frightening to approach her mother and the issue of female identity in this way at the outset of the book. Nevertheless, her mother's words begin and end the story, and it is her mother who has told her of the aunt's existence. " 'You must not tell anyone,' my mother said, 'what I am about to tell you. In China your father had a sister who killed herself. She jumped into the family well. We say that your father has all brothers because it is as if she had never been born' " (*WW*, 3). The conclusion of her mother's story points specifically to connection with her own sex: " 'Now that you have started to

menstruate, what happened to her could happen to you.' . . . Whenever she had to warn us about life, my mother told stories that ran like
this one, a story to grow up on" (*WW*, 5).

But the daughter is not satisfied with her mother's account. "My
mother has told me once and for all the useful parts. She will add
nothing unless powered by Necessity, a riverbank that guides her life"
(*WW*, 6). The daughter wants to know, for example, what kind of
clothes her aunt wore, "whether flashy or ordinary." She wants, in
other words, access to the motivation, the feelings, the personality of
this female ancestor, to "see her life branching into mine"; she wants
"ancestral help." And she senses in the very abbreviation of her
mother's version a duplicity: "The emigrants confuse the gods by
diverting their curses, misleading them with crooked streets and
false names. They must try to confuse their offspring as well, who, I
suppose, threaten them in similar ways—always trying to get things
straight, always trying to name the unspeakable. The Chinese I know
hide their names; sojourners take new names when their lives
change, and they guard their real names with silence" (*WW*, 6).

To name what her mother has left out the narrator employs
imaginative empathy, making up her aunt's story and in that way
coming to know her, to connect with her. Because she conceives of
this aunt as like herself, rebelling against tradition, she identifies
with her: "my aunt, my forerunner," who, "caught in a slow life, let
dreams grow and fade and after some months or years went towards
what persisted" (*WW*, 9). To "get it straight, to name the unspeakable," the narrator must use her own imagination, not her mother's.

It takes the narrator three chapters to apply this technique directly to her mother. This third chapter, "Shaman," stands at the
center and heart of the text. What precedes it is "White Tigers," the
story of the woman warrior, the fabulous Fa Mu Lan, the girl who took
her father's place in battle, the girl with whom the narrator identifies
and into whom she turns herself, the girl who comes at last to stand
for the woman writer.

Once again, impetus for the narrator's imaginative reconstruction of the story of the woman warrior is given by her mother's
version. Now the daughter begins to have some intimation that her
mother's duplicity has a function other than to confuse or conceal.
Chinese culture, as the narrator has described it in "No Name Woman," is strongly repressive of women. Yet, as she says in the opening
lines of "White Tigers," "when we Chinese girls listened to adults
talk-story, we learned that we failed if we grew up to be but wives or
slaves. We could be heroines, swordswomen. Even if she had to rage

across all China, a swordswoman got even with anybody who hurt her family. Perhaps women were once so dangerous they had to have their feet bound" (*WW*, 23). In telling her daughter stories of female heroism that directly contradict many of her other messages about the position of women, the mother shows her daughter another possibility for women that is not revealed in her equally strong desire for her daughter's conformity and thus safety in a patriarchal system. Which, then, is the "true" story?

In "White Tigers," too, the narrator replaces her mother's story with her own, yet at the same time she understands her mother's connection with her own version of the woman warrior, who is also an image of herself:

Night after night my mother would talk-story until we fell asleep. I couldn't tell where the stories left off and the dreams began, her voice the voice of the heroines in my sleep. . . .

At last I saw that I too had been in the presence of great power, my mother talking-story. After I grew up, I heard the chant of Fa Mu Lan, the girl who took her father's place in battle. Instantly I remembered that as a child I had followed my mother about the house, the two of us singing about how Fa Mu Lan fought gloriously and returned alive from war to settle in the village. I had forgotten this chant that was once mine, given me by my mother, who may not have known its power to remind. She said I would grow up a wife and a slave, but she taught me the song of the warrior woman, Fa Mu Lan. I would have to grow up a warrior woman. [*WW*, 24]

Not only is the mother's connection to her daughter acknowledged here but her female power as well, a power specifically associated with her ability to talk-story. In the telling of her own story—with herself as the woman warrior, a hero possessing most of all the power of imagination—a story which is then contrasted to her actual childhood memories of repression and misogyny, the narrator concludes by identifying language as the means by which she can become a woman warrior. The association with her own mother, the woman story teller, cannot be ignored: "The swordswoman and I are not so dissimilar. May my people understand the resemblance soon so that I can return to them. What we have in common are the words at our backs" (*WW*, 63).

In "Shaman" the narrator looks directly at Brave Orchid, the mother whose presence has infused and helped to create the stories that precede it. She tells not one but two stories, however—or tells the story twice: the "truth"—her actual memories of her mother, a laundress in America—and the "fiction"—the story of her mother who in China became a doctor. The fiction includes her own postulation of thoughts and feelings, added to the facts she has been given to create the character of Brave Orchid. But of course both kinds of story, the mother as ordinary woman and the mother as hero, are necessary, both kinds of knowledge, truth and fiction—each a corrective for the other, each a part of the reality of character.

Brave Orchid's heroism, as her daughter tells it, identifies her with the woman warrior, because her success, like the woman warrior's, is based on powers of the imagination. "I learned to make my mind large," writes the narrator, as the woman warrior, in "White Tigers," "as the universe is large, so that there is room for paradoxes. Pearls are bone marrow; pearls come from oysters. The dragon lives in the sky, ocean, marshes, and mountains; and the mountains are also its cranium. Its voice thunders and jingles like copper pans. It breathes fire and water; and sometimes the dragon is one, sometimes many. . . . When I could point at the sky and make a sword appear, a silver bolt in the sunlight, and control its slashing with my mind, the old people said I was ready to leave" (WW, 35, 39). She describes Brave Orchid in similar fashion:

> My mother may have been afraid, but she would become a dragoness. . . . She could make herself not weak. During danger she fanned out her dragon claws and riffled her red sequin scales and unfolded her coiling green stripes. Danger was a good time for showing off. . . .
>
> My mother was wide awake again. She became sharply herself—bone, wire, antenna—but she was not afraid. She had been pared down like this before, when she had travelled up the mountains into rare snow—alone in the white not unlike being alone in the black. [WW, 79, 80]

In China, Brave Orchid is best at vanquishing ghosts, this power symbolic of her becoming a "new woman," a woman doctor. But in America, with its taxi ghosts, police ghosts, meter-reading ghosts, and five-and-dime ghosts, she is mystified, no longer in control. Although she remains brave in the face of these dangers, in her daughter's memory she is no hero but a very ordinary woman.

The factual and fantastic tales of Brave Orchid combine to make of her a complete person in her daughter's eyes, a person with a separate identity both to be proud of and of necessity to reject, to move beyond. The story ends, however, with a more recent memory, one which reminds the reader that it is the connection itself, both uncomfortable and satisfying, that endures, even after the daughter has gone on to her own life.

" 'Aiaa,' sighs Brave Orchid to her daughter, now a grown woman: 'how can I bear to have you leave me again?' " (WW, 118). "Her eyes are big, inconsolable. A spider headache spreads out in fine branches over my skull. She is etching spider legs into the icy bone. She pries open my head and my fists and crams into them responsibility for time, responsibility for intervening oceans" (WW, 126). Yet even as the daughter pulls away from the connection and its corresponding need, she also, on the very next page, finds satisfaction, encouragment, and, yes, a sense of identity in it:

She yawned. "It's better, then, for you to stay away. The weather in California must not agree with you. You can come for visits." She got up and turned off the light. "Of course you must go, Little Dog."
  A weight lifted from me. The quilts must be filling with air. The world is somehow lighter. She has not called me that endearment for years—a name to fool the gods. I am really a Dragon, as she is a Dragon, both of us born in dragon years. I am practically a first daughter of a first daughter. [WW, 127]

The next stage of the book moves onward, however, even if the stories themselves demonstrate that the process in life is not schematic. The next stage of the journey is to leave home, to define the self, or, Kingston says here, to speak for oneself. In the two final stories the narrator learns to talk.

"At the Western Palace" offers the story of female relatives, once again, as the prelude or first step. The association of women with madness is shown as the alternative to their achievement of self-identity. Moon Orchid, Brave Orchid's sister who cannot change Chinese reality into American reality, goes mad. "'The difference between mad people and sane people,' Brave Orchid explained to her children, 'is that sane people have variety when they talk-story. Mad people have only one story that they talk over and over'" (WW, 184). The story of Moon Orchid is expanded upon in the final chapter, "Song for a Barbarian Reed Pipe": "I thought talking and not talking made the difference between sanity and insanity. Insane people were the ones who couldn't explain themselves. There were many crazy girls and women. . . . I thought every house had to have its crazy woman or crazy girl, every village its idiot. Who would be it at our house? Probably me (WW, 216, 220).

The narrator's own childhood silence—"a dumbness, a shame"—comes from the conflict between her Chinese upbringing and the ways of an American school, but in the story she represents it as symbolically caused by her mother (China), who seems to have cut her tongue, slicing the frenum, when she was a child. "'It's your fault I talk weird,'" accuses the daughter, later, to a mother who however has explained, "'I cut it so that you would not be tongue-tied. Your tongue would be able to move in any language. . . . I cut it to make you talk more, not less, you dummy' " (*WW*, 234, 190).

Moving beyond this terrible shyness and silence demands the thing that happens at last, when the daughter starts to talk back. "I had grown inside me a list of over two hundred things that I had to tell my mother so that she would know the true things about me and to stop the pain in my throat" (*WW*, 229). In a fierce tirade against her mother she asserts her own American sense of independence and attacks, specifically, her mother's talk-stories: "And I don't want to listen to any more of your stories; they have no logic. They scramble me up. You lie with stories. You won't tell me a story and then say, 'This is a true story,' or, 'This is just a story.' I can't tell the difference. I don't even know what your real names are. I can't tell what's real and what you make up. Ha! You can't stop me from talking. You tried to cut off my tongue, but it didn't work" (*WW*, 235).

Establishing herself as a talker in opposition to her mother—as American instead of Chinese, a truth teller instead of a liar—makes it possible for her to define herself as separate from her mother. Leaving home at this stage means leaving China, and her mother's Chinese way of talking ("We like to say the opposite"), in order to understand difference: "I had to leave home in order to see the world logically, logic the new way of seeing. I learned to think that mysteries are for explanation. I enjoy the simplicity. Concrete pours out of my mouth to cover the forests with freeways and sidewalks. Give me plastics, periodical tables, TV dinners with vegetables no more complex than peas mixed with diced carrots. Shine floodlights into dark corners; no ghosts" (*WW*, 237).

Yet this way of seeing and talking, this complete sense of separation from her mother, from China, is not the whole truth either, the truth of her identity, and this fact the text itself has revealed. For the text is more complex and fuller of insight than any particular moment of understanding within it. Poised against the linearity of the narrator's progress is the recurrent alternation of movement toward and tugs against connection that takes place within the narrative field, as it were, in which the forward progress occurs. Thus, when the narrator discovers her independence from her mother, that fact is indeed a part of her process toward identity but is not its fulfillment. Independence must be understood in order that connection can occur again, but a connection, finally, between two different people rather than between two people who together make one identity.

The Woman Warrior ends with its narrator's perception of this achievement, with the story of the Chinese woman poet Ts'ai Yen, with a celebration of the woman who is powerful because she can speak, can write. The story is begun by her mother, finished by the daughter. "It translates well" (*WW*, 243). In this way we see how the connection between mother and daughter, both storytellers, both women warriors, has been reestablished, but on terms that now both allow for separation and admit attachment.

China Men is less complicated textually than *The Woman Warrior*. As Kingston says, "the person who 'talks-story' is not so intrusive." Although here, too, the fact of memory is juxtaposed against the fiction of imaginative recreation, the memories are much fewer, and the imagining—the stories of male relatives, of grandfathers, father, uncles, and brother—is no longer urgent, no longer empathetic. These stories, lines thrown out across the chasm of separation, are more idealistic than realistic, more conceptual than kinetic, more parallel than developmental. The richness and tension created by the search for difference in the context of sameness—the mother-daughter relationship—is replaced by the clarity that distance offers, a lucidity that is at the same time monotonal. Only one person, after all, is talking here; narrative movement is in only one direction, not the tug toward and away from the mother but the yearning toward the father that goes so far but no farther, proceeding from anger and ignorance toward knowledge and admiration. The father need not be left, only loved:

> What I want from you is for you to tell me that those curses are only common Chinese sayings. That you did not mean to make me sicken at being female. "Those were only sayings," I want you to say to me, "I didn't mean you or your mother. I didn't mean your sisters or grandmothers or women in general."
>
> I want to be able to rely on you, who inked each piece of our own laundry with the word *Center*, to find out how we landed in a country where we are eccentric people. [*CM*, 9]

Her father's screams, curses, and, especially, his silence produce a profound ignorance that the narrator, whose love for her father is at war with her anger, longs to destroy. The fact of this ignorance is offered as an introduction to the book in a one-page piece entitled "On Fathers." Here the narrator and her brothers and sisters, waiting at the gate for their father to come home, see a man coming around the corner. They think he is their father. "But I'm not your father," he tells them: "Looking closely, we saw that he probably was not. We went back inside the yard, and this man continued his walk down our street, from the back certainly looking like our father, one hand in his pocket. Tall and thin, he was wearing our father's two-hundred-dollar suit that fit him just right. He was walking fast in his good leather shoes with the wingtips" (*CM*, 3).

The parable shows not only the children's lack of familiarity with their father but also the kind of evidence upon which they have based their false sense of knowledge: clothes, shoes, shape of the body. They recognize him from the outside only, from the back, the point being that this is not genuine knowledge. The purpose of the text as a whole is to gain that knowledge by imaginatively entering the father's interiority—something denied to the daughter by actual experience—by replacing opacity and abstractness with concrete particularities, a technique that served the narrator well in *The Woman Warrior* to establish the identity of her mother.

Yet in using this technique the narrator is self-conscious in a way she is not in *The Woman Warrior*. "I think this is the journey you don't tell me," she says as she introduces one version of her father's passage to America, to be followed later by "of course my father could not have come that way. He came a legal way, something like this" (*CM*, 50). Whereas in *The Woman Warrior* the transitions between "fact" and "fiction" occur almost seamlessly, *China Men* bases its structure on the artifice of these transitions and of their very creation. This format helps to make us aware of the "distance" of which Kingston speaks, a distance necessitated by the nature of the father-daughter relationship, which begins in separation and difference, rather than in connection or sameness.

To tell the story of fathers is to tell the story of China's coming to America. Both the mother and the father represent China to the American-born narrator, but there is a difference in their experience and therefore in the aspect of the homeland they embody. While the women were left behind in China, coming afterward to join their husbands, the men were the sojourners who came to America to discover the "Gold Mountain" there. In seeking to know her father the narrator looks as well for the experience of active appropriation, however painful, even humiliating some of its aspects may be, that has been denied to women, who find their power in the imagination, as *The Woman Warrior* shows, not in the public world. *China Men* confronts that public world, as grandfathers and fathers wrestle with nature and society from Hawaii to Alaska, from New York to California.

Yet there is in *China Men* a generality, an abstractness to all this experience that seems to bespeak the impossibility of the narrator's ever claiming male experience as an integral part of her heritage. Each character in the book has his own name, his own adventures, but all are referred to more frequently as "the father," "the grandfather," "the brother," a mode of appellation that is itself indicative of the generic character of the men, their normative function. In reading, it is difficult to keep them separate. They merge into the common maleness, a concept that the prose creates. The following passage can serve as example:

He sucked in deep breaths of the Sandalwood Mountain air, and let it fly out in a song, which reached up to the rims of volcanoes and down to the edge of the water. His song lifted and fell with the air, which seemed to breathe warmly through his body and through the rocks. The clouds and frigate birds made the currents visible, and the leaves were loud. If he did not walk heavy seated and heavy thighed like a warrior, he would float away, snuggle into the wind, and let it slide him down to the ocean, let it make a kite, a frigate bird, a butterfly of him. He would dive head first off the mountain, glide into the airstreams thick with smells, and curve into the ocean. From this mountaintop, ocean before him and behind him, he saw the size of the island. He sang like the heroes in stories about wanderers and exiles, poets and monks and monkeys, and princes and kings out for walks. His arias unfurled and rose in wide, wide arcs. [CM, 95]

What is most significant here is the combination of specific detail with a generalization of consciousness; the combination not only depersonalizes the individual man—in this instance it is Bak Gook, "The Grandfather of the Sandalwood Mountains"—so that he becomes akin to all the other male consciousnesses in the book, but also allows him, regardless of his immigrant status—he is a frequently brutalized sugarcane worker—to become heroic. All the Chinamen are capable of this kind of poetry, the result, I think, of an idealization of masculine experience representative of the daughter's approach to her father. Although the author seeks the humanizing middle ground between the father's generalized curses about the women and the daughter's idealized flights of poetic heroism, she creates such moments infrequently, despite many physical details, and these moments occur more often in actual memories than in imaginings.

These memories, which begin the book and reappear occasionally as the narrative continues, remind us that the search for the father is occasioned by both yearning and fear or anger. "The American Father" begins with memories of "father places": "He also had the power of going places where nobody else went, and making places belong to him. . . . When I explored his closet and desk, I thought, This is a father place; a father belongs here" (CM, 236-37). The father goes places nobody else went, made places belong to him, places that bespeak the Gold Mountain itself as well as the cellars, attics, and gambling hall of this particular father. The passage shows the daughter's yearning for the power of appropriation, heightened, perhaps, by its very inaccessibility.

After her father has lost his job at the gambling hall and becomes despondent, his children respond to his silence with a confusion—"I invented a plan to test my theories that males feel no pain; males don't feel" (*CM*, 251)—that finally turns to anger:

We children became so wild that we broke Baba loose from his chair. We goaded him, irked him—*gikked* him—and the gravity suddenly let him go. He chased my sister, who locked herself in a bedroom. "Come out," he shouted. But of course, she wouldn't, he having a coat hanger in hand and angry. I watched him kick the door; the round mirror fell off the wall and crashed. The door broke open, and he beat her. Only my sister remembers that it was she who watched my father's shoe against the door and the mirror outside fall, and I who was beaten. [*CM*, 252]

Such experiences, informed as they are by powerful unmediated responses to the father's separateness, can be contrasted to the imagined experiences of the men themselves, sympathetic but lacking this intensity, experiences narrated through the creation of a masculine consciousness. Sympathy is not empathy, and the very distance between them seems to influence the nature of the knowledge that is available to the narrator.

China Men demonstrates that finding the father, for the daughter, means finding what one has always known: that distance. Fear and anger may be transformed into love, but it is a love based on knowledge laced with idealization. Over and over in *China Men*, in each of its stories, the daughter begins in ignorance, with silence, and fills the gap or void with the fruits of her own imagination to gain—just that—her own creation. Never having been able to encounter the true interiority of the father, she has, finally, only the stories she has told about him. She finds her identity as a storyteller, a writer, here as in *The Woman Warrior*, but here there is a suggestion that the imagination is less the embodiment of life itself than an alternative to it.

Consequently, the two processes—finding the mother, finding the father—seem less than parallel for the daughter. Regardless of its author's intentions, *China Men* is more of a postscript to *The Woman Warrior* than a complement to it. Because the mother is not only of the same sex but, by virtue of the familial arrangements of society, the infant's first and primary love, she remains at the center of the daughter's search for identity. The familial arrangements of society ask as well that the female be understood in relation to the male—as the word *female* itself suggests—so that Kingston is correct in seeing *The Woman Warrior* as a partial text, an incomplete autobiography. Finding the father may be understood as synonymous with ascertaining the woman's relation to the external world, or the other. Difference and distance, which produce ignorance, fear, and idealization, create boundaries that can be bridged imaginatively but cannot really be destroyed. The yearning to destroy them, perhaps the most important feature of the search, in both its intensity and its frustrations or displacement, propels the text of *China Men* but is also diffused by it. Kingston sees that text as an achievement for herself as a writer—not so "selfish," not so "intrusive." Perhaps she is right. Perhaps this is the success daughters can have with fathers—to displace the yearning for him with the creation of something in his place, to understand that her love must be informed by the knowledge of separateness.

Taken together, the search for the mother and the search for the father allow a person to find home, a place both inside and outside the self, in the way that, for a woman, the mother is always inside, the father always outside. Finding home gives a sense of such boundaries, of understanding not only what is eternally beyond the self but what is eternally within the self. The woman, as in *The Woman Warrior* and *China Men*, establishes her individual identity in this context. Recognizing this context, this meaning for *home*, she can leave it, go on into her life, while she recognizes that home can never be left but only understood.

Telling is the way to understand, so finally both volumes of Kingston's autobiography are about becoming a writer. Taken together, the two texts demonstrate the special power of telling and, especially, of the imagination for women. Traditionally denied access to the outer world by literal appropriation, women can nevertheless follow a different route. Language is symbolic action, and it becomes, in this autobiography, the route and embodiment of female psychological development.

NOTES

1. The understanding of female development that I bring to my reading of literature comes from recent studies in feminist psychology, such as Nancy Chodorow's *Reproduction of Mothering: Psychoanalysis and the Sociology of Gender* (Berkeley and Los Angeles: Univ. of California Press, 1978) and Carol Gilligan's *In a Different Voice: Psychological Theory and Women's Development:* (Cambridge: Harvard Univ. Press, 1982). I make no attempt here to correlate specific ideas of the psychologists with specific literary interpretations, for my point is neither to "prove" the psychological

theories with the literary texts nor vice versa, but rather to show how literature as well as psychology is based in and seeks to articulate such ideas about human experience.

    2. *The Woman Warrior* (New York: Alfred A. Knopf, 1976), 116; hereafter cited in the text as *WW.*

    3. *China Men* (New York: Knopf, 1980), p. 10; hereafter cited in the text as *CM.*

    4. Timothy Pfaff, "Talk with Mrs. Kingston," *New York Times Book Review*, 15 June 1980, 25-26.

    5. Ibid., 26.

A Bibliography of Writings by

MAXINE HONG KINGSTON

Suzanne Juhasz

BOOKS

The Woman Warrior. New York: Alfred A. Knopf, 1976.
China Men. New York: Knopf, 1980.

POEMS

"Restaurant." *Iowa Review* 12 (1981): 206.
"Absorption of Rock." *Iowa Review* 12 (1981): 207-8.

ARTICLES

"Literature for a Scientific Age: Lorenz' King Solomon's Ring." *English Journal* 62 (January 1973): 30-32.
"Duck Boy." *New York Times Magazine*, 12 June 1977, 54-55.
"On Understanding Men." *Hawaii Review* 7 (1977): 43-44.
"Reservations about China." *Ms.* 7 (October 1978): 67-68.
"San Francisco's Chinatown." *American Heritage* 30 (December 1978): 36-47.
"The Making of More Americans." *New Yorker* 55 (11 February 1980): 34-42.
"The Coming Book." In *The Writer on Her Work,* ed. Janet Sternburg. New York: W.W. Norton, 1980, 181-85.
"A Writer's Notebook from the Far East." *Ms.* 11 (January 1983): 85-86.

TONI MORRISON

Mastery of Narrative

Linda W. Wagner

Toni Morrison's narrative accomplishments in her first four novels have won her accolades, prizes, and readers. *The Bluest Eye*, *Sula*, *Song of Solomon*, and *Tar Baby* are perhaps most impressive collectively because, unlike many novelists, Morrison attempts different and usually new techniques with each book, rather than following a traditional pattern of learning from the first novel how to be more effective in the second, as Hemingway learned from *The Sun Also Rises* what not to do in *A Farewell to Arms*; or as Faulkner borrowed a number of tactics and characters from *The Sound and the Fury* as he wrote *As I Lay Dying* immediately following. For Morrison, each book is a new arena, a place to choose structure and craft to achieve a total effect.

Such inspired self-consciousness, in a positive sense, marks the greatest work of the established modern writers. It is particularly impressive coming from Morrison, a woman writer, who must be subject to the anxiety of authorship as is any woman who attempts to excel in the male stronghold of commercial publishing. According to Sandra Gilbert and Susan Gubar, who coined the wonderfully apt phrase in their study of nineteenth-century women writers, women writers must work against a "socialization which makes conflict with the will of her (male) precursors seem inexpressibly absurd, futile, or even . . . self-annihilating."[1] It is difficult to be a woman writer. Yet Morrison seems to overcome that difficulty easily. Even in *The Bluest Eye*, her first novel, published in 1970, hers was expertly written fiction, involving the reader to the greatest extent possible— though with seemingly little conscious effort—hitting hard themes of contemporary social and political life. This paradigm is a major accomplishment in the world of current American fiction.

And as Morrison says emphatically in her 1983 interview with Nellie McKay,

A writer does not always write in the ways others wish. The writer has to solve certain kinds of problems in writing. The way in which I handle elements within a story frame is important to me. Now I can get where I want to go faster and with more courage than I was able to do when I began to write. . . . It seems to me that from a book that focused on a pair of very young black girls, to move to a pair of adult black women, and then to a black man, and finally to a black man and a black woman is evolutionary. One comes out of the other. The writing gets better, too. The reading experience may not, but the writing gets better. I am giving myself permission to write books that do not depend on anyone's liking them, because what I want to do is write better.[2]

Morrison's consciousness of technique, of the way she achieves her effects, permeates all her interviews and her shorter pieces of writing; it seems fitting to read her novels, at least in part, from the perspective of narrative strategies, so long as we consider as well the ways those strategies inform the vision of Morrison's oeuvre.

The Bluest Eye is Morrison's novel "focused on a pair of very young black girls," and her narrative procedure is the attempt in a plethora of ways to recreate their experiences. Claudia and Frieda McTeer provide both the voice and the understanding consciousness for Pecola Breedlove's story, a story that would have been vastly different if told by another kind of observer. The aptness of having the young black girl's story told by her peers, other children for whom life—sexual, political, economic—is as much a mystery as it is for Pecola, becomes clear as Morrison closes the masterful "Autumn" with the sleepy dialogue between Pecola and Frieda, with Claudia listening in:

After a long while she spoke very softly. "Is it true that I can have a baby now?"
"Sure," said Frieda drowsily. "Sure you can."
"But . . . how?" Her voice was hollow with wonder.
"Oh," said Frieda, "somebody has to love you." . . .
Then Pecola asked a question that had never entered my mind. "How do you do that? I mean, how do you get somebody to love you?" But Frieda was asleep. And I didn't know.[3]

Younger sister Claudia, the *I* in this passage, is even more like Pecola than her sister Frieda, who is wiser, older, and more caustic. So it is truly through Claudia that we come to know Pecola's consciousness, a mind that surfaces finally toward the end of the novel but otherwise is portrayed objectively—or through its parallel, Claudia's mind. Morrison chooses an elaborate structure to prevent the novel from becoming just another first-person, child-as-innocent account, even though—somewhat ironically—*The Bluest Eye* derives its power from being exactly that.

Morrison's narrative design keeps squarely before us the perceptions, concerns, and characters of the children who are victims of incest. The novel opens with the repetitions of the Dick and Jane primer, a passage emphasizing home, family, pets, and friends. Several critics have written about the effect of the telescoped lines, but perhaps of more importance than visual appearance is the content of the passage.[4] In some fantasy land, white children live happily with two parents, in a house, playing with pets and friends. In the Breedlove world, where housing is macabre if it exists at all, parents engage in physical battle, do intentional harm to their children, and abuse pets as readily as they do children. The novel is built on these almost unspeakable contrasts, and Morrison's narrative strategy is to show the contrasts, but always ironically and nearly always through the eyes of children.

The chronology of events, too, occurs in an order a child might consider important. The preface to the novel is Claudia's account of their selling seeds, hoping to win a bicycle: the death of Pecola's child, Pecola's loss of sanity, and the end of the Breedlove family are all imaged through the infertile seeds. "The seed shriveled and died; her baby too" (*BE*, 9). And once the novel proper begins, Morrison gives us impressions that reflect the girls' concerns: a stuck-up child, the opening of school, Claudia's being sick and her mother's caring for her. We do not hear about the German attack on Poland because Claudia and Frieda would not have understood any mention of that (although one of the three prostitutes is called Maginot Line). All characterization occurs through childlike recounting of events that are crucial to the children's maturing but are hardly of world-shaking significance. Pecola's menstruation, Pecola's greedily drinking the McTeer milk (so she can enjoy using the Shirley Temple cup), Pecola's coming to stay with Claudia and Frieda because her parents have lost their housing: these are the monumental events of the girls' memories.

And through this seemingly limited means of narration Morrison achieves many aims. We see the McTeer family as unified and protective, practical enough to take on a boarder, sensible enough to get rid of him when he tries to abuse Frieda. We see a loving family, whose values surface in their daughters in the scenes of boys taunting Pecola and Maureen Peale's taking advantage of her. Yet Morrison condemns even the best of these families when it is unable to stand the test of genuine horror, Pecola's pregnancy: "They were disgusted, amused, shocked, outraged, or even excited by the story. But we listened for the one who would say, 'Poor little girl,' or, 'Poor baby,' but there was only head-wagging where those words should have been. We looked for eyes creased with concern, but saw only veils" (*BE*, 148).

In the implicit contrast between the ideal schoolbook society and the lives of the McTeers and Breedloves—and in the further contrast between the McTeers and the Breedloves proper—Morrison creates levels of values that could easily confuse Frieda, Claudia, and Pecola, whose perceptions provide the narrative center of the novel. In fact, much of the dialogue in the early parts of the novel occurs in the form of questions that children would ask. Morrison involves the reader by not supplying answers—so the reader does. The reader also sorts through the families, meanings, situations, and trappings of plot in order to create a mosaic of "story" that seems to elude the girls, who are ostensible narrators even to the end of the book.

But Morrison does more, and in her additions of characters and plot segments that are seemingly separate from the McTeer-Breedlove nexus, she takes her greatest risk. The organized fragmentation of what is basically a four-part seasonal structure, beginning, sadly, with "Autumn" and moving to a "Summer" of death—of seeds and fetuses—gives Morrison a flexible format so that she can add segments, minichapters, that deal with new characters. Part 1, "Autumn," opens, as do all the four sections, with a chapter that is focused on the McTeer family—but on the McTeer family in relation to the Breedlove family. In the first two chapters, Frieda and Claudia are protecting Pecola; the atmosphere is heavy with threatening situations for all the girls. In the first, Mr. Henry comes to board with the McTeers; in the second, he entertains two of the local whores, after bribing Frieda and Claudia to leave the house. In the third chapter, "Spring," Mr. Henry attacks Frieda, and her family reacts virulently to his audacity. Seeking solace, Frieda and Claudia go to Polly Breedlove's place of work with Pecola, then witness Mrs. Breedlove's shameful abandonment of her daughter. Chapter four, "Summer," parallels the preface description of Frieda and Claudia selling seeds and serves as a summary of Pecola's state—violated, pregnant, mad. There might be Frieda but for the awareness of the McTeer family.

These chapters, however, make up less than half the novel. After each of them, Morrison adds the same kind of interchapter used by

John Steinbeck in *The Grapes of Wrath*, naratives sometimes obviously related to the central plot line, sometimes not. In these secondary chapters, Morrison does the following:

• "Autumn" describes the Breedloves' house, an abandoned store—the caption is "Here is the House . . ."—and the Breedloves—"Here is the family." Since the members of the family are enemies, Pecola turns at the end of the segment to her friends, the three loose women.

• "Winter" describes Geraldine, the neat, educated black woman who disowns her race and has perverted her son—"See the cat . . ."—so that he tortures pets and friends alike.

• "Spring" describes Mrs. Breedlove—"See mother"—as she traces her life from girlhood, and it does the same for Cholly Breedlove—"See father." Toward the end of this segment is the rape of Pecola, told in a dreamlike reverie to match the nostalgic account of Cholly's earlier life. The third segment concerns Soaphead Church—"See the dog"—a maverick who pretends to help Pecola in exchange for her poisoning a dog for him.

• "Summer" includes a dialogue between Pecola—highly significant, because it is the only time in the entire novel that she speaks for herself—and an imaginary friend whom she has created in the absence of the people who might have befriended her. The ironic use of the lead-in segment of the epigraph, "Look, look, here comes a friend," is poignant. Much of this dialogue concerns Pecola's new, blue eyes, the bluest eyes possible. It is permeated by Pecola's belief that if she were beautiful—by the standards of the white community, which would include blue eyes—her family would love her and she would have no more problems, leaving the reader with an almost unbearable despair. There is no more emphatic scene of existential loneliness in contemporary literature, but it is loneliness with no hint of self-knowledge as redemption.

For all the intricacies of Morrison's structure—and this is a difficult novel to read—*The Bluest Eye* remains an active narrative. First of all, the reader must be active to follow the literal meaning. Much of the novel concerns episodes and scenes that relate to Pecola only peripherally. *The Bluest Eye*, in fact, shares many of the difficulties of Faulkner's *Go Down, Moses*, a novel in which separate chapters appear to be independent of any main narrative line. But by forcing the reader to accept that these seemingly other episodes *are* related to Pecola, Morrison emphasizes the thematic focus of the book: the child *is* the product of her family's life, the lives of the families tangential to those people, and the lives of the community as a whole.

The bleak ending of the novel reinforces that theme, too, in showing that not one member of Pecola's community would come forward to offer her love, or even attention. She is so bereft in her pregnancy and madness that she creates the imaginary friend portrayed in the halting, brutal dialogue.

The dialogue begins with innocuous interchanges about the blue eyes, but becomes steadily more threatening:

> *Is that why nobody has told you how pretty they are?*
> Sure it is. Can you imagine? Something like that happening to a person, and nobody but nobody saying anything about it? They all try to pretend they don't see them. Isn't that funny? . . . I said, isn't that funny?
> *Yes.*
> You are the only one who tells me how pretty they are.
> *Yes.*
> You are a real friend. I'm sorry about picking on you before. I mean, saying you were jealous and all.
> *That's all right.*
> No. Really. You are my very best friend. Why didn't I know you before?
> *You didn't need me before. . . . [BE, 152]*

The ending of the dialogue, several pages later, shows the now desperate Pecola trying to find the *bluest* eyes, not simply the blue eyes she has supposedly been given. Her recognition that she needs something further weighs even more heavily on the reader, now that the novel draws to its close with this apparently aimless, childish, interchange:

> Here comes someone. Look at his. See if they're bluer.
> *You're being silly. I'm not going to look at everybody's eyes.*
> You have to.
> *No I don't.*
> Please. If there is somebody with bluer eyes than mine, then maybe there is somebody with the bluest eyes. The bluest eyes in the whole world.
> *That's just too bad, isn't it?*
> Please help me look.
> *No.*
> But suppose my eyes aren't blue enough?
> *Blue enough for what?*
> Blue enough for . . . I don't know. Blue enough for something. Blue enough . . . for you!
> *I'm not going to play with you anymore.*
> Oh. Don't leave me. [BE, 157–58]

Morrison's dialogue suggests the second way the reader is drawn actively into the process of reading *The Bluest Eye*, through the creation of anger. As Raymond Hedin says, the "structure [of the novel] has begun to take on a double edge"; because Pecola cannot understand that she should be angry, Morrison creates an anger in the reader: "the careful form of the novel intensifies rather than deflects the reader's sense of that anger." And, Hedin also remarks, the book is without relief, for either Pecola or the reader: "The coherence of Morrison's vision and the structure which parses out its logic into repeating patterns offer the reader no solace, no refuge from Morrison's anger."[5]

Considered in the context of Morrison's later fiction, *The Bluest Eye* becomes even more impressive, for Morrison does not use the elaborate, layered, segmented narrative manner again; she relies instead on a much simpler narrative technique and voice in *Sula*, a novel which in its complex character undermines the ostensible peace suggested by its narrative rhythm. Once again, Morrison manages her storytelling technique to involve the reader in unexpected ways.

Sula is set forth in a seemingly straightforward chronological pattern. It begins in 1919 and moves, through chapters titled as dates—"1920," "1923," "1927," "1937," "1965," and so on—to Nel's realization of what her friendship with Sula has meant. Sula herself has died in 1940. The structure of *Sula* like that of *The Bluest Eye*, creates the full context for the "meaning" of the protagonist's life: the novel does not begin with Sula, but rather with Nel. It begins, in fact, with a quaint explanation of why the blacks in Medallion live in the highlands and why those highlands are called "The Bottom." The first section of the book titled "The Bottom," is not the only section titled by date. As Morrison explains why the uplands are so labeled, she keeps repeating, "A joke. A nigger joke. . . . Just a nigger joke."[6] Similarly, the reader wants to place Sula and her unconventional life in a like setting—no malice intended, an almost unconscious will to observe, a way of enduring, should circumstances allow. In this instance, however, as in *The Bluest Eye*, social norms affect everyone but Sula, who is not allowed to exist on her own terms.

The first chapter of the novel to be titled by date, 1919, with flashbacks to 1917, is focused on Shadrack, the returned soldier, whose contribution to the lore of Medallion is the creation of National Suicide Day, which is January 3 of every year. Again treated comically, both Shadrack's madness and the "holiday" serve as metaphors for the malaise of the community, and of the Peace family. The third section describes Nel's parents, her long journey to the South, where she is made to understand the real position of the black in that culture, and her coming to an understanding of herself with her joyous chant, "I'm me." And because she does now have a sense of self-assurance, she can befriend Sula Peace, whose macabre family is the subject of the "1921" chapter. The legless grandmother, Eva Peace, dominates the novel from this point on—whether actually on stage or not—and the narrator's description of Eva's life and of her relationship with both her daughters and her drug-addicted son, Plum, sets the somber, understated tone of the narrative voice throughout the novel.

Morrison keeps to this narrative voice throughout most of the book; even when Nel attempts to tell the story of Jude and Sula's lovemaking, her voice sounds like the narrator's. One of the few times when Eva does speak, Morrison calls attention to the fact that it is a double-speak kind of monologue: "When Eva spoke at last it was with two voices. Like two people were talking at the same time, saying the same thing, one a fraction of a second behind the other" (S, 71). Eva as indomitable, if insane, matriarch, is in absolute control. When her daughter Hannah, Sula's mother, questions her about Plum's death by fire—and the reader knows that Eva has consciously set him afire—her own death by fire occurs soon after. Eva presents, in answer, a powerful metaphorical monologue, in which she uses the images of the mother's womb and the crippled, drugged child—Plum—attempting to crawl back into it. Because she sees him as an invader, her destruction of Plum, is an act of self-defense. Here is some of Eva's answer:

He was crawlin' back. Being helpless and thinking baby thoughts and dreaming baby dreams and messing up his pants again and smiling all the time. I had room enough in my heart, but not in my womb, not no more. I birthed him once. I couldn't do it again. He was growed, a big old thing. Godhavemercy, I couldn't birth him twice. I'd be laying here a night and he be downstairs in that room, but when I closed my eyes I'd see him . . . six feet tall smilin' and crawlin' up the stairs quietlike so I wouldn't hear and opening the door soft so I wouldn't hear and he'd be creepin' to the bed trying to spread my legs trying to get back up in my womb . . . a big man can't be a baby all wrapped up inside his mamma no more; he suffocate. [S, 72]

This metaphor, of confinement, possession, security, occurs often in the narrative of *Sula*, along with the dream imagery of a bridal dress of red, the plague of robins (a contradiction in connotation), the fur ball. Through her narrative manner Morrison places the reader in a conjure world, a lush, primitive world, but her narrative voice assumes the normalcy of such events and lulls the reader into accepting them. Eva's purposely losing her leg, Sula's cutting off the end of her finger,

Chicken Little's drowning, Hannah's burning: these are all events usually to be told discretely, if at all; instead, they are the conclusive events of Morrison's narrative in *Sula.*

Part one of this novel ends with Nel's wedding to Jude and with Sula's leaving after the reception to seek her fortune in the outside world. Such a division implies that the girls' friendship is the focus of the novel; once one of them is married, their intimacy must change. Part two begins ten years later, with Sula's return and her immediate challenge to Eva; soon, Eva is sent to a home for the elderly, and Sula assumes leadership of what is left of the family—the three foster children (the Deweys) and the drunk Tar Baby. In the first chapter of part two Sula makes love to Jude and breaks Nel's heart. Jude leaves and Nel takes on the burden of raising her three children alone. In the second chapter, "1939," Sula meets and loves Ajax, a free-wheeling man who eventually leaves her because she has begun to care in a possessive, stifling way. In her loss of that affection and passion, Sula knows grief, but she makes no overtures either to the community or to Nel. In the next chapter Sula dies of a painful illness, but Nel's visit and talk bring them close together once again. Strangely, Morrison gives us two more chapters—one describing the fate of Medallion as a community after Sula's death, the other describing a visit Nel makes to Eva Peace, jumping in time from 1941 to 1965. The result of the latter is that Nel realizes the real evil inherent in Eva, and in reconsidering her friendship with Sula, she concludes that the bond between them was the most important thing in her life. And the novel closes, with Nel's words, "'All that time, all that time, I thought I was missing Jude.' And the loss pressed down on her chest and came up into her throat. 'We was girls together,' she said as though explaining something. 'O Lord, Sula,' she cried, 'girl, girl, girlgirlgirl.' It was a fine cry—loud and long—but it had no bottom and it had no top, just circles and circles of sorrow" (S, 174).

The final distinction, the nigger joke at the beginning of the novel, is that bottoms and tops are erroneous, one more way of failing to deal honestly with other human beings. As the narrative manner of *Sula* indicates, most of life follows anything but a linear, progressive pattern. The recurrence of Eva, the repetition of burning fatalities, the circles surrounding Chicken Little's disappearance, the balls, eyes, suns—"Nothing was ever different. They were all the same. All the words and all of the smiles, every tear and every gag just something to do" (S, 146). "Morality," "Justice," "Right": just as Sula questioned Nel in their last meeting, so Morrison questions the reader's right to make judgments about any of her characters. Eva burned her child, but Eva, too, was afraid. Morrison's vexing of simple answers is managed narratively in a montage of locked doors, grotesque injuries—to self and to others—and predictive dreams. Not surprisingly, of all Morrison's novels, *Sula* has occasioned the most disagreement among critics.

For Anna Shamon, *Sula* is a nostalgic look at a black community unable to exist in the definition of a white society; in fact, Morrison allows her characters-to flaunt their differences and shows through Sula that "self definition must precede social responsibility."[7] For Cynthia Davis, *Sula* is a scapegoat story, and Sula—like Pecola Breedlove—allows her community to feel superior and thereby improve their own image and behavior. Whereas Chikwenye Okonjo Ogunyemi sees Sula as a force for good in that society, Davis sees Sula as a less positive force.[8] Her "curiosity" about her mother's burning, her inability to feel any sorrow for the child's drowning, her readiness to succumb to the same possessiveness she has ridiculed in Nel— reviewing these facts Davis concludes that Sula "is not fully heroic. . . . Freedom defined as total transcendence lacks the intention and significance that can come from commitment."[9] And Barbara Hill Rigney sees Sula as "a composite of archetypal scapegoats: Christ, Cain, even Lilith." Yet Sula never chooses her martyrdom, and Morrison's attention is, finally, less on Sula than on the community. Sula's rebellion is against Medallion's conventions, but it has no real "center," no purpose. According to Davis, Sula is "Morrison's version of the Jungian shadow" but without a conscience. If Medallion can be translated as *mandala*, Shadrack seen as a Holy Fool, and Sula as a scapegoat, then the novel is not "a celebration of the heroism of black women, but an indictment of society's immoral and irresponsible need to create scapegoats in the first place."[10]

Rigney makes a strong case for the continuation of these themes into Morrison's third novel, *Song of Solomon*, the book that has won the widest acclaim for Morrison. Partly because it seems to have a male protagonist—although the case can certainly be made for the strong women in the novel, especially Pilate—this novel has been found accessible by a variety of readers. Narratively, *Song of Solomon* is a strangely disproportionate *Bildungsroman*, and in that disproportion lies Morrison's theme. If it is true, as Bruce Michelson writes, that one interest of the critic is "the way in which structure and moral concern connect with the personality of the writer," then Morrison's distinctive use of the traditional form of the *Bildungsroman* carries a great deal of information.[11]

In the conventional *Bildungsroman*, the young man to be educated leaves home and parents to seek learning and fortune in a city. Most of the book charts his adventures away from home. In *Song of Solomon*, however, Morrison devotes much of her attention and space to Milkman's home life, to his existence before his travels begin. To equip Milkman Dead for his journey of discovery takes Morrison most of part one of the novel, and part one is considerably longer than part two. When Milkman travels out on his own, in part two he only reinforces truths learned earlier from his own family, chiefly from the women of his family. As Rigney points out, the Dead women in *Song of Solomon* parallel the Peace women in *Sula*, and Morrison succeeds even in a novel that appears to be about men in suggesting to her readers that "paternity is unimportant . . . and polyandry, whether contemporaneous or successive, is the norm."[12] But Milkman, acting individually or with his double, Guitar, does live at the end of the novel, as he witnesses Pilate's death and assumes Pilate's role in the family as namegiver (like Eva Peace). As Davis says,

By conceiving himself as both free individual and member of the social group, the hero unites his free and factitious natures and becomes part of the historical process by which the struggle for self-definition is both complicated and fulfilled. Thus at the end of *Song of Solomon*, Milkman has restored the names of his family, recovered their song; and he can "fly." But he does not fly away; he flies toward Guitar, his wounded "brother": "For now he knew what Shalimar knew: If you surrendered to the air, you could *ride* it" (*Song*, 341). Only in the recognition of his condition can he act in it, only in commitment is he free.[13]

Again, Morrison's narrative manner—her inclusion of the details of the community, treated almost as an individual, and of each member of the Dead family—signals the reader that Milkman is not an isolate and that withdrawal from community, in a Morrison novel, is never positive. *Tar Baby*, seemingly very different in narrative technique, also conveys this message, and Cyrus Colter, reviewing that novel, points to Morrison's "prodigious technical know-how," explaining that her "floodtide of narrative and dialogue which takes her to the very edge of the language" conveys the improbable yet accurate impression of the wealthy white couple making a houseguest of the hidden, unkempt black, as worlds collide and psychic problems surface.[14] *Tar Baby* is pocketed with long paragraphs of the kind of prose Colter calls "dense, imagerial." The ballast those paragraphs provide to a narrative includes much more dialogue than had *Sula* and it aids the reader in finding Morrison's intention. Consider, for instance, this description of Son, the outsider:

In those eight homeless years he had joined that great underclass of undocumented men. And although there were more of his kind in the world than students or soldiers, unlike students or soldiers they were not counted. They were an international legion of day laborers and musclemen, gamblers, sidewalk merchants, migrants, unlicensed crewmen on ships with volatile cargo, part-time mercenaries, full-time gigolos, or curbside musicians. What distinguished them from other men (aside from their terror of Social Security cards and *cédula de identidad*) was their refusal to equate work with life and an inability to stay anywhere for long.[15]

This description is followed quickly by a conversation between Jadine and son, in which their differences fabricate another layer to Morrison's portrait of Son. This is Jadine:

"You're like a baby. A big country baby. Anybody ever tell you that?"
"No. Nobody ever told me that."
"Well, you are. Like you were just born. Where are your family?"
"Home, I guess."
"You don't know?"
"I haven't been back in a long time."
"Where in Florida are you from?"
"Eloe."
"Eloe? What on earth is that? A town?"
"A town, yeah."
"God. I know it already: gas stations, dust, heat, dogs, shacks, general store with ice coolers full of Dr. Pepper." [*TB*, 172]

In many ways, *Tar Baby* is Son's story more than it is Jadine's, and the tragic account of the white family and their abused child that introduces the Son-Jadine story serves to warn Son of the acculturation that Jadine has undergone. When Son makes his choice at the end of the novel, it is a choice of life-style, loyalty, identity proper, not just a course of action for that moment.

Again, Morrison has included long and perhaps misleading context chapters to open the novel. Even before Son makes an appearance, the reader seems to be much involved with Michael's Christmas visit—which never materializes—and with the relationships of Jadine with her relatives Sydney and Ondine and with Valerian and Margaret Street. Most of this—if the real interst in the novel is the Jadine-Son relationship—is peripheral. But Morrison never feints, and her control is superb. For her to spend so much time on the wealthy atmosphere and perversion of the Streets and their alienation of their only child, she intends the effect to have shaped, if not marred, Jadine's development. Then the subsequent arguments between Son and Jadine about the value of an education, as well as other points at issue, prove what an effect the Streets' values have had on this woman who longs to have everything, both the white and black world—or, rather, a black world with largely white values and appurtenances.

Morrison has recently said that both the title and the imagery of "lickety-split" at the end of *Tar Baby* are meant to reinforce the scene of Son's journey away from the briar patch, Jadine.

I also wanted to suggest that this journey is Son's choice—although he did not think it up, Thérèse did. He said he had no choice, so she manipulated his trip so that he had a choice. On his way back to Valerian's house in order to get the address so he can find Jadine, there is a strong possibility that he joins or is captured by the horsemen—captured by the past, by the wish, by the prehistoric times. The suggestion in the end, when the trees step back to make way for a certain kind of man, is that Nature is urging him to join them.

And then she adds, about her narrative structure, "Close to the opening of the book, Son is going towards the island through the water. In the last part of the book he is doing the same thing, going towards the island through the water. Neither of these sections has a chapter head—they are parentheses around the book."[16]

To read Morrison without attention to her narrative structures and methods is to obscure her always careful relation of character to theme, shape to focus, voice to effect. Whether she frames, uses chapters as parentheses, intentionally misdirects, builds episodes from fragments or relies on the perspective of a child, Morrison moves with steady direction toward her finale. Most of her novels include at least one climactic scene, sometimes handled with understatement and deft placement in the narrative; but few of those climactic scenes embody in themselves the meaning of the novels in which they occur. She speaks of her selection of narrator as a means of suggesting the oral telling of tales, a purposely unnamed and unidentified narrator: "The stories look as though they come from people who are not even authors. No author tells these stories. They are just told—meanderingly—as though they are going in several directions at the same time."[17] And this method of moving a story on several fronts simultaneously can also lead to endings that are far from simple resolutions of plot lines. In emphasizing the oral telling of tales, Morrison reinforces a point manifested in her various narrative modes: no "clear" resolutions. Instead, she plans to whet her readers' imaginations: "I do not want to bow out with easy answers to complex questions. . . . I'm interested in survival—who survives and who does not, and why."[18]

Assuming that the confidence and authority with which Morrison responds to questions in interviews are genuine, the reader is forced to repeat the conviction stated at the opening of this essay:

that Morrison appears to be a woman writer who has grown beyond any need to write in ways that others wish her to write. In her creative adaptations of traditional literary forms and devices, Morrison shows herself to be well aware of her own aims and abilities. She will make literary narrative tell the stories she intends. As she says, confidently, even triumphantly, "We can tell it the way it is. We have come through the worst, and we are still here."[19]

NOTES

1. Sandra M. Gilbert and Susan Gubar, *The Madwoman in the Attic: The Woman Writer and the Nineteenth Century Literary Imagination* (New Haven: Yale Univ. Press, 1979), 49.

2. Nellie McKay, "An Interview with Toni Morrison," *Contemporary Literature* 24 (Winter 1983): 416-417.

3. Toni Morrison, *The Bluest Eye* (New York: Washington Square Press, 1970), 29; hereafter cited in the text as *BE*.

4. For the best discussions of *The Bluest Eye* see Barbara Christian, *Black Women Novelists: The Development of a Tradition, 1892-1976* (Westport, Conn.: Greenwood Press, 1980); Cynthia Davis, "Self, Society, and Myth in Toni Morrison's Fiction," *Contemporary Literature* 23 (Summer 1982): 323-42; Phyllis R. Klotman, "Dick-and-Jane and the Shirley Temple Sensibility in *The Bluest Eye*," *Black American Literature Forum* 8 (Winter 1979): 123-24; Chikwenye Okonjo Ogunyemi, "Order and Disorder in Toni Morrison's *The Bluest Eye*," *Critique* 19, no. 1 (1977): 112-20; and Susan Willis, "Eruptions of Funk: Historicizing Toni Morrison," *Black American Literature Forum* 16 (Spring 1982): 34-42.

5. Raymond Hedin, "The Structuring of Emotion in Black American Fiction," *Novel* 16 (Fall 1982): 35-54. Trudier Harris makes a complementary point in *From Mammies to Militants: Domestics in Black American Literature* (Philadelphia: Temple Univ. Press, 1982), 36, when she describes Polly Breedlove's assuming the role of a classic mammy, "totally identifying with whites and white culture and negating blackness and black culture." The damage she does to her daughter is irreparable.

6. Toni Morrison, *Sula* (New York: Alfred A. Knopf, 1973), 4; hereafter cited in the text as *S*.

7. Anna Shamon, "'We Was Girls Together': A Study of Toni Morrison's *Sula*," *Midwestern Miscellany* 10 (1982): 9-22.

8. Chikwenye Okonjo Ogunyemi, "*Sula*: 'A Nigger Joke,'" *Black American Literature Forum* 8 (Winter 1979): 130.

9. Cynthia Davis, "Self, Society, and Myth in Toni Morrison's Fiction," *Contemporary Literature* 23 (Summer 1982): 333.

10. Barbara Hill Rigney, *Lilith's Daughters: Women and Religion in Contemporary Fiction* (Madison: Univ. of Wisconsin Press, 1982), 17-19.

11. Bruce Michelson, "Huck and the Games of the World," *American Literary Realism* 13 (Spring 1980): 108.

12. Rigney, *Lilith's Daughters.* 61.

13. Davis, "Self, Society, and Myth," 334; see also Joyce Wegs, "Toni Morrison's *Song of Solomon:* A Blues Song," *Essays in Literature* 9 (Fall 1982): 211-23; Dorothy Lee, "*Song of Solomon:* To Ride the Air," *Black American Literature Forum* 16 (Summer 1982): 64-70; Leslie Harris, "Myth as Structure in Toni Morrison's *Song of Solomon.*" *Melus* 7 (Fall 1980): 69-76; and Susan Blake, "Folklore and Community in *Song of Solomon,*" ibid., 77-82.

14. Cyrus Colter, review of *Tar Baby, New Letters* 49 (Fall 1982): 112-14.

15. Toni Morrison, *Tar Baby* (New York: New American Library, 1981), 166; hereafter cited in the text as *TB.*

16. McKay, "Interview," 424-25. Morrison also says about *Song,* "I found that I had to leave the town in *Song of Solomon* because the book was driven by men. The rhythm of their lives is outward, adventuresome" (p. 417).

17. Ibid., 427.

18. Ibid., 420.

19. Ibid., 429.

A Bibliography of Writings by

TONI MORRISON

Curtis Martin

BOOKS

The Black Book. Compiled by Middleton Harris, with the assistance of Toni Morrison and others. New York: Random House, 1974.

The Bluest Eye. New York: Holt, Rinehart and Winston, 1970.

Sula. New York: Alfred A. Knopf, 1974.

Song of Solomon. New York: Knopf, 1977.

Tar Baby. New York: Knopf, 1981.

SHORT STORY

"Big Box." In collaboration with Slade Morrison. *Ms.* 8 (March 1980): 57-58.

ARTICLES

"What the Black Woman Thinks about Women's Lib." *New York Times Magazine,* 22 August 1971, 14.

"Cooking Out." *New York Times Book Review,* 10 June 1973, 4.

"Behind the Making of *The Black Book.*" *Black World,* 23 February 1974, 86-90.

"Rediscovering Black History." *New York Times Magazine,* 11 August 1974, 14.

"Reading." *Mademoiselle* 81 (May 1975): 14.

"Slow Walk of Trees (as Grandmother Would Say) Hopeless (as Grandfather Would Say)." *New York Times Magazines,* 4 July 1976, 104.

REVIEWS

[Review of *Amistad 2,* ed. John A. Williams and Charles Harris; *The Black Aesthetic,* ed. Addison Cayle; *New African Literature and the Arts,* vol. 2, ed. Joseph Okpaku.] *New York Times Book Review,* 28 February 1971, 5.

[Review of *To Be a Black Woman: Portraits in Fact and Fiction,* ed. Mel Watkin and Jay David.] *New York Times Book Review,* 28 March 1971, 8.

[Review of *The Black Man in America, 1791-1861,* by Florence Jackson; *Black Politicians,* by Richard Bruner; *Black Troubadour,* by Charlamae Rollins; *Forward March to Freedom: The Biography of A. Philip Randolph,* by Barbara Kaye; *Gordon Parks,* byMidge Turk; *Jackie Robinson,* by Kenneth Ruddeen; *James Weldon Johnson,* by Harold W. Felton; *Jim Beckwourth,* by Lawrence Cortesi; *The Magic Mirrors,* by Judith Berry Griffin; *The Making of an Afro-American: Martin Robinson Delany,* by Dorothy Sterling; *Men of Masaba,* ed. Humphrey Harmon; *The Orisha: Gods of Yorubaland,* by Judith Gleason; *The Picture Life of Thurgood Marshall,* by Margaret B. Young; *The Rich Man and the Singer: Folktales from Ethiopia* by Mesfin Habte-Mariam; *Sidewalk Story,* by Sharon Bell Mathis; *Soldiers in the Civil War,* by Janet Stevenson; *Songs and Stories of Afro-Americans,* by Paul Glass; *Tales and Stories for Black Folks,* by Toni Cade Bambara; *Unsung Black Americans,* by Edith Stull.] *New York Times Book Review,* 2 May 1971, pt. II, 43.

[Review of *South to a Very Old Place,* by Albert Murray.] *New York Times Book Review,* 2 January 1972, 5.

[Review of *Con,* by M.E. White.] *New York Times Book Review,* 3 September 1972, 6.

[Review of *Hero in the Tower,* by Hans Hellmut Kirst; *Love Songs,* by Lawrence Sanders.] *New York Times Book Review,* 1 October 1972, 41.

[Review of *Who Is Angela Davis: The Biography of a Revolutionary,* by Regina Nadelson.] *New York Times Book Review,* 29 October 1972, 48.

MISCELLANEOUS

"City Limits, Village Values: Concepts of the Neighborhood in Black Fiction." In *Literature and the Urban Experience: Essays on the City and Literature,* ed. Michael C. Jaye and Ann Chalmers Watts. New Brunswick, N.J.: Rutgers Univ. Press, 1981, 35-43.

"Toni Morrison on Cinderella's Stepsisters" [adapted from commencement address given at Barnard College, May 1979]. *Ms.* 8 (September 1979): 41-42.

"Writers Together" [address given at American Writers Congress, New York, 9 October 1981]. *Nation* 233 (24 October 1981), 396.

Presentation of National Medal in Literature to Eudora Welty. Public Broadcasting System, 6 July 1980. [Phonotape, Michigan State University Voice Library, cat. no. M3395, band 11.]

The Double Narrative Structure of *Small Changes*

Elaine Tuttle Hansen

This is the oppressor's language / yet I need it to talk to you."[1] Speaking thus of the equivocal relationship between women and language, Adrienne Rich in the earliest days of the women's movement addressed the central question that female writers and feminist critics still seek to answer. Is the dominant discourse a male construct that women cannot use to represent their experience, or can women control or escape this discourse to speak of and for themselves?[2] In *Small Changes*, more explicitly than in any of her other six novels so far published, Marge Piercy confronts this troubling question. The novel reflects at various levels a profound suspicion of "the oppressor's language," but like Rich, Piercy finally wants to appropriate—with certain modifications—the dominant discourse. Her aim as a writer, she claims, is to communicate, and after all how else to do so: "I need it to talk to you."[3] Affirming that women must simultaneously mistrust and use language, Piercy goes on to explore in *Small Changes*, through its narrative structure, the possibilities and limitations of two different ways in which the female artist can use "the oppressor's" words, as well as his conventional narrative modes, to write—and perhaps even rewrite—female experience.

In *Small Changes*, a profound and pervasive suspicion of the

Photo by Ira Wood

dominant discourse is explicitly articulated by one of the two main characters, Beth Walker. Beth both recognizes and suspects the power of words. In the opening chapter, she tries to suppress her own discomfort and misgivings, as she stands at the altar with Jim, by invoking "magic words that made things happen or go away, recipes like I Love You, and I'm Sorry, and I Pledge Allegiance, and God Bless Mommy and Daddy, and Will You Marry Me, and Fine, Thank You, and I Do."[4] But she cannot hear these soothing formulas "over the roaring in her ears," the sound of an apparently instinctive, inner pulse that prefigures the roars of an anger she gradually learns, in the course of the novel, to acknowledge and express. In the same scene we find that Beth, although untrained in Speech Act Theory, fully understands the performative power of "magic words," as she hears what the clichés really say and demystifies those old recipes.[5] So, for example, she translates her sister's description of her wedding dress, written for a newspaper that will never print it:[6] "Nancy had written 'the train comes away.' That meant the thing that dragged could be taken off, with a little timely help" (SC, 12). Beth's debunking revision frankly emphasizes the oppression of women that the formulaic words conceal: the conventional train of the white wedding gown is in fact a useless burden, "the thing that dragged," symbolizing not elegance—or pretensions to elegance—but woman's lack of power, her need for "a little timely help" to rid herself of obstacles to comfort and freedom of action. Beth's revisionist insight into the way words both reflect and hide the oppression of women continues throughout the novel: again, when Dorine laments her loneliness—"I feel sometimes as if I'll go through life and never belong to anyone"—Beth responds: "But you aren't a dog, why do you want to be owned?" (SC, 88). On her wedding night, "going all the way" with Jim for the first time, she is left completely unsatisfied by his rapid defloration: "they had made love finally, but where was the love they had made?" (SC, 26).[7]

Beth's mistrust of magic words extends to the written word as well. Reflecting on her past, as she tries to find out what is going wrong in her marriage, she notes that she was once an avid reader, first consuming adventure stories for boys and later "a lot of Frank Yerby and Galsworthy," and "all of Aldous Huxley and Iris Murdoch." But she stopped reading as she began to feel the gap between "reality" and fiction: "The books had betrayed her, leading her to want what she could not approach" (SC, 29). She finds the diary she kept in high school and discovers that she, too, wrote words that misrepresented life, lying to herself in order to cover up painful experience with a story of "how it was all supposed to be" (*SC*, 35). Even "Jim," she comes to believe, is "a character made up as she used to make over her daily life for her diary" (*SC*, 37). To escape her depressing marriage to the real Jim, she once again turns to books—to Hemingway and Colette, among others—and to daydreaming. Beth finds something "shameful," however, about this retreat to a fantasy world, "something second rate about an imaginary life" (*SC*, 37). Later, after her first actual escape from Jim and Syracuse, at a point at which she no longer needs to imagine herself taking part in fictional adventures, she picks up some magazines from an old friend's coffee table. With clear sight she analyzes the way they prescribe and distort female life, but she can still feel their power: "The effect of reading them was to feel discontented and sad and vaguely stirred up, as if lacking, as if something were wrong with her. Quickly she put down the magazine" (*SC*, 314).

On her own for the first time, in Boston and on the fringes of academe, Beth learns about another (ab)use of words. The educated men she now meets play a "verbal game," while the women "sat on the sidelines and watched the words go by" (*SC*, 56). Talking for these men is "a kind of playing," like Jim's car races and football games, but this game has serious consequences. Men have the power to name women: just as Jim called Beth "Little Girl," the men in the apartment on Pearl Street call Dorine "Chlorine"; Beth is "Peter Rabbit" and Miriam is "Venus." (Later male epithets for Miriam are even more offensive and destructive: Jackson identifies her with his ex-wife—"You're both cunts" [*SC*, 201]—and Neil criticizes her for her failure to behave as "my wife"—even "a professor's wife"—should.)[8] Dorine consoles Beth for her inability to play the verbal game by arguing that it is just a little harmless sport—"It's jaw exercise. It's Indian wrestling." But Beth sees more: "I think it's their way of putting things in their place and people in their place and keeping them there. . . . They're making a pecking order" (*SC*, 267).

In her suspicion of words and the ways they are used to keep people, especially women, in their places, Beth explores alternative ways of understanding and expressing herself and of communicating with others. She turns first to music, where "sometimes it was people saying things sharper and cleaner than people ever talked to each other in her life . . . great charges of feeling, someone and then someone else talking to her with power" (*SC*, 28). Through music she joins "the heart of feeling" (*SC*, 38) she cannot otherwise enter, and she hears the vague but powerful promise of "something, something" that "hung out there in music and birds, wheeling against the dusk and crickets chirping in the weeds" (SC, 31). She also thinks in images (SC, 42); she studies herself as a turtle in an attempt to understand what she feels and believes. Later she finds alternative outlets for her creativity, first in the children's story that she and the women of the commune collectively invent, and ultimately in the women's theater group. She also continues to talk and listen and write, but always with a marked effort to be honest, to say what she means, and to hear what other people are saying. She replaces magic words that distort, falsify, and oppress with the mottoes she writes on the walls of her room in Back Bay (SC, 47), sayings that use language itself, as Beth always does, to demystify, debunk, and deconstruct the dominant discourse and replace it with words that speak of and for women: "NOBODY LOVES A DOORMAT, THEY JUST WALK ON OVER. THE MIRROR IS THE FIRST DAILY TRAP. CHICK—small, fuzzy, helpless, stupid, cute, lays eggs and in the end gets eaten. CAT— predator, active, alert, tough, independent, mean, quick. The language says one is predator and the other is prey. LOVE IS WHAT WOMEN DO INSTEAD OF KNOWING OR FIGHTING OR MAK- ING OR INVENTING" (SC, 244).[9]

Beth even writes a poem, a self-help piece that ends with a chant of defiance and self-affirmation—"Yes, Beth! Yes, Beth! / Yes"— whose chief virtue is that it makes her feel better (SC, 313). Miriam's perceptive analysis of Beth's surprisingly strong sense of her identity underscores Beth's escape from the dominant discourse that (mis)di- rects and (dis)figures most women's lives: "She seemed to have her own cry that she uttered through the confusions they all lived in" (SC, 244).[10]

But Beth herself understands that "her own cry" is not enough for a woman, and despite her strong distrust of their uses of language, she wants to engage with men in the verbal game. She articulates to Dorine the reason for her apparently contradictory desire to play a game she hates and in which she has no confidence: "I want to be better with words. I want to be able to answer them back. But I don't believe that's how you do anything. I only want to use words as weapons because I'm tired of being beaten with them. Tired of being pushed around because I don't know how to push back" (SC, 267). When Beth says that words, as men use them, are inadequate to "do anything," she is not denying the potency of words; she is voicing, rather, her political belief in action as opposed to a hollow rhetoric that is not useful to women, or to anyone else who wants to change the world. As she puts it later, explaining her distrust of Phil: "He talks too much. He turns everything into words and makes it change in words, but nothing changes" (SC, 441). Without relinquishing this insight into the insufficiency of words, she acknowledges their real power to oppress and wants access to that power, not to join in the dominant discourse, not to play the game as men play it, but to protect herself against oppression. In *Small Changes* Piercy expresses her mistrust of language but does not advocate or sentimentalize silence on the part of women. While women need to seek alternatives and to reject language and literature when they are used to keep women in their place, they cannot allow themselves to be muted; inarticulateness is not a useful weapon.

Other characters and events in the novel support Beth's explicit stance on the troubled question of women and language. Miriam, for instance, who has had more formal education than Beth has had, is always talking and has less suspicion of the dominant discourse, perhaps because she is better at playing the verbal game herself. But while she is seldom at a loss for words, she is also the most oppressed woman in the novel, or at least the one who is most damaged by the epithets and plots assigned to her by men. She uses words to hide—chiefly from herself—the truth about her relationships with men. Her lovers and her husband repeatedly shut her out from their games and refuse to speak, while she tries in vain to understand and communicate: "Still she watched him for a sign, any sign" (SC, 213). Fittingly, like so many women, Miriam has a special facility for language, which is manifest in her interest as a computer scientist in the problems of artificial language. She begins work on a project that will facilitate communication between people and computers and between various incompatible computer languages, but when she marries the director of the project, she is transferred to work on a missile contract (SC, 361-62). Only Phil ever really talks with Miriam, but then Phil is an unusual man, the exception that proves the rule. A hustler with words—as are women (SC, 521)—Phil is beaten down by the establishment, undergoes a conversion, and in the end recants his old phallogocentrism. He gives up writing poetry—whose eternal status he earlier celebrated (SC, 122)—drops out of graduate school, and even distances himself from his friend Jackson because "being with him pushes me into my old way of using words" (SC, 464). He chooses to withdraw from the dominant discourse and becomes a carpenter: "I want to do simple useful things with my hands and keep my rotten fucked-up head out of it. I don't trust how I use words" (SC, 463).

The pervasive and fundamental suspicion of words that separates the sheep from the goats in *Small Changes* may also serve, self-reflexively, to explain and defend Piercy's own characteristic use of language. Critics have repeatedly faulted her novels for their stylistic lapses, their failure to display "the felicities of a decent prose style."[11] A reader might be reminded, however, when reading such criticism, of Virginia Woolf's self-mocking critique of *Life's Adventure*, the imaginary novel by Mary Carmichael analyzed in *A Room of One's Own*: "She had broken up Jane Austen's sentence," Woolf complains, "and thus given me no chance of pluming myself upon my impeccable taste, my fastidious ear."[12] Piercy, in *Small Changes*, as did Mary Carmichael in *Life's Adventure*, insists that we question our standards of taste, our fastidious assumptions about stylistic decency, that we see the political *indecency* of "very very literary literature,"[13] and that we recognize Piercy's effort to communicate with a "popular" audience, specifically one that includes men and women "who don't go into bookstores," as she puts it.[14] There are dangers, of course, in this insistence and this effort. There is a danger, for instance, that Piercy will go unread, or unappreciated, by people who do go into bookstores—people whom she also wants to reach, or so she says. And there is the more serious danger, perhaps, that Piercy's mistrust of language and literature can radically undercut the political message of the novel for any reader. If literature falsifies experience, why should anyone believe what *Small Changes* says about women's lives? If words change nothing, can a novel be "of use," as Piercy wants hers to be?[15]

Such are the questions raised in *Small Changes*, crucial questions for many women writers today, and to my mind they make this novel a particularly exciting document for both the feminist critic and the student of contemporary narrative. This is not the conventional novel or the "merely" popular work that so many critics have plumed themselves on criticizing.[16] Whether it succeeds or fails in the attempt to set new standards and say new things, it raises questions that are on the cutting edge of feminist aesthetics and feminist theory, and it repays critical analysis. One type of analysis, to which some of Piercy's other novels—especially *Woman on the Edge of Time*—might more obviously give occasion, is examination of her narrative technique as a kind of literary manifesto for contemporary women writers. From this perspective, *Small Changes* suggests several by now almost commonplace strategies and principles, including the subversion of conventional narrative openings and closings; the intentionally didactic, oversimplified, even allegorical nature of the work and its characters; the use of what DuPlessis has called "multipersoned or cluster protagonists" to affirm the "feminine" values of "collectivity" and "interdependence"; the rich (even "exhaustive" and "obsessively observed"—details, often associated with stereotypically female interests such as the way space is arranged in various domiciles, or the way "life support" activities are managed.[17]

Along these lines, I want to suggest that the narrative structure of *Small Changes*, built on the stories of two women, can be seen as an experiment, not in "the variety of lifestyles that women in our time are adopting,"[18] but in two alternative ways in which the woman writer can write, can represent the experience of women while using the only language available and the traditional forms and myths available to any writer. I want to suggest, that is, that Piercy, wary like Beth of language, investigates the possibilities and the limitations of two prominent ways in which the woman writer can appropriate the dominant discourse: either by inverting the classic male plot, as in Beth's story; or by revitalizing and perhaps "legitimating" a conventional female form of narrative, as in "the ongoing soap opera" (*SC*, 429) of Miriam's life.[19] *Small Changes* is in this regard not an optimistic novel; it reveals in both modes the difficulties as well as the possibilities of appropriation, the price that women pay, the resistance of the dominant discourse—a system that is not user-friendly, as Miriam might put it, when the user is a woman writing for women and hoping to "do" something with words.

The plot of Beth's story represents an example of the first possibility that is available to the feminist writer: the revolutionary use of a classic male narrative structure to portray a radical female experience. Beth's story is a version—and an inversion—of both the *Bildungsroman* (or even the *Kunstlerroman*, in which Beth is the artist as a young woman, unable to speak) and the melodrama. Endowed only with her seemingly innate feminist sensitivity—"She bruises easily," her mother says (*SC*, 16)—Beth miraculously escapes imprisonment in the perpetual childhood of the married woman. She begins to educate herself, is recaptured, escapes again, and finally after many adventures meets the perfect woman and finds her true identity, both sexual and social, as a lesbian feminist. This plot is clearly presented as a romantic journey from darkness to light, a narrative of revolution and rebirth into a new and higher state. Appropriately, the climax of the story comes when the hero explicitly breaks the law she has already transgressed in private and escapes as nearly as possible, not just from her personal patriarchs, but from the patriarchal state as a whole. At the end of the novel, Beth goes underground, literally creating a new identity and renaming herself and her family. The maleness of this plot, despite its feminist twist, is underscored by the characterization of Beth. The name Jackson gives her—Peter Rabbit—is shown to be apt; although she loves women and is abused by men, she has few traditionally feminine traits and tastes. She is cool and dry, flat-chested and narrow-hipped; she hates to cook, travels light, and refuses to be caught in the reproductive cycle: "I can't be mothered and I won't mother," she tells Miriam (SC, 264). Tellingly—and with the homoerotic overtones characteristic of the central male-male and female-female relationships in the novel—Miriam likes Beth because she seems, like Phil or Neil, more an equal than other women (SC, 222, 229, 352). At the same time, however, Beth's feminine capacity to love and care for others—for Wanda and her sons, in particular, and for the hypothetical patients she will treat if she becomes, as she plans, a paramedic—is validated by the ending of her story. Piercy may be attempting to suggest here what Lee Edwards has recently argued: that the woman hero challenges stereotypical associations of sex and behavior. "Permitted, like others of her sex, to love and nurture, to comfort, to solace, and to please," Edwards argues, "the heroic woman specifies these impulses as human, not just female, and endows them with a value that counters their usual debasement."[20]

Where Beth and her plot, like the classic male story of education and adventure upon which it is built, are basically "simple and contained," Miriam and her story are "vast and yeasty" (SC, 229), hopelessly complicated and and archetypally feminine. The characters themselves suggest to us the specific genre of Miriam's story: as she herself says (SC, 429) and as Jackson later repeats (SC, 508), she is the heroine of a soap opera. Closer analysis confirms and clarifies the significance of this point, as we see how Piercy manipulates narrative structure, point of view, and thematic elements so that Miriam's story corresponds in critical respects to the shape and style of the soaps, and is in sharp contrast to the story of the woman hero. The novel begins, for instance, with "The Book of Beth," in which we are introduced to the protagonist as she learns about herself, and thus we are given a sense, as in the typical *Bildungsroman*, of the freedom and capacity of the central character to grow, to make choices, and to take action. Miriam, by contrast, is first introduced in Beth's book (SC, 50) as just one of a group of people with complex histories and relationships, a small but complete cast of characters whose lives are already—and only, and always—in progress when Beth tunes in. We later see Miriam and Phil but know no more than Beth does about their relationship at this point; in the penultimate chapter and narrative climax of "The Book of Beth," set on the day of the Street Fair,

Dorine and Lennie and Beth walk in on Miriam and Jackson, who are
in bed.

In "The Book of Miriam," which begins shortly thereafter, we are
offered the testimony of Miriam's childhood, college days, and affairs
with Phil and Jackson, in a lengthy reprisal that appears to introduce
us to Miriam in the same way in which we were introduced to Beth.
But when we have finally come again to that same point in narrative
time (SC, 231) where we were in Beth's Book—the day of the Street
Fair (SC, 76)—we already know what is going to happen. Our knowledge makes us perceive Miriam's experience much differently from
the way we perceive Beth's: the soap-opera heroine is caught in
predetermined circumstances, unable to choose or to act on her own.
She is constrained by the narrative structure, and hence by the
reader's foreknowledge, as much as by her own all too predictable desires.

Furthermore, as is that of any character in a good soap opera,
Miriam's story is interrupted by other characters in a way that Beth's
is not. In "The Book of Miriam," two chapters are in fact written from
Phil's point of view; Miriam, who sometimes feels as if she is Phil's
product—or his poodle (SC, 221)—relinquishes control to him even
in her titular story. In the third and longest section of the novel, "Both
in Turn," the reader is farther from Miriam, especially in crucial
scenes such as the party she gives (SC, 445-49), where we see her first
through Beth's eyes, just as, in the last chapter, we see her through
Helen's. The effect is that in general we *see with* Beth, where we often
merely *see* Miriam.[21]

Like a soap opera, and unlike Beth's evolutionary plot, Miriam's
story is also one of continual and unfulfilled anticipation, obsessive
and ungratified desire, and formless repetition. Miriam repeatedly
thinks her dreams have at last come true—first when she meets Phil,
then when she succumbs to Jackson, then when she marries Neil—
but we soon see how blind she is and how little progress she makes.
Again, the narrative structure highlights her self-deception: when
Beth returns to Boston, finds Miriam married to Neil, and asks how it
happened, Miriam clearly represses the all-important meeting in
Washington with Wilhelm Graben (SC, 340); only later (SC, 369-75)
does she reveal to us how much this episode influences her decision
to marry Neil and to have a baby. Her life is presented as a series of
defeats, as her story moves relentlessly from one predictable scene to
the next: Phil gets stoned and lets Miriam down, but makes Miriam
feel that she has let him down; Jackson wins the chess game; Tom
Ryan—or Wilhelm Graban, or Phil, or Neil—has sex with her while

she is drunk, or unable to object, or too sleepy to use her diaphragm; Neil humiliates her for smoking marijuana when she is carrying "his" child, or for talking to the wrong people, or for spilling her drink, or for spoiling or neglecting Ariane. Occasionally Miriam even sees the predictability and shapelessness of her narrative. With Jackson, she feels unable to "shatter the web of myth" (*SC*, 251), and toward the end of the novel, comments on the ironic exchange of roles that she and Dorine have undergone: "It's strange, Beth. As if our lives had no inner shape" (*SC*, 434).

Contrast the exhausting, repetitious, shapeless series of defeats that Miriam experiences with the functional repetition in Beth's plot. When, for example, Jim's detective takes Beth back to Syracuse, and she has to escape from him all over again, what might look like a frustration, even a regression, of her development serves to demonstrate how Beth has in fact grown in moral stature and in heroic resolve. Juxtaposed in this way, the two escapes reveal Beth's development from passive resistance—before, she simply lied and evaded confrontation—to active, even aggressive self-defense, as she now takes up the bread knife and gets herself a lawyer. Whereas she simply boards a plane to Boston the first time she runs away—"She thought she would be less frightened to get on a plane and be in Boston in an hour and a half" (*SC*, 44)—after her second escape she hitchhikes to California and back, exercising her new self-reliance and earning her stripes (she has her first lesbian affair on the way) before returning to the women's house. Literally as well as figuratively the heroine covers much more space—"what a distance she had traveled beyond what she has been raised to" (*SC*, 499-500)—than does the soap-opera heroine, who stays in the same small world—within easy range of Route 128—for the central part of the action.

And as in the soap operas, the predominant concern within Miriam's small world is the life of the emotions. She earns a Ph.D. in computer science from M.I.T. and speaks of the joys of work, but when "she understood that she was in love" with Jackson, she forgets everything else, "plans and projects and curiosities and relationships and speculations" (*SC*, 193). She is not really committed to her career even in the beginning; she dreams of saving half her first year's salary, then taking a leave of absence or quitting to travel with Phil (*SC*, 259). By the time her second child is born—only three years after her "leave of absence" from Logical Systems Development—she feels totally unmarketable. Rationalizing her professional failure, Miriam might speak for all soap opera characters when she says "People are the most important thing to me" (*SC*, 434). Again and again, in long stretches of dialogue or interior monologue, we hear of her obsessive desire to be loved, and we also hear the simple Freudian psychologizing that guides her—and most of the characters—in her thinking about love and sex.[22]

The final and most emphatic similarity between Miriam's narrative and the genre of soap opera is its open-endedness. We do not know exactly what will become of Beth and Wanda, but the effect of the final two-page narrative (*SC*, 531-32) of "Cindy" and "Marie," and their sons, and their dog Dean, is to seal off Beth's story. Our brief glimpse of this happy family sitting down to a meal of potato soup and discussing Cindy and Marie's plan to train as paramedics is as idealized and romantic as the happy ending of the most conventional novel. In our last view of Miriam (*SC*, 533-38), on the other hand, we witness yet another fight with Neil, who is already having an affair—soon to be revealed to us, unbeknown to Miriam—with his secretary. He leaves Miriam, and she sits alone in the dark house, thinking about her dreams, her love, her children, and her connections with Beth, Wanda, Dorine, Phil, Sally—the principal players in the cast. Although we know Miriam is still deceiving herself in her hope that she can regain Neil's love, we are—at least momentarily—invited to believe that the strength of her connections will enable her to survive, to recover her energy, and perhaps even to break the cycle of repeated defeat, not as Beth does in one fell revolutionary swoop, but through "the slow undramatic refounding, single thought by small decision by petty act, of a life: her life" (*SC*, 538). This all-but-final vision of Miriam crouched in the dark, looking out at the streetlights, could encourage the reader to invent a future that takes the character out of a world of endless repetition without insisting that she become a heroine, a superwoman, or a lesbian separatist.

But *Small Changes* does not end with this plausible if limited optimism: instead, underscoring its affinities with the constitutionally endless soap operas, the last brief chapter of the novel—"Another Desperate Soprano (Helen)"—introduces a new heroine, mentioned in passing by Neil in the preceding chapter, and a new point of view. The story, however, is depressingly familiar: Helen is on the verge of taking Miriam's place in the plot, repeating her error, and fleeing gratefully from a hard, lonely life into the deceptive protection of Neil Stone's petrifying embrace. The final word in *Small Changes* implies that for every woman who manages to escape even a little, as Miriam might, there is another soprano waiting in the wings, doomed to reenact a plot that offers no relief from oppression, no freedom from endless anticipation and frustration of desire.

Piercy thus uses the double narrative in *Small Changes* to explore both the possibilities and the limitations of two available narrative structures, one male and one female, for speaking the unspoken and perhaps unspeakable story of women's lives. The feminist *Bildungroman*, built on a culturally male model, facilitates the representation of a certain kind of revolutionary change, of individual growth and development in a woman's life; the soap opera more accurately presents and records ordinary women's experience. Each genre, as used in *Small Changes*, can be deployed to expose the oppression of women and to write stories that diminish the gap, for women, between reality and fiction, stories that do not betray the woman reader as Beth was betrayed by the fiction she once devoured, and stories that enable women to play the verbal game without turning into the oppressors. But neither mode is yet adequate to communicate a truly satisfactory vision of the as yet unrealized future in which no one is oppressed. *Small Changes* does not ask us to trust language and its present forms fully, but to remain wary of the ways in which literary conventions, like the world that produces and is shaped by them, "push women around"; and so from a late-twentieth-century feminist point of view each of the two characters and her story serves as a critique of the other.

Beth's story, the classic male narrative, works for women only if it is inverted to show the radical feminist's escape from rather than reintegration into society; in this way it may also reprivilege individual over collective values and cannot easily accommodate heterosexual relationships. At the same time that Beth's narrative thematically supports female bonding, Beth's individual heroism of necessity implies a rejection of traditional women's culture and, most problematical, of motherhood. Wanda breaks the law in order to keep her children; but if Beth had children, could she sacrifice them to her love for Wanda? Again, only because Beth will not be a mother is she free to act in a heroic plot. Miriam takes as much of a risk as she can to help Wanda because both are mothers—"Suppose they were my children? Of course she has to get them back" (*SC*, 515). But she cannot go underground with her friends. She articulates precisely the limitations of Beth's career, the elitism that radical feminism can seem to perpetuate: "Come on, you call it the women's movement, but what do you have for an ordinary woman? . . . What have you got for me? I love my kids and I don't burn banks down or run around the streets with picket signs" (*SC*, 515).

In response to Miriam's indictment, Beth has no easy answer, but her thoughtful advice in turn exposes the inadequacies of soap opera from a feminist perspective. Above all Beth blames the isolation of woman that is the result of an excessively private life, a total investment of self in the male object of desire, and a mistaken belief that she is solely responsible for, and hence chained to, her children. The soap opera, as others have argued, could be said to affirm the collective character, the community, that the male narrative subordinates to the individual hero,[23] but such a possibility is unrealized as long as the love of a man is the primary source of narrative action, and hence of meaning, in women's lives. Soap operas give narrative space to the experience of women in a way that the male plot cannot, but by replicating the web of myth they also serve to deny an ordinary woman the chance to escape its constraints.

NOTES

1. "The Burning of Paper Instead of Children," cited from *Adrienne Rich's Poetry*, ed. Barbara Charlesworth Gelpi and Albert Gelpi (New York: W.W. Norton, 1975).

2. For a recent discussion of this large and complicated question that includes in its footnotes an excellent bibliographical guide to the debate among feminist writers and critics, see Margaret Homans, " 'Her Very Own Howl': The Ambiguities of Representation in Recent Women's Fiction," *Signs* 9, no. 2 (1983): 186-205. I take the phrase "male construct" from Homans.

3. This is a reiterated theme in Piercy's writings and comments on her work and her political goals, as the reader will discover from considering any of the pieces recently collected in *Parti-Colored Blocks for a Quilt* (Ann Arbor: Univ. of Michigan Press, 1982).

4. Quotations, with page numbers in parentheses, are from the paperback edition of *Small Changes* (New York: Fawcett Crest, 1972), 21; hereafter cited in the text as *SC*.

5. I refer to the by now well-known work of the British natural-language philosopher J.L. Austin. In *How to Do Things with Words* (New York: Oxford Univ. Press, 1962), Austin begins by pointing out what philosophers have long failed to recognize: many utterances are not just "constantive"—that is, they are not simply statements that describe or state and may be designated "true" or "false"; they are "performatives"—they do things. Austin's first example of performative utterance is identical to one of the "magic words" Beth tries to invoke: " 'I do (sc. take this woman to be my lawful wife')—as uttered in the course of the marriage ceremony" (p. 5). He goes on to talk about naming, bequeathing, and betting, then concludes that in fact *all* utterances "do" something, or are "speech acts."

6. At least one reviewer has criticized Piercy in *Small Changes* for forgetting class and racial oppression in her concern with women; see Sara Blackburn, review of *Small Changes, New York Times Book Review*, 12 Aug.

1973, 2-3. But Beth's working-class origins and loyalties are shown to shape her views as a feminist; on the very first page of the novel, for instance, we learn: "They never printed that [the description of the wedding dress] except for people like, oh executives' daughters from the G.E. plant where her father worked at the gate" (SC, 12).

7. There is no significant distance between Beth and the narrating voice that presents her story, so I have not distinguished here or elsewhere between what the character says directly—in quotation marks—and what the narrator says, from the character's point of view, in the free, indirect style used throughout.

8. For analysis of the antifeminist use of epithets "directed against a woman . . . to malign her own relationship to her own gender or to sexuality as men define and enforce it . . . to intimidate her in a particular situation," see Andrea Dworkin, "Antifeminsm," in Right-Wing Women (New York: G.P. Putnam's Sons, Perigee Books, 1983).

9. A remote but interesting parallel may be seen in the use of mottoes—didactic, aphoristic slogans—in the early Christian movement. Robert Wilken speculates that the sententious sayings and maxims that survive in written collections were memorized by Christian intellectuals and used "to bring thought and action into greater unity"; see "Wisdom and Philosophy in Early Christianity," in Aspects of Wisdom in Judaism and Early Christianity, ed. Robert L. Wilken (Notre Dame: Univ. of Notre Dame Press, 1975), 145. Extending Nancy K. Miller's thesis about the "demaximization" of the dominant discourse in certain novels by women is "Emphasis Added: Plots and Plausibilities in Women's Fiction," PMLA 96 (January 1981): 36-48; an effort toward "remaximization" might be seen in Beth's slogans.

10. Compare Toni Morrison's reference in Sula (New York: New American Library, 1973) to Nel's attempt to utter "the oldest cry," "her very own howl" (p. 108), a phrase to which Homans calls our attention in the title of her essay on the ambiguities of representation (see n. 2, above).

11. The critic is Anatole Broyard, speaking specifically about a later novel, The High Cost of Living; see "One Critic's Fiction: 'The High Cost of Living,' " New York Times Book Review, 22 January 1978, 14. Catharine Stimpson is one of the few critics to read Piercy's style as a deliberate and effective strategy: she compares Piercy's "willingness to sacrifice linguistic flair for detail, clarity, and accuracy" to Doris Lessing's; see "Three Women Work It Out," review of Yonnondio: From the Thirties, by Tillie Olsen; Portrait of a Marriage, by Nigel Nicholson; and Small Changes, by Marge Piercy, Nation, 30 November 1974, 567.

12. A Room of One's Own (New York: Harcourt, Brace and Co., 1929), 95.

13. From a recorded panel discussion, "The Ordeal of the Woman Writer," with Toni Morrison and Erica Jong, introduced by Heywood Hale Broun (Norton, 40061, 1974), cited by Susan Kress, "In and Out of Time: The Form of Marge Piercy's Novels," in Future Females: A Critical Anthology, ed.

Marlene S. Barr (Bowling Green, Ohio: Bowling Green State Univ. Popular Press, 1981), 122, n.3.

14. "Interview with Karla Hammond," in *Parti-Colored Blocks*, 25.

15. Consider the title of Piercy's third volume of poetry and such comments as "You live in a social web where other people's work sustains you—and you give back. I think that literary production is real production"; *Parti-Colored Blocks*, 137.

16. See, for instance, Pearl K. Bell, "Marge Piercy and Ann Beattie," *Commentary* 70 (July 1980): 59-61: "Though [Piercy] presents herself as a revolutionary . . . her novels are surprisingly conventional."

17. Kress comments on the beginning of the novel in "In and Out of Time," p. 114. See Rachel Blau DuPlessis, "The Feminist Apologues of Lessing, Piercy, and Russ," *Frontiers* 14 (Spring 1979): 1-8; Du Plessis's discussion is of *Woman on the Edge of Time*. See Bell, "Marge Piercy and Ann Beattie," p. 59; see also Betty Falkenberg, "Plying an Empty Radicalism," *New Leader* 63 (25 February 1980): 18.

18. Diane Schulder, "Two Women," *New Republic* 169 (27 October 1973): 30-31; this quotation is reprinted on the first page of the paperback edition of *Small Changes*. In contrast to my argument here, Schulder praises the novel for "avoiding both flights into political rhetoric and deterioration into soap opera."

19. A classic discussion of the "plot-patterns" available to the woman writer is Joanna Russ's "What Can A Heroine Do? or, Why Women Can't Write," in *Images of Women in Fiction: Feminist Perspectives*, ed. Susan Koppelman Cornillon (Bowling Green State Univ. Popular Press, rev. ed., 1973), 3-20. For some recent discussions of the soap opera that have influenced my analysis of the genre here, see, for instance, R.E. Johnson, "Dialogue of Novelty and Repetition: Structure in 'All My Children,'" *Journal of Popular Culture* 10 (Winter 1976): 560-70; F.I. Kaplan, "Intimacy and Conformity in American Soap Opera," *Journal of Popular Culture* 9 (Winter 1975): 622-25; R. McAdow, "Experience of Soap Opera," *Journal of Popular Culture* 7 (Spring 1974): 955-65; and especially Tania Modleski, "The Search for Tomorrow in Today's Soap Opera: Notes on a Feminine Narrative Form," *Film Quarterly* 33 (Fall 1979): 12-21.

20. *Psyche as Hero: Female Heroism and Fictional Form* (Middletown, Conn.: Wesleyan Univ. Press, 1984), 5.

21. There are rare exceptions to this rule; see for instance p. 222.

22. Pearl G. Aldrich, in "Daniel Defoe: The Father of Soap Opera," *Journal of Popular Culture* 8 (Spring 1975): 767-74, suggests that "the unifying theme of twentieth-century soap opera is ultra-conservative Freudian psychology" (p. 770).

23. As Modleski suggests in "The Search for Tomorrow."

A Bibliography of Writings by

MARGE PIERCY

Elaine Tuttle Hansen & William J. Scheick

BOOKS

Breaking Camp [Novel]. Middletown, Conn.: Wesleyan Univ. Press, 1968.
Going Down Fast [Novel]. New York: Trident Press, 1969.
Hard Loving [Poems]. Middletown, Conn.: Wesleyan Univ. Press, 1969.
Dance the Eagle to Sleep [Novel]. Garden City, N.Y.: Doubleday, 1970.
4-telling [Poems]. With Bob Hershon, Emmet Jarrett, and Dick Lourie. Trumansburg, N.Y.: New Books, 1971.
Small Changes [Novel]. Garden City, N.Y.: Doubleday, 1973.
To Be of Use [Poems]. Garden City, N.Y.: Doubleday, 1973.
Living in the Open [Poems]. New York: Alfred A. Knopf, 1976.
Woman on the Edge of Time [Novel]. New York: Knopf, 1976.
The High Cost of Living [Novel]. New York: Harper and Row, 1978.
The Twelve-Spoked Wheel Flashing [Poems]. New York: Knopf, 1978.
The Last White Class: A Play about Neighborhood Terror. With Ira Wood. Trumansburg, N.Y.: Crossing Press, 1979.
Vida [Novel]. New York: Summit Books, 1979.
The Moon Is Always Female [Poems]. New York: Knopf, 1980.
Braided Lives [Novel]. New York: Summit Books, 1982.
Circles on the Water [Poems]. New York: Knopf, 1982.
Parti-Colored Blocks for a Quilt [Selected prose]. Ann Arbor: Univ. of Michigan Press, 1982.
Stone, Paper, Knife [Poems]. New York: Knopf, 1983.

SHORT STORIES

"An Excerpt from Maud Awake." *December Magazine* 4 (Winter 1963): 184-90.
"Crossing over Jordan." *Transatlantic Review* 19 (Fall 1965): 72-73.
"An Excerpt from Maud Awake." *The Bold New Women*, ed. Barbara Alson. (Greenwich, Conn.: Fawcett, 1965. [Reprinted in *Modern Girl* 1 (August 1971): 22-27.]
"Love Me Tonight, God." *Paris Review* 43 (Summer 1968): 185- 200.
"A Dynastic Encounter." *Aphra* 3 (Spring 1970): 3-10.
"Do You Love Me?" *Second Wave* 1, no. 4 (1971): 26-27 + .
"And I Went into the Garden of Love." *Off Our Backs* 1 (Summer 1971): 2-4.
"The Happiest Day of a Woman's Life." *Works in Progress*, no. 7 (1972): 284-304.
"Somebody Who Understands You." *Moving Out* 2, no. 2 (1972): 56-59.

"Marriage Is a Matter of Give and Take." Parts 1 and 2. *Boston Phoenix* 11 (3 and 10 July 1973): 1+.
"Like a Great Door Closing Suddenly." *Detroit Discovery* 4 (March/April 1974): 45-50.
"Little Sister, Cat and Mouse." *Second Wave* 3, no. 1 (1973): 9-12.
"God's Blood." *Anon* 8 (1974): 50-59.
"The Retreat." *Provincetown Poets* 2, nos. 2 and 3 (1976): 9+.

POEMS

[Individual citations of more than 450 poems that Piercy has published in periodicals since 1956 are not given in this bibliography. Most of these poems have been published—either before or after their appearance in periodicals—in one or more of the eight volumes of poetry listed under "Books."]
"Magic Mama." *Women of Power* 1 (Spring 1984): 71.

ARTICLES

"Beginning to Begin to Begin." With Bob Gottlieb. *Radicals in the Profession Newsletter*, June 1968. [Pamphlet.]
"The Foreign Policy Association: 50 Years of Successful Imperialism." *Caw*, February 1968: 7-10.
"The Grand Coolie Dam." *Leviathan.* Sommerville, Mass.: New English Free Press, 1969. [Pamphlet.]
"Women's Liberation: Nobody's Baby Now." *Defiance* 1 (1970): 134-62.
"Tom Eliot Meets the Hulk at Little Big Horn: The Political Economy of Poetry." With Dick Lourie. *Triquarterly* 23-24 (Winter-Spring 1972): 57-91.
"Getting Together: How to Start a Women's Liberation Group." With Jane Freeman. Sommerville, Mass.: New England Free Press, 1972. [Pamphlet.]
"Books for the Daughters." *Margins* 7 (August/September 1973): 1-2.
"Margaret Atwood: Beyond Victimization." *American Poetry Review* 2 (November/December 1973): 41-44.
"It's High Time." *Provincetown Advocate*, November 21, 1974, 17.
"Through the Cracks: Growing Up in the Fifties." *Partisan Review* 41 (July, 1974), 202-16.
"The White Christmas Blues." *Provincetown Advocate*, January 9, 1975.
"Symposium: A Chapbook on Poetry Readings." *Some*, 1977: 26-29.
"A Fish Needs a Bicycle: Responses to a Questionnaire on Marxism and the Arts." *Minnesota Review*, N.S., 9 (Fall 1977): 43-44.
"Feminist Perspectives 1978." *Sojourner* 4, no. 5 (January 1979).
"The City as Battleground: The Novelist as Combatant." In *Literature and the Urban Experience: Essays on the City and Literature*, ed. Michael C. Jaye and Ann Chalmers Watts. Newark, N.J.: Rutgers Univ. Press, 1981, 209-17.
"Mirror Images." In *Women's Culture: The Women's Renaissance of the*

Seventies, ed. Gayle Kimball. Metuchen, N.J.: Scarecrow Press, 1981, 187-94.

"Starting Support Groups for Writers." In *Words in Our Pockets: The Feminist Writers Guild Handbook,* ed. Celeste West. San Francisco: Bootlegger Press, 1981.

"A Symposium Response: From the Sixties to the Eighties." *Cultural Correspondence,* nos. 12-14 (Summer 1981).

"Inviting the Muse." *Negative Capability* 2 (Winter 1982).

"Fame Fortune." *New Boston Review* 6 (February 1982).

"Forward." In *The Zanzibar Cat,* by Joanna Russ. Sauk City, Wis.: Arkham House, 1983.

"On Being a Jewish Feminist." *Women's Review of Books* 1, no. 5 (1984): 5-6.

"The Turn-on of Identity." *Ms.* 12 (February 1984): 46-48.

"Jewish Identity." *Shmate* 2, no. 8 (Pesach 1984): 25-26.

"Poets on Poetry." *Literary Cavalcade* 37 (October 1984): 24-25.

"Autobiography." In *Contemporary Authors Autobiography Series,* ed. Dedria Bryfonski, 1: 267-81. Detroit: Gale Research Co., 1984.

REVIEWS

[Review of *Children of Crisis,* vols. 1 and 2, by Robert Coles.] *New York Times Book Review,* 13 February 1972, 1 +.

[Review of *Daughters of the Moon,* by Joan Haggerty; *Memoirs of an Ex-Prom Queen,* by Alix Kates Shulman.] *Second Wave* 2, no. 1 (1972): 46.

"Asking for Help Is Apt to Kill You" [*Women and Madness,* by Phyllis Chesler]. *Village Voice,* 30 November 1972.

[Review of *Monster,* by Robin Morgan.] *New* 21 (Spring/Summer 1973): 64-67.

"Gritty Places and Strong Men" [*The Diviners,* by Margaret Lawrence]. *New York Times Book Review,* 23 June 1974, 6.

"Agnes Smedley: Dirt Poor Daughter of Earth" [*Daughter of Earth,* by Agnes Smedley]. *New Republic* 171, 14 December 1974, 19-20.

"Writer's Choice" [*Science Walks on Two Legs; The Jane Poems,* by Kathleen Spwack; *Voices from Wounded Knee; New Days,* by June Jordan]. *Partisan Review* 42, no. 1 (1975), 156-57.

"From Where I Work: A Column" [Audre Lorde]. *American Poetry Review* 5 (March/April 1976): 11-12.

[Review of *Meridian,* by Alice Walker]. *New York Times Book Review,* 23 May 1976, 5 +.

"A Rich Gift for Us" [*Of Woman Born,* by Adrienne Rich]. *Sojourner,* December 1976.

"From Where I Work: A Column" [Joanna Russ]. *American Poetry Review* 6 (May-June 1977): 37-39.

"A Fuller Life" [*The Woman and the Myth,* by Bell Gale Chevigny]. *Seven Days,* 6 June 1977: 34-35.

[Review of *Stories*, by Doris Lessing.] *Chicago Tribune Book World*, 14 May 1978, 1.

"Contemplating Past Youth, Present Age" [*Now and Then Poems*, by Robert Penn Warren]. *Chicago Tribune Book World*, 10 September 1978.

"Shining Daughters" [*The Two of Them* and *Kittatinny*, by Joanna Russ]. *Sojourner*, October 1978: 14.

"Other Planets, Other Cats" [*Motherlines*, by Suzy McKee Charnas; *Watchtower*, by Elizabeth Lynn; *Godsfire*, by Cynthia Felice]. *Sojourner*, April 1979.

"The Feminist Gospel According to Adrienne Rich" [*On Lies, Secrets, and Silence*, by Adrienne Rich]. *Chicago Tribune Book World*, 15 April 1979, 1.

"A Touching Detective Story" [*Rosie: An Investigation of a Wrongful Death*, by Ellen Frankfort]. *Chicago Tribune*, 11 June 1979, Sec. 2, 6.

"A Lot of Strange from Lessing" [*Shikasta*, by Doris Lessing]. *Washington Post*, November 1979, 5.

[Review of *The Queen of Egypt* and *The Bible of the Beasts of the Little Field*, by Susan Fromberg Schaeffer.] *Chicago Tribune Book World*, 27 January 1980, 3.

"Hellman Twilight: Memories of a Dramatist" [*Maybe*, by Lillian Hellman]. *Chicago Tribune Book World*, 11 May 1980, 1.

"Tom Robbins with a Bad Case of the Cutes" [*Still Life with Woodpecker*, by Tom Robbins]. *Chicago Tribune Book World*, 14 September 1980, 3.

"The Mills of Fate" [*Emmeline*, by Judith Rossner]. *Washington Post Book World*, 14 September 1980, p. 3 + .

"A Historian Obsessed by Ghosts" [*The Chaneysville Incident*, by David Bradley]. *Chicago Tribune Book World*, 26 April 1981, 4.

[Review of *You Can't Keep a Good Woman Down*, by Alice Walker.] *Washington Post Book World*, April 1981, 11.

[Review of *Who Killed Karen Silkwood?* by Howard Kohn.] *Sojourner*, December 1981.

[Review of *A Mother and Two Daughters*, by Gail Godwin.] *Chicago Tribune Book World*, 10 January 1982, 3.

[Review of *Zami: A New Spelling of My Name* and *Chosen Poems, Old and New*, by Audre Lorde.] *13th Moon* 7, nos. 1 and 2 (1983): 187-90.

[Review of *Keeper of Accounts*, by Irena Kelpfisz.] *American Book Review* 5 (September/October 1983): 12.

[Review of *Mysteries of Motion*, by Hortense Calisher.] *Washington Post*, 31 December 1983, Sec. C, 2.

"Caught in a Tangled Web of Stories" [*Swallow*, by D.M. Thomas]. *Chicago Tribune*, 25 November 1984, Sec. 14, 35.

[Review of *Van der Steen's Cats*, by J.R. Bruckner.] *New York Times Book Review*, 3 February 1985, 36.

(continued)

MISCELLANEOUS

"Marge Piercy: Poems" [Recording, twelve poems, some recorded in 1968, some in 1969]. New York: Radio Free People.

"Laying Down the Tower" [Recording, a sequence of eleven poems, recorded in 1972]. New York: Radio Free People. [Included in *Black Box #1* (cassette magazine), 1972.]

"Reclaiming Ourselves" [Marge Piercy reading her poems in 1973, sometimes alone, sometimes with guitar accompaniment, and Painted Women's Ritual Theater, with Jeriann Hilderly, performing some of her songs]. New York: Radio Free People.

"Reading and Thoughts" [Recording]. Women's Studies Series. Deland, Florida: Everett/Edwards.

"The Ordeal of the Woman Writer" [Recorded panel discussion, with Toni Morrison and Erica Jong]. Introduction by Heywood Hale Broun. New York: Norton, 1974.

"At the Core" [Cassette]. Washington, D.C.: Watershed Tapes, 1976.

"Memory Annex" [Excerpts]. In *Ariadne's Thread: A Collection of Contemporary Women's Journals*, ed. Lyn Lifshin. New York: Harper and Row, 1982, 58-61.

"Interview with Ira Wood and Marge Piercy." *Pulp* 8, no. 1 (1982).

Compilers' note: We would like to thank Marge Piercy for her assistance in compiling this bibliography.

Notes on the Writers

Ann Beattie was born 8 September 1947 and grew up in Washington, D.C. She earned a B.A. in English at American University in 1969 and a master's degree at the University of Connecticut in 1970. She has taught briefly at the University of Virginia, and at Harvard as Briggs Copeland Lecturer in English. Beattie writes primarily about the era of the 1960s and 1970s in America, but she resents critical reduction of her works to statements about these times. The recipient of a Guggenheim grant and an Excellence Award from the National Academy and Institute of Arts and Letters (1980), Beattie has lived in New York since 1980.

Annie Dillard, born 30 April 1945 in Pittsburgh, Pennsylvania, received a B.A. (1967) and an M.A. (1968) in English from Hollins College. She has taught writing at Western Washington State University and was distinguished visiting professor of English at Wesleyan University from 1979 to 1981. Her writing has been termed "existentialist" and "transcendentalist," and critics remark on her keen observation and imaginative use of empirical data. Dillard is contributing editor to *Harper's* magazine and a member of the Authors' Guild, the P.E.N. Poetry Society of America, and Phi Beta Kappa. Her awards include the New York Presswomen's Award for Excellence (1975), the Washington State Governor's Award for Literature (1978), and the Pulitzer Prize for general nonfiction (1974) for *Pilgrim at Tinker Creek.*

Maxine Hong Kingston, born 27 October 1940 in Stockton, California, graduated in 1962 from the University of California, Berkeley. For a while she taught English and mathematics at various high schools in California and Hawaii. In 1977 she was visiting associate professor of English at the University of Hawaii. Kingston wrote even as a child, telling her parents that she was "just doing homework." She is especially interested in writers such as Mark Twain, Gertrude Stein, and Virginia Woolf whose works reflect sensitivity to patterns and rhythms of oral storytelling. Kingston has won the National Book Critics Circle general nonfiction award (1976), the *Mademoiselle* magazine award (1977), the Anisfield-Wolf Race Relations Award (1978), the American Book Award for nonfiction (1981), and the Stockton, California, Arts Commission Award (1981). In 1980, Kingston was named "Living Treasure of Hawaii."

Toni Morrison, who reports that she began to write seriously only after age thirty, was born in Lorain, Ohio, on 18 February 1931. With a B.A. (1953) from Howard University, where she was sometimes involved in theater, and an M.A. in English from Cornell University (1955), Morrison taught English from 1955 to 1957 at Texas Southern University in Houston. In 1957 she returned to Howard as a faculty member and remained there until 1964. Since then she has taught black literature and techniques of fiction writing at Yale University and Bard College. As a senior editor for Random House, Morrison enjoys advancing the careers of other black writers. She is the recipient of the National Book Critics Circle Award (1977) for *Song of Solomon* and of two awards from the American Academy and Institute of Arts and Letters (1978, 1981). She is a member of the National Council on the Arts and was featured in the PBS series "Writers in America."

Cynthia Ozick has spent most of her life in New York City, where she was born 17 April 1928. She graduated from New York University in 1949 and received a master's degree from Ohio State University in 1950. Poet, critic, fiction writer, and translator of Yiddish poetry, Ozick reports that she never ceases to be pleased that other people enjoy reading what she so much enjoys writing. Ozick's works have attracted much attention. She is the recipient of the B'nai B'rith Jewish Heritage Award (1971), the Edward Lewis Wallant Memorial Award (1972), the Jewish Book Council Award for fiction (1972), and an O. Henry Short Story Award (1975). She has also received grants from the National Endowment for the Arts and from the Guggenheim Memorial Foundation. *Newsweek* listed her among the best of American short story writers.

Grace Paley was born 11 December 1922 in New York City and grew up in the Bronx. From 1938 to 1939 she attended Hunter College and New York University. Politically active all her life, she terms herself a "pacifist" and an "anarchist"; during the 1960s she was involved in anti-Vietnam War activities, and she continues to be a committed anti-militarist, feminist, and advocate of prison reform. Paley currently lives in Greenwich Village and teaches at Sarah Lawrence College. She has also taught at Columbia University and Syracuse University. Awards presented to Paley include a Guggenheim fellowship in fiction (1961), a National Council on the Arts grant, and a National Academy and Institute of Arts and Letters award for short story writing (1970).

Marge Piercy was born 31 March 1936 in Detroit, Michigan. She graduated from the University of Michigan in 1957 and received a master's degree in 1958 from Northwestern University. Piercy was very active in the 1960s civil rights movement and as an organizer of Students for a Democratic Society. Around 1969 she transferred her allegiance to the women's movement, where it remains; she hopes that her works will help raise the feminist consciousness of women who are not yet involved in women's issues. Piercy has won several awards for fiction and poetry writing from the University of Michigan, the (Massachusetts) Governor's Commission on the Status of Women literature award, the Borestone Mountain Poetry Award (twice), the Orion Scott Award in Humanities, and a national Endowment for the Arts award (1978).

Anne Redmon was born 13 December 1943 in Stamford, Connecticut. She spent most of her life until age twenty-one in the northeastern states, and in 1964 moved to England. She attended the University of Pennsylvania from 1962 to 1964. In addition to being a full-time writer, Redmon enjoys traveling. She has been a book reviewer for the London *Sunday Times* and for the BBC. For *Emily Stone,* Redmon won the *Yorkshire Post* prize for a best first work; *Music and Silence* has been translated into several languages.

Anne Tyler, born 25 October 1941 in Minneapolis, Minnesota, earned a degree in Russian from Duke University in 1961 and attended graduate school at Columbia University from 1961 to 1962. Until 1965, she was a librarian at various universities. She currently lives in Baltimore, a city of which she is especially fond. Tyler is a member of the P.E.N. Authors' Guild, the Authors' League of America, and Phi Beta Kappa. Although she "disowns" her first two novels, her later works have won her a *Mademoiselle* magazine award (1966), the American Academy and Institute of Arts and Letters award for literature (1977), the Janet Heidinger Kafka prize (1981), and the P.E.N. Faulkner award for fiction (1983).

Alice Walker was born 9 February 1944 in Eatonton, Georgia. She attended Spelman College from 1961 to 1963, then went on to graduate from Sarah Lawrence College in 1965. Since 1968, Walker has taught writing and black studies at Jackson State College and Tougaloo College. She was lecturer in literature at Wellesley College and at the University of Massachusetts, Boston, in 1972 and 1973. In 1982, she was distinguished writer in Afro-American studies at the University of California, Berkeley, and later that same year was Fannie Hurst professor of literature at Brandeis University. Walker is an editor of *Ms.* and the recipient of numerous awards: she was Breadloaf Writer's Conference scholar in 1966; and in 1967 she won first prize in the *American Scholar* essay contest. Most impressive among a variety of other awards are the Pulitzer Prize and the American Book Award for *The Color Purple* in 1983.

Notes on
the Contributors

Daniel Cahill, professor of English at the University of Northern Iowa, Cedar Falls, has compiled many bibliographies of contemporary writers and has written a large number of articles for such journals as the *North American Review* and the *Chicago Review.*

Susan Currier, assistant professor of English at California Polytechnic State University, San Luis Obispo, has a special interest in Cynthia Ozick's work, on which she has written an article for the *Dictionary of Literary Biography.*

Elizabeth Fifer, assistant professor of English at Lehigh University, has had many poems and six critical studies published in such journals as *Contemporary Literature, Texas Studies in Literature and Language,* and *The Journal of Narrative Technique.*

Elaine Gardiner, associate professor of English and assistant dean of the College of Arts and Sciences at Washburn University of Topeka, has translated numerous works and is the author of several critical studies, including one on Kate Chopin in *Modern Fiction Studies.*

Elaine Tuttle Hansen, assistant professor of English at Haverford College, is the author of eight articles that have appeared in such journals as *Speculum* and the *Journal of English and Germanic Philology.*

Suzanne Juhasz, associate professor of English at the University of Colorado at Boulder, is the author of four books, including the recent *The Undisclosed Continent: Emily Dickinson and the Space of the Mind* (Indiana Univ. Press), and of numerous articles and poems.

Curtis Martin, a teacher at the Air Force Academy, is completing his doctoral dissertation on Toni Morrison at Michigan State University.

Ellen Pifer, associate professor of English and comparative literature at the University of Delaware, is the author of *Nabokov and the Novel* (Harvard University Press) and of a number of articles that have appeared in such journals as *Modern Fiction Studies* and *Studies in American Fiction.*

Carolyn Porter, associate professor of English at the University of California at Berkeley, is the author of *Seeing and Being: The Plight of the Participant Observer in Emerson, James, Adams, and Faulkner* (Wesleyan Univ. Press) and a number of essays, including one in *The Virginia Quarterly Review.*

Catherine Rainwater, lecturer in English at the University of Texas at Austin, has had articles published in such journals as *Southern Literary Journal, Essays in Literature,* and *Resources for American Literary Study* and is the coeditor of *Three Contemporary Women Novelists: Hazzard, Ozick, and Redmon (Texas Studies in Literature and Language).*

Mary F. Robertson, assistant professor of English at the University of Texas at Austin, is especially interested in postmodernist fiction. Her work has appeared in such journals as *Contemporary Literature, Texas Studies in Literature and Language,* and *Modern Philology.*

William J. Scheick, professor of English and editor of *Texas Studies in Literature and Language* at the University of Texas at Austin, is the author of numerous articles and five books, of which the best known are *The Slender Human Word: Emerson's Artistry in Prose* (Univ. of Tennessee Press) and *The Half-Blood: A Cultural Symbol in Nineteenth-Century American Fiction* (Univ. Press of Kentucky).

Ronald Schleifer, associate professor at the University of Oklahoma and editor of *Genre,* has edited two books and has had twenty articles published in such journals as *Modern Fiction Studies* and *Modern Language Notes.*

Linda Wagner, professor of English and editor of the *Centennial Review* at Michigan State University, is the author of thirteen books, including two on William Carlos Williams (Wesleyan Univ. Press), and the editor of nine books. Her countless articles have appeared in such professional journals as the *Southern Review* and *Contemporary Literature.*